America by Design

Spiro Kostof

America by Design

Based on the PBS series
by Guggenheim Productions, Inc.

Oxford University Press *New York Oxford* 1987

OXFORD UNIVERSITY PRESS   Oxford, New York, Toronto, Delhi,
Bombay, Calcutta, Madras, Karachi, Petaling Jaya, Singapore, Hong Kong,
Tokyo, Nairobi, Dar es Salaam, Cape Town, Melbourne, Auckland
and associated companies in Beirut, Berlin, Ibadan, Nicosia

Copyright © 1987 by Oxford University Press, Inc.

Published by Oxford University Press, Inc.,
200 Madison Avenue, New York, New York 10016

Oxford is a registered trademark of Oxford University Press

Library of Congress Cataloging-in-Publication Data
Kostof, Spiro.
America by design.
Includes index. 1. Architecture—United States.   2. City planning—
United States.   3. Parks—United States.   I. Title.
NA705.K64   1987   720'.973   86-12787
ISBN 0-19-504283-2

9 8 7 6 5 4 3 2 1
Printed in the United States of America

For J.W.

Preface

The scope of this book is both presumptuous and modest. As conceived, the book presumes to scan the fabric of manmade America, from its houses to the grand configurations of the continent at large. How did we mark the land with farms and towns and railroad lines, it asks, and what does all this activity say about us—who we are, what we have been? An agenda of this magnitude, intended religiously, would consume a lifetime and call upon a store of specialized knowledge in several fields.

I don't have such resources. What I set out to do here, and in the television series which preceded the book, is much more limited. I wanted to see America as one design, made out of whole cloth, and to review some of the enduring themes in its history which determined the main features of its landscape: the detached house on its plot of land, the factory and the office tower, the National Survey grid, the tracery of fields, and the layered palimpsest of streets and roads.

This setting of our collective career, it goes without saying, is not a steady, unchanging pattern. We redefine it constantly, so that, at any single moment, the pattern that contains our present activities also preserves the memory of where we have been as a people, and conditions to an appreciable degree the course of our development. What motivated both the series and the book was, in fact, a curiosity about that process without end—the ways in which our landscape shifts and adjusts according to the rhythms of our days, the interventions of clients, designers, and users, the forces of an impatient future.

I was curious about everything around us—street pavements, air field ramps, suburban patches and treelined avenues, Civil War monuments, long-span bridges. And I wanted to think about what we could no longer see. What was it like to travel on the Pennsylvania Main Line Canal or Cumberland Road, clear a farmstead in the forests of Vermont or the tallgrass ripples of Illinois?

But what I would settle on was quite selective, and the selection in large measure arbitrary. There was never any thought, and, given the nature of the project, never any call, to be either exhaustive or scholarly. The series was meant to address a general audience, and to do so lightly. The book has the same goal. The five essays it consists of are expanded versions of the scripts, tighter in structure and less conversational in tone. They do not propose a thesis, or present findings of original research. Their substance is culled from observations in the field, and from a great amount of reading.

I read indiscriminately—everything I could find. Because of the all-embracing nature of the inquiry, this meant reading architectural historians and cultural historians, geographers, anthropologists, planners, reformists and politicians. Though the book could not support the apparatus of footnotes, I thought it important to give a full account of my sources in an annotated bibliography. It will show interested readers how much there is to be had on the subject of our surroundings; but it may also mislead them into thinking that we know enough. On the contrary, I was often frustrated as I went along. I could find little on sidewalks or the origins of Elm Street or the physical layout of farms; a lot on the architecture and technology of skyscrapers, but little on their use; volumes on Louis Sullivan, but almost nothing on the creator of the early TVA dams, Roland Anthony Wank. Much remains to be written on the planning of cemeteries and the Bureau of Reclamation, on Mississippi levees and the architecture of our great irrigation systems. In one sense, the book reflects the unevenness of the published material.

Throughout, I tried to help people *see* America, and not take anything they saw for granted. I had two major inadequacies for this task, which, in the end, turned out to be advantages. I am not an Americanist by training, first of all; and I am not a native-born American, so I could not hope to know what it was like to grow up in Oconomowoc or Brooklyn.

But there is much to be said for approaching a subject as a relative outsider, free from having to assume conventional postures. I came to this country like millions of others to find new roots, and so my search had a special urgency—the need to know what I had hitched my fortune to. And as a practicing historian I had developed over the years professional attitudes that decided how I was to approach the subject. I have come to understand architecture to mean, quite simply, all buildings, the standard and the fancy, and their arrangement into landscapes of form. I am interested in uses and users—that is, in the social content of architecture. And I have grown to believe that the primary task of the architectural historian, behind all the sophisticated research and the erudition, is to recreate and convey the actual processes of designing, building, and using the manmade landscapes of the past—to think, what was it like for a determined group of English settlers to clear a site in the forested wilderness of seventeenth-century New England, survey the land and distribute it, put up a meeting house, and activate a town as a living covenant with God?

The experience of roaming the continent for many months to learn how we shaped it will remain unforgettable. There is a bonus history in that adventure, a history of people and happenings, that is not part of this book. I will remember fondly all those who welcomed and entertained us, those who confided precious local wisdom about the places and buildings we had come to study, and those many others who looked on quizzically as we worked, proud of what they had but uncertain of the nature of our curiosity. I will also remember, with gratitude and fondness, my traveling companions—the several crews who smoothed my pilgrim's progress and expertly monitored my performance.

To the director and producer of the series, Werner Schumann, I am profoundly beholden; we toiled together hard and long, and it is a measure of his professionalism and his humanity that he sustained unfailingly what I sought to accomplish and did so in a spirit of genuine camaraderie. His photographs, taken in the field, contribute substantially to the effectiveness of the book. The field notes of Jeff Howard, Mary Jane Lucchetti, and Brian Horrigan were useful in the early stages of the project. I also profited tangibly from the overseeing of the advisory board: Stanford Anderson, Lois A. Craig, Everett L. Fly, Dolores Hayden, Rai Y. Okamoto, Michael Pittas, and especially its chairman Henry A. Millon, and the peerless John B. Jackson who feels the design of America more deeply than I ever will. Over us all hovered the sheltering influence of Charles Guggenheim. For his encouragement and good fellowship I express heartfelt appreciation.

My colleagues at Berkeley merit a special grant of thanks for their sympathy and patient tolerance of my long absences. Professor Dell Upton read much of what I produced and generously gave me the benefit of his superior knowledge. Others who reviewed segments of the manuscript include Professors Richard G. Carrott and Paul Groth. My research assistant Douglas MacDonald stayed the course; along with Karen Lundeen and Joan Bossert at Oxford University Press and Jennifer Moffitt at Guggenheim Productions, he deserves the credit for the organization of the visual material. Greg Castillo prepared the index. My editor Joyce Berry will join me, I know, in a sigh of relief.

May 1987   S. K.
Berkeley, California

Contents

Color illustration section follows page 276

America by Design

1

The American House

On a coastal knoll set against the Santa Lucia Mountains, midway between San Francisco and Los Angeles, sits a remarkable California house. The two ornate Spanish towers of its main front announce its presence from below, as you drive along Highway 1. On the way up, along the winding road that leads from the little village of San Simeon to the knoll crest, you see zebras, tahr goats, and Barbary sheep roaming freely in the lush landscape—a reminder of the zoo that was once part of the estate. Then you are there.

The twin-towered front belongs to the Casa Grande, the main house on the estate. Clustered around it are three palatial guest houses and two pools—the indoor Roman Pool lined with Venetian glass tiles and the 104-foot long Neptune Pool dug out of the hillside, which has a Greco-Roman temple for a backdrop. The Casa Grande itself has thirty-eight bedrooms, two libraries, a movie theater, and a grand assembly hall where guests—Hollywood stars, singers, politicians—would gather every evening to await the arrival of their host.

The Casa Grande at Hearst Castle. Hearst Castle (1919–40) was designed by Julia Morgan, the first woman to graduate from the architecture school of the Ecole des Beaux Arts, Paris, and the first woman to practice architecture in California. (See also color section for a detail of Casa Grande.)

He was William Randolph Hearst, a gritty mining and ranching tycoon and the head of a vast publishing empire. Hearst called the estate La Cuesta Encantada, the Enchanted Hill. And so it was, this once barren, rocky hilltop, when he was done with it. For twenty-seven years, from 1919 onward, a small army of workers and artisans toiled under the direction of a strong-willed woman, the architect Julia Morgan, to give shape to Hearst's fantasy. They shaped the land and made it fertile. They made roads where only cattle trails had been, hauling up rich topsoil from the lowlands. They piped in water from mountain springs five miles away. They cut stone and finished it, carved moldings, and laid tile. Steel, iron, and cement arrived by coastal steamer at the resurrected port

Refectory, Hearst Castle. The hall is lined with fifteenth-century Spanish choir stalls. On the wall is a Flemish Gothic tapestry with scenes from the life of the prophet Daniel, and at the end is a French Gothic fireplace.

Living and dining rooms of a suburban home, Alexandria, Virginia.

of the old whaling village of San Simeon. And so did cargo of a more precious sort: hundreds of works of art—old European fireplaces, entire ceilings, sculpture, tapestries, Oriental rugs—which were kept in warehouses until their place was ready on the Enchanted Hill.

Besides the main buildings, Morgan designed hothouses and kennels, bear and lion pits, an elephant house, a switchboard and a newspaper office, and a pergola on vine-covered concrete pillars that curved around the hill for more than a mile starting at, and returning to, Casa Grande.

A family doing yardwork in the frontyard of their home, Lorain, Ohio, 1948.

Above, left. *A farmhouse in the Midwest.*

Above. *Spanish Colonial Revival style houses, Oakland, California, ca. 1938.*

This is how one American lived in the early decades of this century. Here he dined in state with the famous of his day, surrounded by masterpieces from abroad that lent him dignity and expressed the values he held dear. In these rooms he relaxed and slept and enjoyed the intimacy of close friends.

These domestic rituals all of us hold in common, far removed as our lives may be from the splendors of the Enchanted Hill. Every house, however modest, is for its occupants a public stage and a private sanctuary. It frames our lives for a spell of time, projects our identity and self-worth, gives us a chance to express ourselves, while we dream of that ideal house, the house we hope to own one day and might, the house we hope to own and might not. This is what makes Hearst's castle kin to the farmhouse out in the Midwest, the one-story bungalow and the suburban tract house, the shingled, wood-sided mobile home moored on the rented lot of a trailer court.

For most Americans today the ideal house means something quite specific. Whatever its exterior look—Georgian, Cape Cod, split-level or ranchlike—it means, first of all, a detached structure standing on its own lot in the company of other freestanding houses. It means, secondly, that its occupants hold title to it or are in the process of making it their own. And this stress on private posses-

Single-family houses and their frontyards, Alameda, California.

sion coincides with our image of its occupants. The house is the proper place to nurture married life and bring up children. This is the true meaning of the American house, whether it is small or grand, old or just off the developer's line.

You can see this freestanding, privately owned, single-family house everywhere you go—in the small towns of Ohio and California and Kansas, in big cities like Chicago, Houston, and Atlanta, in suburbs all across the country. It is set back from the street; it has a frontyard with a lawn and a tree or two, a garage or carport, and a backyard for barbecuing. The lawn extends from house to house, uninterrupted by fences; there are miles of blue-grass front lawns in midwestern towns and suburbs, stretching on both sides of the street for blocks on end. The backyard is more private. It usually is fenced in, and might have a picnic table, a toolshed, a barbecue pit. Whatever the external trim, inside, the houses are not very different from one another. Each has two or more bedrooms, at least one and a half bathrooms, a family room with the main television set, and a kitchen equipped with dishwasher, electric range, and refrigerator.

Today we take this house for granted; for us it is as common as the ubiquitous skyscraper, fast-food outlet, or department store.

To those raised in other cultures, however, the average American house must seem an extravagant domestic setting, in its spaciousness, the specialized uses of its several rooms, the mechanical systems, and labor-saving devices. Even to European visitors, the American house is distinctive, and peculiar in a number of ways.

To begin with, the freestanding house itself is a rarity in Europe. Europeans are by and large dwellers of apartments and rowhouses. And for an intended occupancy of one family, two to six people, American houses are very big—enormous, in fact, by European standards.

Moreover, the house is peculiar in that it is built of wood in an overwhelming number of cases. Europe exhausted its forests long ago and uses timber sparingly. The structure is light—thin boards extending the full height between floors. Some parts have been precut at the factory and assembled on the site. Fixtures are standard. There are double-glazed sliding windows and doors in light, aluminum frames.

The house is likely to be rather new—not only by European standards but even in terms of American history. Only a handful of houses, comparatively speaking, go back a hundred years or more. Older ones, when they have miraculously survived, are looked upon as national monuments. Fully seventy percent of our total housing stock has been built since the Second World War. It was built in great patches, laid out at one time by merchant builders over fields, meadows, and hillsides. One day it was open country; the next, a residential neighborhood had sprung up intact, with roads and lawns and driveways, and stood there, in the middle of nowhere, waiting for life to well up inside it.

Although meant to be urban or suburban, the house is isolated from public life and from the workplace. Zoning laws protect it from the encroachment of businesses and manufacturing, so there is no commercial life to speak of on its street. Little happens by way of public celebration or public display that would envelop the house in ritual manifestations of community. The house is self-contained. The occupants may choose to interact with their neighbors or not as they please.

How did we come to create this domestic ideal for ourselves? We can be sure that it is not in the least accidental or "natural."

It has been in the making for at least two centuries: the handicraft of a broad consensus of politicians, reformers, ministers, builders and architects, and average Americans themselves. This American house is at the core of our national existence. It is the vehicle through which immigrants complete their acculturation, which starts in the crowded urban settings where many first settle. It expresses the structure of our society as we have come to see it— a structure based on the sanctity of the nuclear family and long-entrenched male and female roles (the male provider, the female homemaker), on notions of self-sufficiency and the inviolable right of property.

So the American house is much more than a house. It is a home, a sacred hearth. It is the American dream. And even though its premises and reality have come into question lately, for many, many people it remains the American dream. If they have not yet attained it, it will be the reward of hard work, proof of one's social worthiness, the promise of security. If they have, they will struggle to hold on to it, or go it one better.

But where did it all begin?

Colonial Roots and Republicanism

This domestic ideal had always been with us—so we would like to believe. And we have Williamsburg to prove it. Almost three hundred years ago it was laid out with rows of detached single-family houses, not unlike our own residential neighborhoods. There it was, at the beginning, what our Colonial fathers seemed to have prescribed for us, and so we took to imitating the style of those houses in our own speculative tracts and even in our trailers.

But is Williamsburg a fair blueprint of that American dream ensconced in the quiet stretches of suburbia? Let us set aside the obvious difference that Williamsburg was created as a capital city, with public buildings and formal streets—not to mention the red-light district in the slums out toward College Landing. No trees lined the streets back then and there was only white sand for pavement. Let's just look at the houses.

Some are very modest, others ample indeed. The wealthy plan-

Duke of Gloucester Street, Williamsburg, Virginia. The town was begun in 1699. Its preservation and restoration, which included eighty-eight original buildings from the eighteenth and nineteenth centuries, began in 1928.

Interior of the Geddy Silversmith shop, Williamsburg, originally built about 1750.

tation owner and the modest artisan lived side by side here in the sort of social mix that is largely unknown in our neighborhoods. Also, unlike today, here the rich and the not-so-rich used their house as their place of business as well. The James Geddy family, for example, lived in a two-story house. It had a hall and parlor on the ground floor and a third room in a rear ell. Geddy and his sons practiced their trade in the shop attached to the house. They set up forges and made guns, cutlery and silverware, clock parts

Tayloe House, Williamsburg. John Tayloe bought the house in 1759 from James Carter, a surgeon. The building with the bell-shaped roof may have been the original doctor's office. The Tayloe family also owned the famous Octagon House in Washington, D.C.

The kitchen of the Wythe House, Williamsburg, Virginia.

and shoe buckles. The premises were littered with ironworking waste and slag.

Colonel John Tayloe's townhouse is almost twice that size, even though Tayloe used it only when the legislature and general court were in session; his principal residence was a great stone mansion called Mount Airy, situated on his plantation in Richmond County, on a ridge with a broad view of the valley of the Rappahannock. The part-time townhouse had a number of dependencies. One was a storehouse; another was the smokehouse, and it stands there still, the door hung on the original hinges, the old rim lock in place. There is a small office building in line with the front of the house, and like all Williamsburg houses the kitchen is in a separate outbuilding—which tells us one more thing about this would-be prototype of the American dream. These Virginians had servants, slaves that is, to do their housework. This slave population, and some free blacks too, introduced a racial mixture to the streets, unequal though the two races certainly were, a mixture that you would not find in the covenanted suburb of this century.

And one further difference. A good deal more was determined by law about the appearance of Williamsburg houses than we would

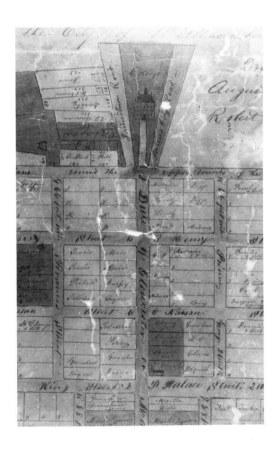

The Buck-Trout-Lively map of Williamsburg, 1867, detail.

probably put up with today. The size was prescribed, depending on the importance of the street, the wall height, the brick chimney. On the main avenue, Duke of Gloucester Street, with the Capitol at one end and the College of William and Mary at the other, the houses had to "come within six foot of the street, and not nearer," and had to "front alike." The lot had to be enclosed "with a wall, pails, or post and rails" within six months after the building was complete, so that even when there were ample side-yards, which was uncommon, the fences held the line of the street and defined the boundary between the private and the public realm.

Here is a specific instance. In a deed of 1749, one Benjamin Waller sells the butcher Stephen Brown two adjacent lots in York County near Williamsburg, on which Brown must build within three years, "one good dwelling house—containing sixteen feet in width and twenty feet in length at the least with a brick chimney thereto; the said house to front in a line with the row of lotts in which it stands at the distance of six feet from the extreme southern bounds of the said lotts . . ." And so on.

Thomas Jefferson, 1743–1826.

Jefferson's home, Monticello. After more than thirty years of work, the house took its finished form in 1809. The house is part of a larger complex, which encompasses underground passages connecting the service wings with the main house. Jefferson's law office and estate office were at the ends of the wings.

So Williamsburg is not really what we would like to believe it is. Despite the familiar dormers and doorways, the almost suburban look of some of its streets, the Colonial town was very different, physically and socially, from our own residential communities. But there is one thing, a crucial thing, the two have in common—the belief that every family should possess a piece of land with a house of its own upon it.

This is what Thomas Jefferson, the most illustrious Virginian of the time, would have approved of about Williamsburg, the town that served him as state capital during his term as governor. Yet he did not think much of the town's architecture, which he found "insubstantial and uncouth." Jefferson's ideas about architecture derived from the Classical tradition. To him it was a style appropriate for a democratic society, and he peopled the emerging nation of America with independent farmer-citizens who lived in simple cottages on their own plots of land. "The small landowners are the most precious portion of the state," he wrote. Here the woman of the house would enjoy the company of her husband,

care for her children, and occupy herself with the arrangement of the rooms and the improvement of the grounds.

Acquiring and possessing property was a civil right of surpassing importance to Jefferson. Liberty was always threatened by the propertyless. He saw a country divided neatly into equal portions settled by freeholders—his answer to the unjust feudal society of the Old World, with its small collection of powerful landowners and the vast multitudes of landless peasants. He laid down a rational grid upon the land—at the level of his own farmland, which he divided into forty-acre square fields, and at the national level, where the squares were to be sixteen times this size, comprising square townships.

Commerce and manufacturing were simply an aspect of this all-pervasive agricultural economy: they did not need big cities. Instead of crowding and polluting cities, American industry would spread over the countryside, in farmhouses and along clean streams. So Jefferson lived in his "cottage" in Monticello, the independent, self-sufficient lord of his domain. He tilled his land and ran a nail factory. The house he designed and ceaselessly modified sat on its knoll, in plain view of the Blue Ridge Mountains, with superb command—the beacon of tamed nature, of human order on the land.

This notion—the individual property owner as the hallmark of republicanism—is one of the most enduring influences on the shape of our built environment and the character of the American house. Walt Whitman, for example, fifty years after Jefferson, voiced the very same sentiment: "A man is not a whole and complete man unless he *owns* a house and the ground it stands on." The Homestead Act of 1862 merely made into law what had already been established long before as a principal expectation of all Americans. "The laborer ought to be ashamed of himself," preached Henry Ward Beecher on the centennial anniversary of Independence Day, "who in twenty years does not own the ground on which his house stands." Frank Lloyd Wright would restate this national creed in the 1930s in his Broadacre City, where citizens would be assigned holdings of one acre so that they could exercise what he called man's "social right to his place on the ground."

Jefferson did not think much of towns, certainly nothing larger than Williamsburg, which at its height had about 3,000 inhabitants. What he passionately disapproved of were cities, on the model of those of Europe, those centers of commerce and industry, which spawned inequities and compromised virtue. He was certain that "the country produces more virtuous citizens," and he did not want the American people to "get piled upon one another in large cities, as in Europe, [and] . . . become corrupt as in Europe." Cities were "sores on the body politic."

Downing and the Dawn of Suburbia

The city, then, was the enemy of this Jeffersonian vision of America, and he never stopped railing against it. Yet what Jefferson feared was already beginning to materialize toward the end of his life in the seaports of the East Coast. Brisk overseas trade and the opening of the American interior had brought prosperity to Boston and Baltimore, New York and Charleston. By mid-century these ports were teeming with immigrants and farmfolk who had swept in to find employment. They lived in rented houses or parts of houses. Well over half of all houses in the nation's large cities were in fact not owned by their occupants.

One outcome of this urban congestion was the rising popularity of rowhouses. There is no doubt Jefferson would have disapproved of them. The rationale was to fit as many houses as possible onto one street. So they were built against each other in series, defining closed street corridors. The rowhouse, though still intended for one-family occupancy, made for more crowded living. Front and sideyards were gone, and the attached houses tightly framed the channel of the street.

Many of these houses were built as speculative developments by landowners and builders. And they were meant for all social classes. For the rich, who might have a house in the country too, these were "townhouses." In medium- and high-priced rows the service alley and backyards formed a courtyard behind the houses, but in inexpensive rows the houses were back to back, so that the only light and air came from the street side.

The practice of building rowhouses, if we discount the very

early exceptions of Jamestown and New Amsterdam, started in earnest in Philadelphia and Boston in the first half of the eighteenth century. A generation or so after Independence, they were being built in Baltimore and New York, and not uncommonly they were being planned in groups that formed unified architectural compositions.

The model came from Georgian London, where rowhouses had been standardized and had become popular. But the American version staged its own variations. In layout at least, Baltimore's rowhouse was the closest to the Georgian prototype. The service functions were relegated to a narrow rear wing, and the plain brick exterior was touched up with marble accents. You could see hundreds of houses in straight rows going up and down hills, their white marble steps (white wooden steps in the inexpensive rows) pleating primly down to the sidewalk. In New York, where

Rowhouses along Elfreth's Alley in Philadelphia. The alley gets its name from Jeremiah Elfreth who owned land on both sides of one end of the alley in the 1750s. At that time the word "alley" meant a residential street, not the commercial or service thoroughfare we associate with alleys today.

Rowhouse construction along Commonwealth Avenue, Boston, 1870s.

the exterior could be very ornate, the service rooms were on the ground floor toward the front, and they were entered below a stoop.

An early surviving example of rowhouses is Elfreth's Alley in Philadelphia. The houses, thirty in all, date from 1713 to 1811. The first occupants were mostly people who drew their livelihood from the sea—shipwrights, boatbuilders, blacksmiths, river pilots, sea captains. They were succeeded by tradesmen, artisans, and small shopkeepers. The oldest houses were three bays wide and two stories high, with an attic under the gable that drew light from a single dormer. The ground floor often included a shop facing the street. After Independence, the shape grows narrower and a story taller, and in the latest house of the alley, which replaced an earlier house with a frame shop in 1836, the dormered attic is turned into a fourth story with a flat roof.

By mid-century rowhouses were everywhere—in New Haven and Georgetown and Savannah. They were Baltimore's and Boston's model form of residential buildings, and they were even copied, both in brick and wood, in peripheral towns like Roxbury and Charlestown where density was not a main problem. The choice, therefore, had ceased to be one of necessity: the townhouse had become fashionable.

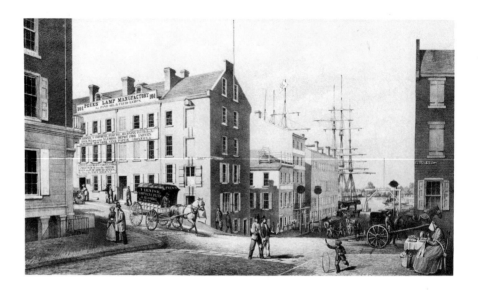

Intersection of Front and Walnut streets, Philadelphia, 1855.

By then a great urban revolution had been set in motion, and its reverberations are still felt today. There were two interlocked cycles to this epic. One had to do with the movement out of the urban centers; the other, with the establishment of suburbs as the new ideal of domesticity.

The story, a complicated one, can be simply told. First, the downtowns became progressively commercialized. This sent the urban middle class further out, in search of quieter and less cluttered living. And *this* was possible to do because of new methods of transportation—regular ferryboat service; the passenger train, commercially inaugurated in 1830 by the Baltimore and Ohio Railroad; and then the streetcar, with its more frequent stops.

The new commuting class left behind their townhouses, which were now taken over by working-class people and the urban poor, most of them immigrants. Where a single family once lived, there were now several families of renters. Filled to capacity and managed by landlords who lived away, the housing stock deteriorated and became easy prey for expanding business premises. The long-term result was that the inner city lost much of its early character; the traditional mixture of dwelling and work began to come undone, since the new transportation systems made it possible to live some distance away from your place of employment. The downtown now consisted of an intensively built up business center, surrounded by decaying neighborhoods of poor renters camping vulnerably in the carcasses of once decent, even gracious, townhouses.

Further out, beyond a zone of warehouses, came the suburbs. At the end of the day, the commuter stepped down from the train or the streetcar into a world that was a world apart from the urban scene he had worked in. For one thing, it looked different. It was green, nestled in what seemed like open countryside. And then it was entirely free of commercial and industrial activity. But there was more to it than that. Here you could associate with neighbors of your own kind. So suburbs were exclusive communities that harbored a special way of life; there was method to them, even when they were not elaborately planned. They were not random or mindless extensions of the downtown.

The suburban ideal of the nineteenth century still determines the way most Americans today think of home and neighborhood and the raising of a family. And one man, more so perhaps than any other, articulated this faith of the suburbs and supplied its imagery.

His name was Andrew Jackson Downing. He came from a laborer's family, but he had higher ambitions for himself. First he married well; his wife was the great-granddaughter of John Adams, the second president of the United States, and a close relative of John Quincy Adams, the sixth president. He learned landscape design from an English landscape painter and became the snobbish admirer of English country gentlemen and their ways. His circle included landscape painters, writers, and the wealthy patrons of large estates along the Hudson Valley.

The image of these estates, in their beautiful natural sites, became Downing's most immediate inspiration. That is what he wanted Americans to emulate. "It is the solitude and freedom of the family home in the country which constantly preserves the purity of the nation, and invigorates its intellectual powers," he wrote. Applied to those who were not wealthy, this meant a suburban cottage, "a snug and economical little home in the suburbs of a town." This was the kind of house occupied by "industrious and intelligent mechanics, the bone and sinue of the land, who

DESIGN 11
SMALL BRACKETED COTTAGE

PRINCIPAL FLOOR
Fig. 10

Andrew Jackson Downing,
1815–1852.

Page from A. J. Downing's The
Architecture of Country Houses, *1850.*

own the ground upon which they stand." He published two immensely popular books to spread this gospel, *Cottage Residences* in 1842 and *The Architecture of Country Houses* in 1850.

Both Downing and Jefferson before him were against the physical and social order of cities. But Jefferson's attachment to the country had nothing to do with living a "natural" life in picturesque settings. The aim of his agrarianism was economic independence. He set out to occupy and control nature, and the symbol of this occupation was the Classical house—white, columnar, symmetrical. What he sought to make evident on the land was a political order.

Downing's love of the countryside, on the other hand, was apolitical. It had an aesthetic and moral basis. And *its* symbol was the Gothic cottage, and other such evocative house types like the "Italian villa," which stressed irregularity in plan, varied massing, and natural colors like russets, greys, and roses. This picturesque, romantic house had steep pitched roofs with floridly ornamented gables, sharply pointed dormers, board-and-batten siding, and in the Italianate style, overhanging eaves on brackets and flat-roofed towers.

A handsome specimen of the Gothic cottage is the Rotch House in New Bedford, Massachusetts. It was built in 1846 by one of Downing's associates, Alexander Jackson Davis, for a prominent citizen, William J. Rotch. Rotch's father found the design "disgusting"—and no wonder. His generation was accustomed to living in white Classical houses, like the one a few blocks down, built for his own father when the old man remarried at age 75. Downing said of the Davis design, "The character expressed by the exterior of this design is that of a man or family of domestic tastes, but with strong aspirations after something higher than social pleasures." (See color section.)

To Downing, the house is a refuge first of all. It is the receptacle of domestic virtue, a private place, a Christian place, a church for the family. "The mere sentiment of home," he wrote, "with its thousand associations, has, like a strong anchor, saved many a man from shipwreck in the storms of life." Here, he said, "the social sympathies take shelter securely under the shadowy eaves, or grow and entwine trustfully with the tall trees or wreathed vines that cluster around, as if striving to shut out whatever of bitterness or strife may be found in the open highways of the world." The house should be intensely personal and full of "feeling." And "feeling" comes across with bay windows and vines, lacy eaves and bargeboarding, porches and balconies.

And this house must look as if it belonged with the land. Rootedness was extremely important to Downing's circle. The time was one of restless mobility. Fifty years earlier, Alexis de Tocqueville had remarked on the curious willingness of Americans to build houses and then move on before living in them, or to plant fields for someone else to harvest. Since then this rootlessness had become pervasive—part and parcel of the American way of life. One apposite phenomenon was the flight into the newly developing suburbs. Another was the great westward movement across the country. A house was seen by many as a temporary shelter, with a life expectancy of a generation or less. It had to be built quickly and cheaply, which meant of wood, and it had to allow for easy modification and even dismantling and moving. And a new way of building houses which was just beginning to come in seemed, if anything, to reinforce this impermanence.

The traditional house was heavy and rigid. The structural frame was made up of sturdy vertical posts and horizontal beams, and it was stiffened with diagonal bracing. The timbers, rough-hewn on the site, were fastened together with rather labored carpentry joints, carved with small hand tools like mallets and chisels. In Downing's day this rigid Colonial braced frame had become lighter, less massive, but the basic structural principle and the nature of the carpentry joints would have been much the same. The siding, which in the earlier period was fixed to the frame with a few large handmade nails, would now make use of machine-made nails which were beginning to be mass-produced about this time. This siding was either the traditional clapboard, or the board-and-batten that Downing preferred because it expressed the vertical timbers of the braced frame supporting the structure.

When cheaply made nails were brought together with another product in the 1830s and 1840s, a major breakthrough in house building took place. That product was the "two by four" stud—thin, uniform strips of lumber, cut at the sawmill, and easily shipped to the building site. With these, and plenty of cheap nails, it was possible to put up a light, efficient frame. No elaborate joints; no separate bracing members. The vertical studs ran continuously, from the sill through the second-floor level to the rafters, with floor plates nailed to their backs. The siding provided what bracing was needed by this light frame of precut members.

Some people thought it was a little too light. They called it, jokingly, balloon-frame construction. But the system was fast; it was cheap; it required no special skills; and it worked. It revolutionized the construction industry. Today, one hundred and fifty years later, this is still the basic construction system we use most commonly to put together houses. It is now called platform framing because the studs no longer reach the full height of the house, but rather join floor platforms laid down at every story. But the principle is much the same—at least in the use of precut parts and light nails.

An even simpler type, the box house, had no frame at all. It was made of wide boards that formed a single-thickness wall. There was no foundation, no interior insulation. It suited the transito-

Frontispiece from Edward Shaw's The Modern Architect; or, Every Carpenter His Own Master, *1855. On the left, in the background, a balloon frame is under construction and, before it, a load of precut lumber arrives in a cart. The architect and builders are in the foreground.*

Construction of a platform frame house, San Fernando, California, 1986.

riness of the frontier, and it was common for lumber company towns and railroad camps.

It is against this prevalence of the house as commodity that reformers like Downing now began to fight. They argued that frequent changes of residence were "destructive of much of that home-feeling which is essential to the education of the affections and moral sentiments," as *Harper's Magazine* put it in 1865—not to mention its being wasteful. J. H. Hammond, the author of a builder's manual for farmers and "mechanics," wrote in 1858 that "a constant moving from house to house causes one to acquire thriftless habits, and is opposed to the practice of a wise and judicious economy."

The sign of a settled life had to be something solidly built. To Downing, this meant brick or stone, but since he recognized that modest cottages could only afford wood, he prescribed vertical siding in the name of structural truthfulness. This concern for durable, honest construction was a requisite of anyone committed to the single dwelling place. And then came the responsibility to have the house "nestle in, or grow out of, the soil"—which meant walls covered with wisteria, trumpet vine, and ivy, a landscaped garden, or more specific, a lawn with no fence around it, and "large and massive trees," preferably forest and not fruit trees. With its ideal rural milieu, this vision of "smiling lawns and tasteful cottages" begins the tradition of garden suburbs.

Open lawns had special meaning for Downing. Traditional house plots were used sensibly; they were plowed and given over to vegetable-growing and medicinal herbs. At a time when animals freely roamed the country roads and town streets, this producing garden was routinely fenced in. But Downing's frontyard was not intended to be utilitarian. It must serve instead to make the transition between the architecture of the house and wild nature. Hence the appropriateness of a lawn, more so than a formal garden of gravel walks and flowerbeds—a lawn that had just the right kind of texture, "grass, not grown into tall meadows, or wild bog tussocks, but softened and refined by frequent touches of the patient mower, till at last it is a perfect wonder of tufted freshness and verdure." In this transition, fences were clearly out of place. A rustic stone wall, old-looking and vine-covered, might be permis-

View of Glendale, Ohio, ca. 1858–65. Glendale was built on the site of a labor camp for the Cincinnati, Hamilton, and Drayton Railroad. The first house was erected in 1852 and the village was incorporated May 22, 1855. (See also color section for a detail of this view.)

sible, and hedges too had their uses, but the common wooden fence was "an abomination of which no person of taste could be guilty." This was the public prospect of the house. Private functions would now be banished to the backyard, where behind a screen of hedges or a board fence, you could tend your vegetable garden and fruit trees and hide a tool shed or even a barn. So much for Jefferson's self-sufficient freeholder and his plot of land.

The first suburb to be designed in sympathy with Downing's writings was probably Glendale, Ohio, midway between Cincinnati and Hamilton. Glendale was a suburb for the well-to-do. It may well be the first commuter village to be laid out with curving streets. The designer, Robert C. Phillips, took advantage of the contour of the land to lay out a scheme that allowed for irregular lots of one to twenty acres.

This was in 1851. The plan included four small parks and a lake, churches, a police station, a village square with a tavern and a grocery store on it, and of course the train depot which served also as social center, voting place, and jail. So the arrangement responded perfectly to the aim of a suburb, which was to combine the benefits of town and country, or as Frederick Law Olmsted was to put it later, "sylvan surroundings . . . with a considerable share of urban convenience."

But it was the houses that mattered, still gracious today after more than a century. They were generously sited, and they had long verandas across the front and outdoor privies. There was often a barn attached, and a carriage house for the horse and carriage that met the train and brought you home. The traditional front-yards, now no longer fenced in, were pleasantly landscaped. Their flowing lawns stressed the sense of a community cut of one cloth and inhabited by one sort of people, the sort—large store owners, brokers, prosperous lawyers, manufacturers, wholesalers—who would move their place of residence away from the city to shun contact with that melting-pot population of immigrants.

And this image quickly became popular. At Riverside outside of Chicago, for example, Olmsted, the most accomplished of Downing's followers, and his partner Calvert Vaux, worked hard to change a piece of flat prairieland into a romantic landscape. They were creating, in their words, "a village in a park" designed for "urban villagers." Thousands of trees were imported to give a more forested look, and they were grouped in irregular clumps. The streets were curved deliberately, despite the level topography, in sympathy with the curves of the Des Plaines River. This sinuous pattern avoided sharp corners and shaped soft-edged lots; but it was also meant to "suggest and imply leisure, contemplativeness and happy tranquillity"—this in contrast to the ramrod town streets which implied "eagerness to press forward, without looking to the right or left." A restrictive covenant would keep the house at least thirty feet back from the front lot line, and the developers made sure that no house cost less than $3,000, a respectable sum at the time of the Civil War.

Yet the Downing formula was also applied to the rectangular frontage lot of the city edge and the gridded subdivisions of the less affluent suburbs. And for the lower middle class, just barely out of the downtown congestion, suburban paradise came in the form of very small single houses and two-family houses, and toward

Triple-deckers in Dorchester, Massachusetts.

the end of the century, in towns like Boston, triple-deckers, tall narrow detached buildings of three apartments, one to a floor. Hardly a rural picture, but at least it did make possible home ownership for many, instead of tenancy. (Such multiple-family houses began to be forbidden by covenants in this century, and zoning laws further restricted nonfamily occupancy.)

Changes Within

The early balloon-frame decades coincided with another dramatic change in domestic design. Machines had started taking away from the craftsman and artisan the ancient tasks of furnishing and em-

Parlor of the Asa Packer mansion. The furniture was machine made by the Philadelphia firm of George Henkel and appeared in 1861 in Homestead Architecture *by the architect Samuel Sloan. Sloan's text describes the sofas and chairs as "one of the grandest Drawing-room suits that can be made. It is very finely and elaborately carved in solid rosewood. . . . The style is now called the 'Napoleon.'" Asa Packer (1805–1879), industrialist, politician, and philanthropist, may have designed the house himself based on Sloan's books.*

bellishing the house. House fittings and appliances, ornament for both exterior and interior, were now made in bulk in factories, and sold in specialty shops or shipped directly to homeowners. For the porches and the dormers and the roof trim, there was a rich choice of milled parts that could turn carpenter Gothic licentious; for parlor and bedroom, there was wall-to-wall carpeting, colorful wallpaper, plush upholstered furniture. Machines laminated, bent, and glued wood into sinuous shapes. Movable saws pierced it into lacy decorative carvings. Playful new furniture types were being invented—love seats, for example, and a kind of spring chair that is the ancestor of the modern revolving, tilting desk chair.

The prices encouraged a mass market and everybody entered the buying fray. You shopped for taste. You leafed through catalogues to put together an image of domestic refinement once open only to wealth and class. Even the very rich were caught up in this excitement of the new machine age.

When Asa Packer, the Pennsylvania coal-mining magnet and founder of Lehigh University, built his mansion in Mauch Chunk (now Jim Thorpe) in the 1860s, he ordered most of his beautiful rosewood furniture from George J. Henkels, the famous Philadelphia cabinetmaker. One of the richest men of his day, Packer was not at all reluctant to avail himself of these machine-made pieces. On the contrary, you feel that he was anxious to be in tune with his time, a modern man who believed in progress and was knowledgeable of recent advances. In the parlor most every piece—the sofa, the side chairs and armchairs, the *étagère*—was straight out of a plate in an architecture book that included illustrations of Henkel's high-quality furniture. With the help of the machine, this furniture was now able to imitate even such complicated handiwork as that of the French Renaissance masters of the sixteenth century.

This was the age of plenty, when rooms were filled with ornamental bric-a-brac and bodies sank in sumptuous, yielding sofas and chairs that the invention of the spiral spring made possible. Gone now was the sober traditional look of house interiors, with their hardwood floors and painted walls, their firm and decorous furniture.

For the housewife, the machine age had even broader implications. By the time of Downing's books, the "age of homespun" was coming to an end. The house had long been a center of production. Women made candles and soap, spun yarn and wove cloth, and stocked the kitchen shelves with butter and cheese and preserved garden vegetables. The house was thought of as "a factory on a farm." But now spinning wheels were becoming obsolete. There were ready-made clothes and blankets to be had. Commercially prepared food and canned goods were no longer a novelty.

So the role of housewife was shifting. She was being released from the traditional chores of home industries, and yet she could not put this newfound freedom to use outside the house since she was almost wholly excluded from the workplace of industry and agriculture. A woman's place was still the home. Her energies were therefore now devoted to being a professional domestic and,

Catharine Beecher, 1800–1878.

with so many ready-made products to choose from, a skilled consumer. She was in charge of a much more complicated physical plant than ever before, and that required specialized planning.

The most influential designer of this domestic environment was a woman—Catharine Beecher, the spinster daughter of a famous New England minister. Beecher believed in and strongly advocated the strict social separation of American life into the male world of work and aggressive competition and a pious, tranquil, female-operated home environment, preferably suburban. So she wasn't much of a feminist in our sense of the word. But in the home, the Christian housewife was to be in full charge of the spiritual and physical well-being of her family—minister and manager in one. Since by this time servants were really out of the question except for the very rich, and even then something of an intrusion into the intimacy of family life, the updated household had to be planned for maximum efficiency and filled with mechanical equipment.

The parlor now became the "home room," the dining room was renamed the "family room." A movable partition—a screen on rollers—transformed a main corner room into a variety of settings as needed. All heating, plumbing, and closets would be concentrated in a central unit in the middle of the house, freeing the edge for light and air. Coal-fired cast-iron stoves had already replaced wood-fired open hearths. Beecher showed how the whole house could be artificially ventilated by a system of flues connected with the stove. The stove room and a compact kitchen were separated by glazed sliding doors that shut out heat and odors, yet let in light.

The greatest changes Beecher envisioned were to take place in the kitchen. She called it the workroom, and systematically rearranged and streamlined it into compact, functional, single-surface work spaces—efficient and sanitary—with cleverly engineered counters and sinks. If the concept could work in a ship's galley, she wondered, why not in the house. In her book, *The American Woman's Home,* she wrote referring to one of her house plans:

The cook's cabin in a steamship has every article and utensil used in cooking for two hundred people, in a space not larger than this stove room [which measures 9 by 7 feet], and so arranged that with one or two steps he can reach all he uses. In contrast to this, in most large houses, the table furniture, the cooking materials and utensils, the sink, and the eating-room, are at such distances apart, that half the time and strength is employed in walking back and forth to collect and return the articles used.

Her design became accepted as the national model by thousands of families. The kitchen she planned for the Hartford home of her sister Harriet Beecher Stowe, her collaborator on *The American Woman's Home* and author of *Uncle Tom's Cabin,* has recently been recreated. It is pleasant, filled with light, and with easy access to the outside. In this kitchen of more than one hundred years ago, we have the beginnings of that standardized modern American kitchen with which we are all familiar.

In the short span of twenty years, then, between 1840 and

The kitchen in Harriet Beecher Stowe's house laid out according to the principles of Catharine Beecher's Woman's Home Companion.

1860, mechanization and the efforts of a handful of reformers like Downing and Beecher brought about a fundamental redefinition of the American house.

Until that time, the basic arrangement of the American house, its general layout, had remained fairly stable. In the harsh, untried new land, at the start, the memories of home and hearth that the European immigrants brought with them had to be forced into local molds. For the Spaniards out West, there was the simple one-story adobe house with dirt floors—not the sparkling tiled patios that we later rather romantically ascribed to them. In the hot riverbands of the South, the French settlers lift their living spaces above the ground and wrap breezy galleries around them.

In the English colonies, the basic house had two rooms, a hall and a parlor, and a chimney in the middle, or in Virginia, chimneys at the two gabled ends bracketing the house. This so-called

I-house, with a second story added to it and a front gallery, would spread south and west, and become associated in time with the well-off rural family. Farther north, there is the familiar New England Colonial house, with its two rooms, an entrance vestibule, and a massive chimney that rivets the house to its site; sometimes a file of secondary rooms is added across the back, in the form of a lean-to which continues the line of the roof.

In the eighteenth century, we have the type of house called "Georgian"—a blocky two-story house, the one-room deep I-house, and the two-room deep house with a central passage running through it. In the two-room deep version, if we remove the pair on one side of the passage, we would have the standard, modest family house of the countryside, which will be with us well into the twentieth century. In fact, here we also have the core of the urban rowhouse, formally speaking, except that it would have to lift itself up in the crowded site and push back from its narrow urban frontage; we can imagine a whole row of these attached houses with similar or identical facades on one or two sides of the street. And without the passageway and the chimney, we are left with the shotgun house of the rural black in the South: two rooms, sometimes more, narrowly stretching away from the street, with the doors and the passageway staggered through the middle of the rooms.

With the likes of Downing, in the middle of the nineteenth century, came an important change. The taste was now for the picturesque, and so the house was reshuffled. The main rooms were arranged in two wings, which were then put together perpendicular to one another, either to form a basic L-shape, with a rakish juxtaposition of gables, or a T-shape with a tower at the crook, so that we get an animated silhouette on the outside. And internally too, the attempt was to break away from the block with bay windows, perhaps a small veranda on the entrance side, a little back porch—all those things that gave the house "feeling" in Downing's discourse.

This preoccupation with letting the house spill out onto its site will only increase as the century goes on, and toward the end of the century we will have in large houses long, elaborate verandas on one or more sides, and projecting wings or bays; and in-

*American house types and
their internal layout.*

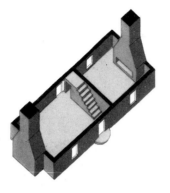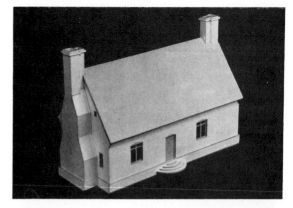

*Two-roof house with end chimneys,
typical of the Colonial South.*

*Hall-and-parlor house with central
chimney, typical of Colonial New
England.*

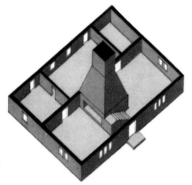

*The same house with lean-to
addition.*

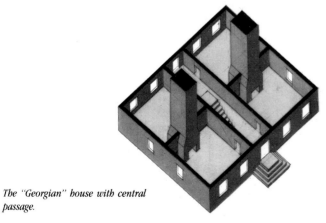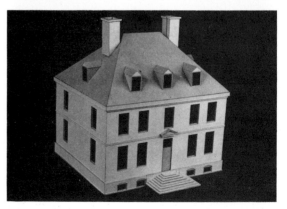

*The "Georgian" house with central
passage.*

Shotgun house.

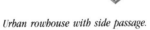

Urban rowhouse with side passage.

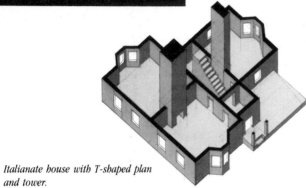

*Italianate house with T-shaped plan
and tower.*

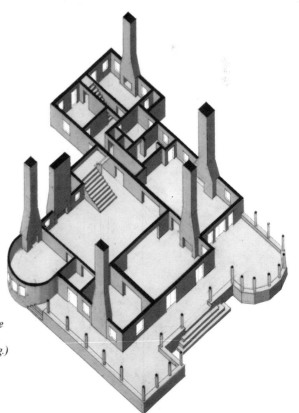

*The "open-plan" house of the late
nineteenth century. (See also the
illustration immediately following.)*

Isaac Bell House, Newport, Rhode Island, 1881–83. A well-known example of the Shingle Style by the firm of McKim, Mead & White.

ternally, space will flow freely between rooms, the partition walls now pierced with wide openings. The sliding door, which had been a component of American house design as early as the 1820s, now comes into its own along with folding doors. And the back of the house, on the garden side, also begins to develop a living terrace, at ground level or very close to it. So by the turn of the century we have all the ingredients of the preferred house arrangement, with the rooms grouped in long rambling wings.

Even in the humble bungalow, for low-income people in the middle and artisan classes, these traits we have singled out find their expression. The word "bungalow" derives from the native Hindustani term for the single-story houses with verandas put up for the British administrators in India. In this country, the bungalow as a year-round house was at first considered suitable only to southern California, but builders soon adapted it for harsher climates. By 1910 it had turned into a national phenomenon, and there are acres of bungalows in Canada as well, Vancouver especially, and in Australia. They were small houses, one story high, often with attics used as sleeping rooms. They sat on very narrow lots, but tried to look woodsy anyway, with rose bushes and vines against a natural-looking, dark-hued skin of plain or stained shakes and clapboarding. No entrance hall, no parlor. You went through a tiny porch or veranda right into the large living room; this was called the "family room," and was connected through an arch with a small dining area—if the dining was not absorbed altogether in the family room. The kitchen was compact, fully equipped with modern conveniences, and planned for efficiency. Often it featured a built-in breakfast nook.

Bungalows often had low, flat-pitched roofs, a fireplace, and plain, sturdy ornament. Since they were cheaper to build and easier to use, they became an exceedingly popular alternative to the standard suburban middle-class dwelling of two stories; and even though there was a rough, do-it-yourself, populist tone about them, they were also appropriated by fancy architects who built grand, costly versions for the well-to-do.

Bungalows along Griffin Avenue, Highland Park, Los Angeles.

While this loosening up, this casualness, characterized the inside all during the second half of the nineteenth century, architects were brilliantly manipulating the exterior dress of the house. All kinds of historical styles were called into service, mixed, and improvised upon. There were Renaissance and Second Empire, Queen Anne and Eastlake, Romanesque and Norman, Shingle Style and Georgian Revival, Mission and Tudor. The houses now no longer depended for their effect on fancy landscaping and a large lot, but rather tended toward a public presence by favoring a large shape on a relatively small lot. Accordingly, most of the styles they employed avoided the romantic, rural look of earlier decades, and strained for a more public, more imposing look.

And something else too: the difference between the dwellings of the wealthy and the not so wealthy was much greater now than it had ever been. Until 1880 or thereabouts, Americans on the

Left page. *The Allen House, Des Moines, Iowa, 1865–69. This example of a French Second Empire style house was designed by W. W. Boyington.*

At left. *Detail of the Peter Davis House, Noank, Connecticut, built ca. 1852. Noank was a center of shipbuilding in the early nineteenth century. Peter Davis was one of four brothers, all sailors and carpenters, who built houses above the harbor.*

whole steered clear of showy, monumental houses that could be called palaces or mansions. The scale, of course, varied between upper-class neighborhoods and those of the middle class, but the general tone of the residential landscape stayed much the same. Ostentation had its place indoors. Downing had made the case against conspicuous grandeur in relation to country houses: we were not to aspire to "those old manor-houses and country halls of England" because ours was a republic and our homes had to remain unostentatious and moderate, "large enough to minister to all the wants, necessities, and luxuries of a republican, and not too large or too luxurious to warp the life or manners of his children." At century's end these sentiments were only faintly echoed. Amassed wealth and extravagant fortunes advertised openly. The decorous house of the well-to-do could now lapse without embarrassment into the gaudy or the grand.

The Legacy of Wright

There was one architect, however, a man of genius in Chicago, who scorned this mood of exhibition, the great eclectic gaggle on suburban streets. He asked why it was that the house, which now sheltered a new, modern way of life, could not find a modern architectural solution that would be consistent throughout. His name was Frank Lloyd Wright, and that name was to dominate American architecture for almost sixty years. During his long and sparkling career, Wright was to design some great American houses but, more important, he would supply builders with a vast wealth of ideas for the revision of the common house—things like a heated concrete "floormat" which sits on a drained gravel bed for insulation, the carport, deep overhanging eaves, and long narrow window bands.

He set up shop in Oak Park, in suburban Chicago, in the 1890s. And for the next twenty years he filled the area with the most extraordinary family of houses—rich, creative, infinitely varied. To see the freshness and courage of this work, you should remember that it went up in the midst of a wild variety of pic-

Frank Lloyd Wright (seated at the right) and his family outside their Oak Park home, 1890.

The Frank Thomas house in Oak Park, Illinois, Frank Lloyd Wright, 1901. This is Wright's first prairie house in Oak Park.

turesque exteriors—what Wright contemptuously described later as "Gables, dormers, minarets, bays, porches, oodles of jiggered woodwork ruthlessly painted, poking in or peeking out of piles of fancified stonework and playing idiotic tricks with each other . . ."

But his own houses were not meant to shock or to be aggressively revolutionary. Wright was then a respectable family man, and so were his clients. In fact, while the prairie house he created was his attempt to ameliorate what he called "the pernicious social fabric so excruciated by ornament," it was at the same time, this house type, a summation of the anti-urban trends of the previous one hundred years, from Jefferson onward, and a very original reaffirmation of the suburban ideal.

There is in Wright, foremost, the Jeffersonian belief in the independent family on its own plot of land. And in him you can detect Downing's romantic streak for natural setting and natural materials, even though Wright treats these things differently. The masses of the prairie house are low and spreading, the horizontality reflecting the earth-lines of his native Midwest—hence the name "prairie house." And he works nature right into the facade of his house with plant-filled urns and built-in window boxes, at the same time that he uses these to emphasize the rectangular shape of the suburban lot.

The house at Riverside, Illinois, designed in 1907 for Ferdinand Tomek, who made wooden moldings, shows how uniquely Wright interpreted contemporary trends toward the open plan and the blending of indoor and outdoor spaces. He did away with what remained of the boxiness of the traditional house. He made the main floor one continuous open space in which living, dining, and other common rooms are made to flow into each other. He wrote at the time: "There need be but one room, the living room, with requirements otherwise sequestered from it or screened within it by means of architectural contrivances." This interpenetration of volumes was emphasized by continuous horizontal trim both inside and out.

And yet the cellarless prairie house sitting on its concrete slab foundation is anything but open and public. The overhanging eaves protect the narrow window bands that are Wright's trademark; the doors and windows are not readily apparent from the outside. All this, and the low ceilings of the rooms that make for a cozy interior ambience, stressed the suburban ideal of the house as a private world sheltering the family against all intrusions. Frederick C. Robie said of the house Wright designed for him in 1906 that it enabled him to "look out and down the street to my neighbors without having them invade my privacy." And looking back on this early work in his older age, Wright himself would write that *"Shelter* should be the essential look of any dwelling."

The Dana-Thomas House at Springfield, Illinois, built in 1902–4 and now a state museum, was for a very wealthy socialite, Susan Lawrence Dana. So it's much grander, more lavish than the other prairie houses. It has a cruciform plan and a two-story-high living room. Hundreds of stained glass panels were used in windows and skylights, lamps and cabinet doors, and they shaped glassed corridors and hallways that connected the main living and entertainment spaces. Their design stylized sumac, wheat, butterflies, and other flora and fauna of the prairie. All these fittings, and all the furniture of fumed red oak, were designed by Wright and executed by an exceptional group of artisans and craftsmen whom he had brought together. Under his watchful eye, Richard W. Bock did terracotta sculpture for the vestibule and the reception hall, and George Niedecken painted murals for the dining room that were respectful of the architectural frame. They point up another aspect of the prairie house as a design in tune with the progressive trends of its time—and that is its emphasis on preindustrial imagery and a crafts-oriented aesthetic.

The reaction against the industrial world, against the flood of machine-made accessories that had transformed the traditional house, was fairly widespread in the late nineteenth century. One sign of this reaction was the popularity of the Colonial revival which was spurred on by the Philadelphia Centennial Exposition of 1876 and would reach full maturity in the Twenties with the restoration of Colonial Williamsburg through the sponsorship of John D. Rockefeller.

Along with this nostalgic look back at an innocent period of our past came the rejection of factory products like wallpaper and the return to hardwood floors, simple, sturdy "homemade" fittings, and built-in furniture. This is the reason for the purposely cultivated "natural" look of bungalows—the stress on exposed wood, on the heavily crafted detail, the ponderous Stickley furniture. Wright appropriated this retrospective mood. You see it in the massive fireplace that rivets the long low wings of his prairie house, in the prominently exposed beams of his ceilings, the stained and waxed wood detailing, the exquisitely made furniture that he designed specifically for the individual rooms. But even though Wright hated the machine-made world of contemporary interiors, he never rejected the machine itself. He believed that in the hands of the able architect it could be made to add to the quality of the work, and even to help create texture, pattern, ornament. He wrote in 1908:

The machine is here to stay. It is the forerunner of the democracy that is our dearest hope. There is no more important work before the architect now than to use this normal tool of civilization to the best advantage instead of prostituting it as he has hitherto done in reproducing with murderous ubiquity forms born of other times and other conditions and which it can only serve to destroy.

But a nagging problem remained unresolved: How to reconcile the idea of the house as a free expression of its owner-occupant and still create a disciplined general order that would signify a harmonious community. Wright experimented with various groupings of his houses. In 1901 he published the "quadruple block plan" in *Ladies Home Journal,* which showed how variations of the same prairie house scheme could be grouped in fours, straddling the suburban streets. He built duplexes in Milwaukee, basically one house on top of another, and arranged three in a row. This was meant to serve as a model for such compact housing. Another model is the so-called Suntop Homes at Ardmore, Pennsylvania, these from the early Thirties; here Wright created a cloverleaf pattern by combining four, single-family houses into a cross formed by two perpendicular party walls, and he could still give each unit the privacy of a detached house. The units are three stories high, with a double-height living room, three bedrooms, a carport, a private garden, and ample balcony and terrace space in the upper floors. The type was what he called "Usonian," the successor to the prairie house—an inexpensive dwelling fit for the Depression years. It was designed on a module, relying on economy measures like bathrooms with standardized fixtures, or wood "sandwich construction" which eliminated the need for plastering and decoration.

Wright even stretched this Ardmore solution into a tall apartment house for New York, even though he had no love for this kind of dwelling. It was to go next to the church of St. Mark's-in-the-Bouwerie in the East Village. What Wright conceived was a freestanding tower, treelike in its organization, rising abruptly from the ground. In the center he put a hollow concrete shaft which contained utilities. Four fins projected from this shaft and supported interlocked two-story apartment floors which cantilevered out and were sheathed in glass and copper. The apartments were lavish, with private elevators and fireplaces. At entry level was found the kitchen with the dining and living areas; upstairs, off the diagonal balcony that overlooked the living room, were a bedroom, a boudoir that could double as a second bedroom, and a bath. The project remained on the boards. A version was finally built in 1953 at Bartlesville, Oklahoma, as Price Tower where

St. Mark's Tower, New York, designed by Wright in 1929. Nine years later the architect wrote of the design: "This building, earthquake, fire and soundproof from within, by economics inherent in its structure weighs less than half the usual tall building and increases the area available for living by more than twenty percent. It is a logical development of the idea of a tall building in the age of glass and steel, as logical engineering as the Brooklyn Bridge or an ocean liner. But the benefits of modernity such as this are not merely economic. There is greater privacy, safety, and beauty for human lives within it than is possible in any other type of apartment building."

Suntop Homes, Ardmore, Pennsylvania, 1939. The buildings are divided into quarters, each quarter with two living stories, a basement, and a sunroof. Only one unit was built at Ardmore, although four were originally planned, each angled differently to allow for greater privacy.

only one corner in each pair of floors was apartment space; the rest was devoted to offices.

St. Mark's Tower—"dignified as a tree in the midst of nature, but a child of the spirit of man," Wright said of it—was as different from the contemporary New York apartment blocks as was his prairie house in the eclectic company of suburban domestic architecture. The multistoried apartment block had established itself in the more populous cities of America by 1920 as an inevitable outcome of density. New York had discovered the apartment house first, in the 1870s—in Paris. In fact, the building type was called "French flats" at first, and the room names on plans were given in French. The impetus came of course from the phenomenal overcrowding of Manhattan which more or less doomed single-family townhouses. In Chicago, where there was plenty of room to spread, the fashion started with the Great Fire of 1871, after which more people wanted to live along the lakeshore than could be accommodated in private houses.

The initial draw to apartment living was that you could have centralized services and the latest in technology applied to domestic comforts—central hot-water heating, central gas mains for lighting, central vacuum-cleaning systems, switchboard operators, fully equipped bathrooms for every unit, and a garbage chute from the kitchen to a common incinerator. You could dine in elegance at the public dining room and have clothes done in steam laundries in the basement. A little later on, internal privacy began to be emphasized instead of centralized services, and luxury and fantasy invaded the exterior. Majestic, opulent, dense blocks were now put up, like the Dorilton on West Seventy-first Street—"The sight of it makes strong men swear and weak women shrink affrighted," the *Architectural Record* noted at the time— or the Ansonia nearby, on West Seventy-third Street and Broadway, which is really a standard apartment building or resort hotel in France blown to immense proportions. And there were other differences besides the obvious one of scale between our massive highrises and the usual five- to six-story apartment building in Paris. Our model was generally residential. In Paris we would find ground-floor stores with their elegant merchandise on display and sidewalk cafes out front.

The interior of the "Fountain Room" in New York's Ansonia apartment building, ca. 1910.

The apartment houses, which were slow getting started, had found a sizable clientele in the early years of this century when the Dorilton and the Ansonia were going up. They were especially popular with the newly married, bachelors, and widows—"the newly wed and the nearly dead," as the saying went. Plans for about fifty of these residential towers per year were filed from 1900 on. Many offered a variety of units, from efficiency bachelor apartments to large family units with parlor, library, and servants' rooms. But the pitch was to the wealthy. There were frequent descriptions of how the French lived in luxurious apartments, often in preference to villas or private houses, when in reality the occupancy of Parisian apartment houses was socially mixed, with the upper stories relegated to moderate incomes and lowly folk tucked away in the attic. And this catering to those most conscious of social status had its effect. We read of people like Mrs. E. F. Hutton, for example, who had a fifty-four room apartment on three floors at 1107 Fifth Avenue that made up for the townhouse on this site she had agreed to sell the builder! Even the middle

The Ansonia, built between 1899 and 1904, originally had shops in the basement, a roof garden, and two swimming pools. Its apartments had a diversity of rooms, including round reception rooms and parlors and oval dining rooms, some with semicircular sculpture niches. The heavy fireproof interior partitions between apartments soundproofed the building making it particularly attractive to musicians, who could practice without disturbing neighbors. The musical celebrities who lived there include Enrico Caruso, Lauritz Melchior, Enzio Pinza, Lily Pons, Igor Stravinsky, and Arturo Toscanini.

class began to respond to publicity. In Chicago the luxury high-rises were emulated in the so-called flat buildings—three-or four-story rowhouses, often grouped together in E- or U-shaped blocks—that had of course far fewer amenities and simpler, less ornate exteriors.

At the beginning, the rooms in these New York apartments were arranged in rows opening out of long, long corridors. In time, the preferred layout featured the foyer as a principal circulating space, from which you could move directly to the living room or the library. At least one architect, the Parisian-born Philip Hubert, insisted that his apartments were "small private dwelling houses." He used sturdy masonry construction to isolate and soundproof his apartments. The vertical arrangement of the rooms on two floors eliminated a major objection to apartment-living— that it was improper to have the bedrooms on the same floor as the parlor.

Still, in the public eye there was something racy, something bohemian about apartment-living. The *Architectural Record* in January 1903 chided the spread of this mode of living beyond its tolerable uses—by bachelors, businessmen, and New York families who lived most of the year in the country but needed a pied-à-terre in the city. Apartment-living, they editorialize, is

the consummate flower of domestic irresponsibility. It means the sacrifice of everything implied by the word "home." No one could apply such a word to two rooms and a bath. A "home" is a place in which the joint life of a married couple has some chance of individual expression; it is more particularly the centre around which the interests and activities of a woman's life are grouped. But a woman who lives in an apartment hotel has nothing to do. She resigns in favor of the manager.

For some women at least, this was exactly the appeal of apartment-living—that it promised the release from domestic chores and child-rearing. All occupants associated their mode of housing with efficiency and modernity. They lived near restaurants and theaters— many apartment houses were on or near Broadway or Fifth Avenue—and had a grand edifice, identifiable by its size and unique style, to call home.

This perception has kept the luxury apartment alive until the present, despite the overwhelming American preference for the single-family house. After the Second World War it embraced the metal-and-glass purity of the modernist idiom. The German émigré Ludwig Mies van der Rohe perfected a rarified version of this new apartment building, and his school filled the Gold Coast and other lakeshore areas of his adopted city, Chicago, with light and gleaming Miesian towers which, contrary to their substantial predecessors fully occupying their block and breathing through an interior courtyard, sat back from the street on an airy frame of piers.

The Red Hook Houses, a housing project in New York City (Brooklyn) 1939–40.

The Postwar Decades

At about the time when the rich in New York and Chicago were being sold on the idea of the apartment house, the same tall massive blocks, now barren and minimal, were being raised for the very poor—at the edges of the residential fabric. These subsidized model tenements, or projects as they came to be called, sometimes managed a decent look, but in the end they only helped to institutionalize poverty. They became the gathering place for unskilled indigents who had little chance of bettering themselves.

What to do with the poor in a country of plenty became a national problem back in the 1830s, with the first waves of mass immigration from abroad. There had always been poor people of course who had to make do. They improvised their own shelters out of scrap materials, and still do—minimal shacks that run afoul of building codes and health ordinances and often defy established patterns of ownership. But in the big cities where many thousands were beached and had to stay, this sort of improvisation did not go very far. Something had to be done about the vast numbers of people who could not afford a house, and who were not socially acceptable in neighborhoods with decent rental property because of color or ethnic identity.

They crowded together with their own kind, where they could or were allowed to. In pockets of the inner city, on the rim of the central business district, they turned into steamy ghettoes the property vacated by homeowners, or comfortably well-off renters who moved out for better urban or suburban locations. Or a ghetto might start from scratch in some unfavorable margin, like the deteriorating edge of an industrial zone or along an affordable transportation line.

Ethnicity and slums always went hand in hand. The dominant element of society was never happy with the prospect of sharing their neighborhoods with alien folk. But the picture of these hemmed-in subcultures did not always look the same. Even today the spectrum ranges from New York's Harlem to San Francisco's Chinatown. The first is the more familiar image. We have been taught to recognize as a slum an area of crumbling and burnt-out buildings, of idle people hanging out in littered streets, of visible congestion and vacant lots.

In San Francisco the few picturesque streets north of Union Square so appealing to tourists—pagoda-shaped street lamps, curved eaves and painted balconies, shops with exotic wares and foods—are also unenviable. Behind the brightly colored facades live thousands of people, at least one-half of them elderly, crammed into the tiny single rooms of residential hotels. The small square city blocks are built up to their maximum capacity; there is scarcely any open space. Outside Manhattan this may be the densest residential quarter of the country. And the heartless overcrowding is the result of a long history of restrictive measures and discrimination against the Chinese.

The wretched conditions of New York's slums in the nineteenth century were well known to contemporaries. We have the classic photographs of Jacob Riis, the journalist and social reformer, and the comments of notable observers to remind us. Charles Dickens left a searing description of an early tenement called Five Points:

. . . lanes and alleys paved with mud knee-deep, underground chambers, where they dance and game . . . ruined houses, open to the street, whence, through wide gaps in the walls, other ruins loom upon the eye, as though the world of vice and misery had nothing else to show.

In response to the horror of these settings, the Tenement House Act of 1867 ushered in some basic improvements. A tougher law, passed in 1901, set strict standards of ventilation, sanitary facilities, and low density. Private enterprise virtually stopped building tenements since the law had made them unprofitable, and this happened precisely at the time when immigration was peaking. That is why the municipal authorities reluctantly stepped in.

The federal government, mindful that subsidized housing was vehemently opposed by public opinion, did not become involved

One of the thousands of homes and farms foreclosed during the Depression.

in a big way until the Thirties. And then it insisted on a "no frills" design, which led invariably to a drab uniform barrenness; and on standard unit plans, which killed any individualizing variety. The prosperity that followed the Second World War was enough to elevate most low-income workers to the ranks of the middle class. Public housing, consequently, came to hold only dropouts and the unemployed. Furthermore, those who managed to rise above a minimum wage level were disqualified as public housing tenants and had to leave. During this time, "problem families" were routinely evicted. This attitude on the part of the authorities, the belief that public housing was a form of charity that can be withheld and not an urgent necessity, caused bitter resentment among its beneficiaries. They were stigmatized by those empowered to provide for them. By the Fifties, unsurprisingly, the projects had turned into battlefields of crime and vandalism.

Meanwhile the federal government was busy subsidizing homeownership. This effort had overwhelming support. The truth is that apartment-living was never considered a genuine choice by either the rich or the poor. It never found general acceptance as the American way. To own a house remained the American dream. But for most Americans until the Second World War that is all the single-family house was—a dream. In 1920 only one in three families owned houses. In the Thirties the situation became worse. Now even those who had houses were losing them. More than a thousand mortgages were foreclosed every day.

So an earnest search got under way in the public and the private sector to see how the American dream could be made accessible to a greater number of our citizens. The campaign to extend homeownership advanced along two fronts. One of these fronts mobilized the financial sector. The Federal Housing Administration and the Veterans' Administration were established as agencies that insured long-term loans with low-interest rates, and the interest on mortgages was soon made tax free. This laid the ground work for an unprecedented national commitment to homeownership. Today, statistically at least, two-thirds of all American families live in their own houses, although it goes without saying that this proportion is much lower for some ethnic minorities.

The second front engaged the building industry. It was im-

Construction of a prefabricated house, in Pacolet, South Carolina, 1941.

perative to produce cheap, affordable houses, which meant that ways had to be found to mass-produce them, somewhat along the lines of automobiles. Standardization of some machine-made parts, practiced at least since the invention of the scroll saw, was simply not enough. Whole houses, or sections of houses, had to be prefabricated.

This was not in itself a new idea. Prefabricated balloon-frame houses were shipped along railroad lines during the decades of Western expansion. By the end of the nineteenth century, mail-order houses could be purchased from Sears and Montgomery Ward at prices ranging from less than $1,000 to $2,500. The precut materials for these sturdy wooden houses arrived in railroad boxcars and were taken to the site by horse and wagon. The package included all the members of the frame, notched and mitered and numbered to identify their place in the house, but also built-in cabinets, nails by the keg, and varnish for floors and trim. Only the foundation, the chimney, and the stuccowork had to be produced locally. In time Sears was operating large lumber mills in Cairo, Illinois, Port Newark, New Jersey, and Norwood, Ohio, and was busy introducing building innovations like Goodwall Sheet

Plaster, an early form of drywall board used as an alternative to plaster lath, and asphalt shingles. In 1900 Sears could boast in its advertisements that "Enough houses have been built according to our plans and with our materials to shelter a city of 25,000 people." Between 1909 and 1937 they had sold 100,000 mail-order "Honor Bilt" houses. Many of them are still around. Hellertown, Pennsylvania and South Plainfield, New Jersey have dozens each, but the record, 192 in all, is held by Carlinville, Illinois, where the Standard Oil Company erected them for its employees.

Some experiments were also made with new materials and new building methods. The aim was to speed up production and lower housing costs. Concrete blocks found their use in the minimal housing for agricultural laborers, but they could also be upgraded by being covered with stucco. There was metal lumber after the Second World War and aluminum siding. There was the proposal of a man named Grosvenor Atterbury, in the second decade of this century, to put up precast houses of concrete: one- to three-ton concrete panels that would form the walls, floors, and roof of the house could be transported by truck to the site and lifted into place by a crane that, traveling along a track, could work on several houses in a row. The panels would then be worked over with a wire brush, to bring out the texture of the gravel aggregate and lend aesthetic interest to the surface. Dormers, entrance porches, and vines would make the thing look homier. Some of these houses were actually built in the new community of Forest Hill Gardens on Long Island. And then there was Buckminster Fuller's Dymaxion House of 1927—a mass-produced circular structure made of aluminum, glass, plastic, and rubber, built around a central aluminum pole. The house was portable, filled with gadgets like a self-activating laundry unit, a humidifier, and pneumatic beds, and had its own electric generator.

Fuller ridiculed the convoluted and archaic process of designing and building a house in the conventional way by describing what it would be like if we acquired our automobiles in the same way. It would be, he wrote, as if the man wanting to buy an automobile

were to visit one of five thousand automobile designers in New York City, equivalent to New York's five thousand architects, and were to commence his

A California tract under construction, mid-1950s. Left, *after pouring the house and garage foundations;* right, *the houses nearing completion but before any landscaping.*

retention of the designer by the limitation that he wanted the automobile to resemble outwardly a Venetian gondola, a jinricksha of the Tang Dynasty, a French fiacre, or a Coronation coach of Great Britain . . .; and he and the "designer" were together to pick and choose (from automobile accessory catalogues, advertisements, and "shows") motors, fly wheels, fenders, frame parts offered in concrete, brass, sugar cane fiber, walnut, *etcetera,* and succeeded in designing an automobile somewhat after the style of some other fellow; and they were then to have the design bid upon by five local garages in Queens

Village . . .; and the local bank, in loaning the money to the prospective "owner" . . . had some practical man look over the plans so that, guessing at the cost, he might base a loan thereon, incidentally insisting on the replacement of several parts and methods by others in which the bank was "interested" . . .

But all attempts to produce houses like cars on an assembly line came to nothing. To have any estimable success with that process, you needed a huge buying public and the techniques of mass production. But mass acceptance was not there—for a number of reasons. The factory-built house was the natural enemy of conventional lending agencies and of unions representing our craft-oriented labor practices. Besides, the diversity of local building ordinances and codes made the regional or national distribution of mass-produced houses extremely difficult. As for buyers, they insisted on the traditional custom-tailored look, shying away from prefabricated houses that veered too far from that image. What they wanted were familiar styles—and Frank Lloyd Wright notwithstanding, the eclectic taste of the consumer for exteriors that carried historical associations was still much in evidence. Then too, the buyer's idea of a reasonable quality house had more to do with the neighborhood, the view, the landscaping, than it had with the speed and cost of construction.

It was after the Second World War that mass production found its chance. When the veterans returned by the millions, conditions were finally right. There was a huge market for houses, and New Deal financing policies made borrowing easy. Enterprising merchant-builders like Levitt, Eichler, and Henry J. Kaiser organized on a big scale and started producing standardized, or rather "semi-prefabricated," houses that were near-perfect replicas of traditional site-built houses. The veteran had gone to fight for home and family, and he was now back to claim a fitting reward—a house of his own. Armed with a VA loan, he could see his dream materialize in no time at all. There was still plenty of cheap land in the vastness of the country, and it seemed inexhaustible. The houses were transported to the site on trucks and put up in rows in an efficient process that resembled the assembly line. The great builders could put up houses at the rate of about one hundred and fifty a week. Buyers could choose from several models, and appliances like washing machines or, later, built-in television sets, included in the mortgage loan, made the houses more attractive. On the whole, the East Coast stuck by traditional styles like the Cape Cod, the saltbox, the Colonial, while the West Coast experimented more freely with houses that had a modern look.

So they started to spread like crabgrass, those patches of suburbia housing people of the same generation, in the same financial bracket. In 1947 the first Levittown got going, in Hicksville, on the Long Island flats—four-and-a-half room identical houses, six thousand of them occupying only twelve percent of their 60-by-

Mobile home construction at the Friendship Industries Mobile Home Plant, Napanee, Indiana, 1986.

100-foot lots. Then came Levittown in Bucks County, Pennsylvania. Meanwhile across the country, in California, Eichler homes were blanketing Palo Alto at the annual rate of 300 to 400 units, and were soon spreading to Sacramento and Los Angeles. These were not true prefabricated houses of course, since a good bit of building was still done on the site. Prefabrication as such has not prevailed. We have settled for the next best thing—full standardization. Today, building a house entails the assembling of standard parts into traditional shapes. We use standard materials in standard sizes, standard doors and windows, standard heating, standard bath and kitchen components. But the whole thing is still put together on the site by hand. Each one of us still likes to think of our new house as something personal, responsive to our own family's requirements and ambitions.

But there is one experiment where prefabrication has paid off—the trailer. Trailers are indeed produced like cars and financed like them. Today one of them can be assembled in the factory in just three days, and they come off the line fully equipped and furnished. Divorced from bondage to a piece of land and the crippling cost entailed, and exempt from property tax, the mobile home is a bargain for those who will not give up the Jeffersonian vision of the independent freeholder in his cottage, but cannot afford the real thing.

Actually, mobile homes have little to do with mobility—the lure of being able to pick up and go whenever the spirit moves you. The only trip for most mobile homes is the first one, from the factory to the site. There the wheels are removed, the fake brick flap is lowered to ground the vehicle visually, or other kinds of "skirting" are resorted to in order to mask the underside. Soon

Newly arrived mobile homes, Almond Heights, Palmdale, California.

Mobile home, Palmdale, California.

lean-to porches, terraces, and gardens are added to root the trailer with symbolic forms and make it look like an authentic home.

And the neighborhood is also simulated. Mobile homes cluster in parks across the country, the largest among them capable of holding as many as 700 homes. Trailer parks like Brookview in Concord, California, are really not distinguishable from ordinary suburbs. They even have community facilities, most prominent, a recreation building which holds meeting rooms, game rooms, and sometimes even a library with a massive fireplace. With all this the attitude toward the mobile home is fast changing. The industry now prefers to call it "the manufactured house"; a conventional mortgage loan for it is becoming accessible; and restrictions are being eased on where within a town's limits it is allowed to stand.

It is a poignant symbol, the trailer, of those abiding conflicts of American existence—to seek freedom and mobility and yet yearn for roots; to treasure privacy but seek the reassurance of neighbors; to accept all sorts of modern gadgets and conveniences and yet insist on the traditional messages of a public presence—shutters and Colonial doors and pitched roofs.

But the remarkable spread of trailers in the Seventies, especially among young married couples without children and the elderly retired, raises something more immediate. The postwar tide

The Smith house, 1965–67, Darien, Connecticut, Richard Meier, architect. The house is made of wood, with a brick chimney. The glazed wall shown here looks out over Long Island Sound.

of suburban expansion, reaching into virgin stretches farther and farther out from metropolitan concentrations, appears to have been stemmed. For one thing, more and more people in the last fifteen years have been discovering the inner city. The decaying neighborhoods are being rehabilitated and occupied by a more affluent population, typically young professionals. Then too, large numbers of young people today do not live as married nuclear families, for which the suburban ideal was intended. Since 1970, the number of unmarried couples living together has more than tripled. What is more, a majority of married women now hold jobs that compete with their traditional role as "the minister of home." Without that long-established casting of homemaker and provider, the American dream is beginning to come undone.

Most detrimental of all is that the dream is not affordable for many in the customary middle-class housing market. Builders and lending agencies, fixed on the model they have been providing for more than one hundred years, will not let go. They stall by devising schemes of "creative financing," and by marketing tiny houses and something called a condominium, a word which connotes

Lakeshore Drive Apartments, Chicago, 1950, Ludwig Mies Van der Rohe, architect.

"shared control." Condominiums are commonly multifamily houses made up of units of similar or identical design. Owners of both condominiums and cooperative apartments share responsibilities for the maintenance of the building and for services. Meanwhile, the old residential neighborhoods zoned for single-family houses are readjusting in an ad hoc way with in-law apartments, internal subdivisions, and the return of work to the house. The pressure is on to relax zoning restrictions and regain some measure of mixed use based on the model of our pre-suburban cities.

Whatever its present troubles, however, the dream is not likely to go away. There are obvious advantages, of course, to living in your own house, with breathing space between yourself and your neighbors; that kind of freedom and privacy you don't give up easily. But that's not the end of it. We have before us the example of the past, the comfort of belonging to a country which through the years has made it possible, however selectively and with all the familiar inequities, for most of its people to have a house of their own, and probably no other modern country quite matches that record. The family homestead has been our national faith and its church is the house—the house we own and protect, keep up and add to, an ell here, an extra room there. In the swift shifting currents of our day, then as now, this is the rock that sits fast: this is the one bit of America we hold title to.

And then, of course, the most human want of all—the want to be visible, to stand out and be counted. It's the shingle house on the corner, we say, with the big elm out front, you can't miss it, it has a green door and brown trim. And that want is surely more basic, more deeply felt, than all the reasonable arguments that point to the task of creating alternative American dreams.

To do that sort of thinking, to reassess in earnest the two fundamental beliefs that have shaped the American house since the days of Jefferson and Downing—home ownership and the single-family detached house in the suburbs—would involve a change of attitude toward things we have long held sacred. It would mean, for example, considering more seriously the possibilities of partial or cooperative ownership. It would mean broad acceptance of apartment living as a permanent type of residence, and this acceptance must be buttressed by financial inducements like the tax relief traditionally enjoyed by mortgage-paying homeowners but not by tenants. It would mean that we would have to learn not to see every criticism of the American dream as an attack on the American family. And finally, it would mean that we would have to acknowledge the presence, and needs, of Americans who are single, widowed, or unmarried and living with partners, and that we would stop considering this vast population as abnormal.

Only with that kind of broad reeducation will politicians, builders, and the public search for alternatives to the gilded American dream. Only then will the home be an affordable place of comfort and peace, a flexible frame for the coexistence of the sexes, and not the gauge of our success or the anachronistic shrine of that long-time religion of the male provider and the female homemaker.

But while the future finds its course, we can look back and treasure the range of American houses—the grand mansions and urbane rows, the simple honest shelters and the dazzling abstractions of our gifted architects, the wood or stone or stucco elegances of Olmsted subdivisions, California bungalows, Miesian glass

House in Belvedere, California, 1957, George Rockrise, architect.

Two Worlds Condominium Complex, 1981, Mountain View, California. The complex marks a return to the design of mixed-use spaces that combine house and workplace.

A 1970s suburban housing development in South San Francisco.

boxes, the hip-roofed cluster houses of Puget Sound, and the shingle marvels of Newport and Nantucket. And as we admire and treasure this wealth, we can expect to add to it ourselves. Our houses, individually, will always express the intimate bond that exists between humans and the places where they are born and raised, where they quarrel and love and age. Cumulatively, our houses have been, and will continue to be, the fullest record we have of our existence as a people, of our collective memories, our hopes and our reach.

2

The American Workplace

Saco, Maine: when the first textile mill was built here about one hundred and fifty years ago, it provided employment all of a sudden for hundreds of men and women. They came from far away to operate the bale breakers, pickers, carding machines, the spinning frames, and looms; they burled the woven cloth and bleached or dyed it; they brushed and napped it, steamed it to make the colors fast, washed and stretched it on tenter frames, folded it and packed it for shipment. At the end of their long day, they walked across the bridge over the canal, to houses put up for them by the company. This was where they belonged; this was where they would end their days. Through all the toil and hardships, they saw themselves as one large family that worked and lived together, industriously and decently and proudly.

They are there in great numbers—old textile mills by fast-flowing New England rivers, their great millyards empty, the red brick buildings along the water's edge abandoned and rundown. The looms are junked: the rooms that held them are stripped down to their elemental frame—hardwood floors, rows of cast-iron

Saco, Maine, interior of an abandoned textile mill.

posts, the walls punctured end to end with large contiguous windows. If you listen carefully, you might still hear the sounds of the last century echo in these rooms, sounds of the coming of the industrial age.

Dearborn, Michigan: the Ford Motor Company on the River Rouge, not far from Henry Ford's home at Fair Lane. Daily, for more than fifty years, this has been a place of work to tens of thousands of workers. They came by streetcar, in private busses and jitneys, and in the Model A's, the T-birds, the Mustangs they were here to manufacture. They spread out to fill over forty buildings in an area that was a mile and a half long and three-quarters of a mile wide. They stoked the furnaces, manned the rolling mills and presses; they machined hundreds of individual parts; they stood in the assembly line and, with smart teamwork and split-second timing, they put together cars at the rate of more than fifty an hour. This awesome setting was a triumph of Henry Ford's hope to "lift," as he said, "drudgery off flesh and blood and lay it on steel and motors."

The Ford Motor Company at River Rouge, Dearborn, Michigan.

Chicago, Illinois: the Sears Tower on Wacker Drive. Its 110 stories are piled in a series of setbacks and rise almost 1,500 feet above ground. It is the tallest private office building anywhere and headquarters of the largest retail business in the world. Twenty-five thousand people file in and out of this building every day. They come to man the telephones, typewriters, and computers; to analyze and plan; to debate and decide. And what they decide in this lofty nerve center of a modern corporation will affect 450,000 company employees across the country and beyond.

These are some of the workplaces of America. For over two hundred years they have left unforgettable monuments like these on the face of the nation—monuments that mark the cities and the countryside as grandly and fatefully as pyramids and New Kingdom temples mark the Nile fringes, or cathedrals the townscapes of Christian Europe. New England mills, industrial plants of all kinds, the grain elevators of the Great Plains and the warehouses of St. Louis, the office towers of Chicago, Houston, and New York that celebrate the energies of urban America—all bear witness to the range and long success of American enterprise. For the world outside they stand as symbols of the American way of life. And for those millions who have spent their days in these great buildings, and do today, they represent that special bond between work and self, our place in the scheme of things, a bond that is at once restrictive and nurturing.

Working Close to Home

For most of us today, the workplace is the place we travel to every morning. It may be within walking distance from where we live or, as likely, at the end of a long bus or subway ride, or a crowded, slow-moving commute by car. But there was a time, during our early years on this continent, when house and workplace were one and the same.

For its first two hundred years, America was a nation of farms— the land the most common of American workplaces. Family mem-

The Sears Tower, Chicago.

Quiet Valley Living Historical Farm in Snyderville, Pennsylvania. This working farm also operates as a museum, with live animals, a large kitchen garden, and two demonstration plots for grain growing.

bers were the labor force with perhaps an extra "hand" in pressing times. The closest neighbors lived a mile or two away but they banded together for jobs requiring joint labor—log rolling and roof raising, harvesting, corn husking and corn shelling. The tasks were much the same on every farm, and so were the buildings. Simply made and functional, they were scattered about the farm-yard. There was the smokehouse, the wagonshed, the woodshed, a corncrib, a pigsty, a chickencoop, a dairy house for making cheese and butter—and sometimes separate sheds for things like meat-curing and cider-making.

Besides the house, the barn was the most important building. Every region had its own type. The common barn of the English colonies was a single-level building with a threshing floor, stalls for the livestock, and a hayloft. In upstate New York barns commonly had a stone basement for the livestock, and the threshing floor and hayloft were in an upper level. Bank barns were built against a hillside or a ramp, so that the upper level, where the hay and grain were stored, could be entered directly from the outside. The New York bank barn commonly had an upper level entered on the end. In Pennsylvania, the bank barn had a forebay overhanging the livestock entrance on the downhill side. The feeder barn of the Midwest had two open ends, with lean-to sheds on either side for the animals and the equipment. A gambrel roof framed of light timber provided a large clear space to store loose hay.

The corncrib had sides with cracks between the boards to let air in and dry the corn. For efficient air circulation, the width had to be kept down. Before mechanical elevators, the ears of corn, husked by hand, were loaded into the crib by a scoop shovel; so the height of the building was also restricted, usually to about twelve feet. If you needed to increase the capacity, you had to make the building longer or add another one a few feet away. Once mechanical loading became possible, two cribs would be built facing each other at a distance of ten to twenty feet, and the lean-to roofs would be extended to form a single gable roof. The upper portion of the central space was then enclosed and used as a granary, and at ground level you could store machinery and equipment. Both granary and cribs would be filled through a cupola on the roof.

Like the farmer, the townsman also worked at home. The main unit of the economy was the one-man shop—and that was lodged in the house. Artisans, merchants, shopkeepers were all individual entrepreneurs. They plied their trade in the large front room: the shoemaker made shoes and sold them here, the merchant prepared his orders and did his accounting. And there was an extraordinary freedom of employment. Unlike the strict occupational system of Europe with its craft guilds, the trades in American towns eschewed rigid control. You could practice what you wanted and move from one craft to another as you wished.

So in those days a man would get out of bed in the morning and walk down the stairs or across the farmyard to go to work. This coziness was possible in the world of small Colonial towns and family farms. Even so, some businesses required more organized effort, and specialized workspaces were set up for distilling, brick- and rope-making, lime-working, and tanning. One man by himself could not make rope, let alone a ship. People had to come together to make certain things, and in this simple sense America's first factories got their start quite early. But these were

Shops along Duke of Gloucester Street in Williamsburg, Virginia. In the foreground is Hunter's store, built sometime after 1772. Little is known about its history, but today it has been reconstructed and is operated as an eighteenth-century grocer's store.

always small enterprises: the production unit did not exceed five or ten people.

These specialized workplaces often took their shape from the nature of the task at hand. Ropewalks, for example, were long buildings stretched out like the long fibers that were twisted into rope. There is a late one in Charlestown near Boston, from the 1830s, built of fine granite. Early ropewalks were simpler, nothing fancier than long sheds. Ironworks, like the early one of the Saugus River in Massachusetts from about 1650, housed various functions in separate frame buildings: in the furnace, the raw materials for making iron—the bog ore from swampy areas and ponds, the dark rock with calcium carbonate, and the charcoal for fuel—were fired; in the forge, the long wrought-iron merchant bar was made; in the slitting mill, the bars were turned into nails and building materials like flats and rods. Shipyards were open spaces with a service shed to one side. In Annapolis, Maryland, the first shipbuilding and repair operation of one Thomas Todd, in what is now the downtown, soon graduated to the Ships' Carpenters' Lot, a public place on the north side of the dock reserved for the construction of ships.

Tobacco was the main export of Annapolis, and it came in from the plantations of Maryland and Virginia. Their docks and landings along the rivers of these states—the Patuxent and Potomac, the James, the York, the Rappahannock—and all along the deep inlets of Chesapeake Bay spoke of organized labor of a very special kind.

The plantation was a unit of commercial farming based on cheap unskilled labor—indentured servants from England working to pay off their debt, and slave labor imported from Africa, the latter especially after about 1675. We can think of the plantation as a small, independent work village. It had its own wharf and served as a commercial center where common planters from round about would bring their modest crop to be shipped to Europe, and where they could purchase imported goods. There would also be a school kept by the owner for the education of his own and other children, and a cemetery.

The Ropewalk, Charlestown Navy Yard, Charlestown, Massachusetts. The ropewalk was designed by Alexander Parris and built in 1834–36. This quarter-mile-long building began operation in 1838, and until it was closed in 1971, most of the U.S. Navy's rope was made here. Before the introduction of machinery which coiled rope as it was made, the length of rope was limited by the length of the building in which it was manufactured, hence the building's shape.

Housing for field hands on Jefferson Davis's plantation, as it appeared in 1866.

Outbuildings at Tuckahoe Plantation, Goochland County, Virginia. The plantation was established in the early eighteenth century. On the right is a mid-nineteenth-century slave house. The building on the left was originally a kitchen. It was used as a slave house in the early nineteenth century and after the 1860s was made into a stable.

The focus of the plantation was the big house, and not far from it, but often hidden from immediate view, were the laborers' quarters—rows of cabins for the slaves, or else barrack-like buildings of several rooms, plus toolsheds, the mule barn, the blacksmith shop, and the tobacco house. There were gardens where the slaves grew produce for their own use or as barter for things or services they needed. The slave landscape also included the nearby woods where some private leisure could be sought. Later accounts of plantation life mention religious meetings held in the woods.

The agricultural land was laid out in large fields and worked by gangs of Negro slaves and mules under the watchful eye of the planter or his overseer. In the bigger plantations these fields were actually semi-independent farms, distinct enough to be treated as separate economic units, each with its own Negro quarters. At the drying sheds the tobacco was packaged into hogsheads made of heavy wooden planks banded with straps of iron and rolled to the wharfs along paths that were known as rolling roads. Some of these still exist. One is in the eighteenth-century town of Urbanna, Virginia. Another begins southwest of Baltimore at the Patapsco River, near the crossing of U.S. Route 1, and is in fact called Rolling Road.

At Tuckahoe, in Goochland County, Virginia, outside Richmond, you can still get a feel for these early Southern plantations. Tuckahoe belonged to a branch of the great Randolph family of Virginia. Thomas Jefferson spent his boyhood here; he and his cousins, the Randolph children, learned to read and write at the little school building east of the big house which was once the plantation office. On the other side were the kitchen and the dairy, the stable, the smokehouses, and the quarters for the house slaves. These stood along one side of a cedar-lined street on axis with the main house, balanced on the other side by the vegetable garden. South of the rather plain H-shaped house, the ground fell sharply toward the bank of the James River.

The slave houses are frame buildings that enclose two one-room family units separated by a chimney, each with its own exterior door. The single-room unit, sometimes with an additional loft, was a standard type of slave housing. A unit was often no larger than twelve by eight feet and held from six to twenty-four people. Built singly or as duplexes, like the ones at Tuckahoe, these houses—of wood, brick, or whitewashed logs—represented the most substantial accommodation for slaves and, in appearance at least, were not much different from the single-room houses that most white planters lived in. The great bulk of slave housing did not measure up to this relatively decent standard.

Besides the tobacco plantations of Virginia and Maryland, there were rice and indigo plantations in South Carolina, and in time sugar plantations in Louisiana. By the end of the eighteenth century the staple crop of the South became cotton. By then holdings of 5,000 acres and more were not uncommon.

Often romanticized in movies and legend, the plantation was for many a beautiful but cruel workplace. Its days numbered, it would give way in time to another kind of farming—farming made possible by the appropriation of new prairie lands and the invention of the steel plow. The slave system actually failed as early as 1800. Once-wealthy owners abandoned their plantations to tenant farmers. Slave labor would be revived again during the three decades before the Civil War. But by then the scene of intensive agriculture had moved far beyond the tobacco fields of the South and the villages of rural New England.

A Change of Pace

Between 1820 and 1860, the size of our settled lands inflated. The opening up of the Midwest and the Great Plains offered vast new territories to the American farmer. From the start, in these stretches of tallgrass prairie and the untamed, unforested wilderness beyond, he was dependent on others for what he needed. The railroads were his lifeline; the commercial market was the changing house of his sweat. To pay for what you needed, you had to produce a surplus. You had to exploit your holdings to the maximum and turn in vast quantities of produce to the commercial market.

The prairie landscape fanned out from the Great Lakes to the northwest and southwest. It stretched from Canada to Texas, from Indiana to Kansas, flat or with a gentle roll, and blessed with rich alluvial soil. You could till it with mechanical equipment—something you could not do on the uneven and rocky fields of New England. It is for this reason that a sudden leap will occur in the middle of the nineteenth century in the prairies of the Midwest—a leap from native wilderness to an advanced mechanized agriculture without going through any of the intermediate stages. It is

George Hoag's Steam Threshing Outfit and Crew Setting New One-day World's Record, *a lithograph of 1878 by Andrew Putnam Hill.*

because of this loamy humus of several feet, the moderately pleated land, and the railroads that big entrepreneurs would initiate a land industry called "bonanza farming," a specialized process that used machines like the McCormick reaper and a hired labor force to produce wheat in bulk for a national and foreign market.

Bonanza farming started with a man named Oliver Dalrymple, who was the agent of a railroad company, the Northern Pacific. Railroad companies were awarded huge chunks of public land from the government in return for opening up new territory. When the Northern Pacific suspended its work on new lines in the depression of the mid-1870s, company officials redeemed their railroad bonds with portions of its land in the Red River Valley. Dalrymple contracted to manage these holdings in North Dakota and Minnesota. He divided the land into administrative units of 500 acres, and on each of these units he put up a house for the superintendent, a boardinghouse for the hired hands, a stable, a granary, a blacksmith's shop, and a machine repair shop. He used steam tractors and plowed furrows several miles long. This was a far cry from the small family farm.

Indeed the new farming slowly undermined the traditional culture of the countryside. Its landscape was different. There were no fences or gardens, no churches, no schools or villages. Left behind, when the land was exhausted and the profit-making apparatus moved elsewhere, were the gaunt barracks of the all-male labor force, empty sheds, and of course the great silos where the grain was stored waiting to be shipped—wooden ones first, since the 1870s, beginning in Maryland and Michigan; then, after the turn of the century, silos made of concrete or hollow tile; and later still, trench and bunker silos. In the long run, these profiteers—the big land companies and owners of large estates—would destroy a stable society moored economically, socially, and politically on farming and a rural way of life. In 1850 the farm population was just over fifty percent of the country's total population and accounted for sixty-five percent of the national labor force. Today we are down to three percent on both counts.

Yet this land-grab was still a long way in the future when the first generations of settlers, hard-working families, often of im-

Left page. *Horse-drawn wagons loaded with wheat arrive at the railroad depot and grain elevator in Mandan, North Dakota, ca. 1900.*

At left. *A local bank in a nineteenth-century farming community.*

migrants, arrived determined to make a go of it in the treeless grassland of the prairie-sea. They bought their small farms with the help of a bank or some other lending agent. The house you could build in the old way, or you could order it and it would come in by railroad within thirty days, precut at the sawmill and ready to assemble. To furnish it and get the tools and machinery for the farm, you would pore over a mail-order catalogue and make your choice, or make your way on foot or by cart to the nearest town along the tracks; there on the block or two of Main Street what could not be grown or made at home—salt and nails, blankets and shoes—could be found.

So the small trackside town of the countryside, with its land office, its merchants, its lawyers and bankers, its post office, and the grain elevator where you took your surplus to be weighed and credited, as much of it at least as could be spared after setting aside what was needed to feed the livestock in the winter—this small town became an extension of the family farm, its mainstay. And beyond the small town there was now the mechanized work-

Hog-Slaughtering and Packing, *Cincinnati, in a panoramic painting of 1873. The modern assembly line probably had its origin in the meat-packing houses of Cincinnati in the late 1860s. After the hog is killed, scalded, and scraped, it is hung from an overhead rail and then moved past a series of stationary workers, each of whom performs a single operation in cleaning out the internal organs.*

place of the factory and the industrialized city—that is, the organization and efficiency needed to meet the new demands of these settled lands of the interior.

Like the slow erosion of the family farm, in the city too, and more drastically, changes in the economy affected the early ties between the house and workplace. The time of the one-man shop was running out. People now needed to come together in large numbers to make and distribute things. So for most townfolk the workplace was now quite distinct from the neighborhood of houses. Men now worked in offices, stores, and shops away from home, and the old front room they vacated was turned into a parlor. The old crafts began to break down into new specialties—shoes would be made in one place now, but sold in others. And many more shoes were made than were needed for the townsfolk. Out there, beyond the bulging cities, a regional market sprang up, which by the time of the Civil War was tied in to a full-fledged national market. Canals spawned bustling new cities far away from the Eastern Seaboard. The cutting of the Erie Canal in 1825, for example, put Chicago on the map, and the extension of the system west to the Mississippi River turned the city into the largest emporium of the Midwest, the hub of the most extensive system of inland waterways in the world. And when the railroads started

operating on a national scale, from about 1840 onward, they made Chicago a great junction for a network that embraced 10,000 miles of line.

To meet this tremendous new opportunity, the scale of manufacturing increased dramatically. Hours of work were longer, the pace faster, and a streamlining of tasks anticipated the modern assembly line. Specialized concentrations drew together the garment industry, furniture and leather-making, locomotive building. A new breed of entrepreneur came of age—the wholesaler. He was the middleman who facilitated the flow of these plentiful goods from the manufacturer to the user, and so in a real sense supervised the distribution of trade.

All of this activity was breeding a new kind of townscape. The look of the old towns was being transformed as this nation of farms started on the road to becoming a nation of factories. There were entire manufacturing districts now. There were warehouse districts like Laclede's Landing in St. Louis, where the goods were stored in large, roomy warehouses built in close proximity to the waterfront and the railroad lines.

Spare, functional buildings, with stacks of open floors or lofts, these warehouses were built with an eye to being as nearly fireproof as possible. They had large openings at the sides and rear, through which goods could easily be moved to the adjacent waterway or onto railway spurs. The construction used cast-iron members, which did not resist heat very well and would give way after a certain point, or the more preferable system of massive, thick

Switzer Licorice Company Building, 1874, Laclede's Landing, St. Louis, 1870s. Next to the Switzer Building is an arch of the Eads Bridge, built across the Mississippi in 1874. This light manufacturing and warehousing area deteriorated in this century, and by 1974 its buildings were ninety-five percent vacant. Although the warehouse of old has lost much of its importance today, its open, unencumbered interiors are being readapted.

timbers that would char rather than burn. With the invention of the automatic sprinkler in 1879, the buildings became resistant to common fires. The only remaining improvements would be the development of a system of reinforced concrete construction, invented by the Minneapolis engineer Charles A. P. Turner in 1905, and, at about the same time, the accommodation of the freight car inside the building, which ensured all-weather loading and unloading.

Thousands of traveling salesmen fanned out from these warehouse districts into the territories that wholesalers served. They brought the manufactured products of the city to the farms of the Midwest and brought the bounty of the farms—the wheat and the beef—to the cities, and to lands beyond the American shores. Scores of hotels and Travellers' Clubs went up to accommodate the new class of working men when they came into town.

The task of keeping track of what hammers were shipped to Keokuk and what shoes to Peoria produced a lot of paperwork. Buildings designed exclusively for rentable office space began to take over the downtowns. They were rather nondescript struc-

United Drug Company warehouse interior, ca. 1900.

tures, walkups of five to six stories, and they went up at the expense of townhouses which began to prove far too uneconomical on this very desirable downtown land that was becoming more precious every year. The more the downtown became commercialized in this way—occupied by warehouses, offices, and banks—the more those urbanites who could took to the suburbs in order to avoid the clamor and the residential crunch.

Reliable and cheap transportation now let them do that. Streetcars would bring them to work every morning and back again at the end of the working day. This commuting would make final the separation of house and workplace that had set in as an urban trend during the early part of the century.

The Company Town

For some businesses, commuting was not the answer. You had to go where the action was. In mining, for example, this meant remote and often harsh environments where makeshift towns would

Bodie, California. On the left is the Dechambreau Building, 1879, used for the Post Office, and later Grandma Johnson's Rooming House and the Dechambreau Hotel. Next to it is the Bodie Odd Fellows Lodge. H. Ward built it in 1880 and used the bottom floor for his undertaking business. On the right is the Miner's Union Hall, built in 1878. (See also color section for another view of Bodie.)

spring up in the shadow of the headframe that supported the hoisting sheaves. The pattern was common everywhere—in the iron and coal-mining regions, at golddiggers' camps. Simple houses, often put up by the managing company, would be scattered about the site or would line up in orderly rows at the mouth of the shaft mine. Streets were nothing but beaten paths. There would be a general store and a saloon at the very least, perhaps a lodge and a schoolhouse, a small rustic church. When the mine ran dry, the town died overnight. The elements moved in where people once lived and worked. You can see them still, these instant ghost towns, especially out West—the weather-beaten houses, the scarred land, ugly piles of waste, rusting railroad tracks.

These company towns all started abruptly, without plan. When a mineral deposit was discovered, men flocked to the site and put up tents and shacks in a hurry; the more optimistic built log cabins. In California the big gold rush started in 1848; in 1849 gold was struck in Colorado and silver in Nevada's Comstock Lode. Mining camps established themselves in these far-flung frontier regions before there were any other settlements, railroad lines, or good roads. Leadville, Colorado; Helena, Montana; Deadwood, South Dakota; Central City, Colorado—these were isolated islands of people surrounded by wilderness. And these camps were the germs of cities. The first arrivals defined the district boundaries and staked out the claims. For a while, in the fever of panning and digging, the camps were left to grow as they would; but as things cooled off a bit, the plat of the village was recorded, with the size of the blocks, lots, and streets marked upon it. Occasionally the original settlers formed a town company. To secure title, they would either go to the federal government for a town patent or request a survey to settle contested ownership of property. Organization would foster pride. Community life would move beyond survival and the comforts of saloon and church. There might be a laundry, even a theater or opera house, like the fancy Tabor Opera House in Leadville, Colorado. The contrast of a rough-hewn camp and these urban civilities was affecting. A source describes coming upon "a very pretty conservatory, attached to a neat cottage" in Central City, Colorado. "It was something strangely cheering, yet touching, in the universal dreariness."

Roads were important. Initially the towns built these on their own, or relied on toll roads built for profit by private companies. "It is a lamentable fact," a newspaper of the time writes, "that one can hardly travel twenty miles in a mining region without being confronted by the toll gatherer." Wagons and pack trains arrived at the camps along these roads. The railroad was a late-comer; not until the Seventies and Eighties was its impact felt, and by then the peak of mining had been reached in the Rockies and rapid decline had set in.

The end was sudden and final. Here is a late account of Elizabethtown, New Mexico, written in 1882, a decade after the town's boom:

It makes one lonesome to walk the streets of Elizabethtown. Although not an old place, it is deserted, and instead of the crowded streets, or crowded houses, rum shops, gambling saloons, and hourly knock downs of a few years ago, a sort of grave yard stillness, deserted buildings, . . . a good deal of broken glass, and other fragments of former prosperity [are] left, but the pith, the vitality of the village life ha[s] departed . . .

To have stable communities that would endure, you had to hitch your fortune to a more dependable natural resource. Water,

Waterwheel of the Slitting Mill, Saugus Iron Works, Saugus, Massachusetts, 1650s. Water from the Saugus River was fed via canals into the sluiceways. By adjusting the sluicegates at the end of the sluiceways, the speed of the waterwheel was regulated.

at the early stages of America's history, was the only feasible source of energy for the manufacturing and processing that needed machines. In old Eastern cities on the fall line, rivers could be harnessed for manufacturing. But very often, adequate waterpower was found only in remote wilderness sites, where the topography included fast running streams broken by waterfalls.

This is where mills planted themselves—early gristmills and ironworks; sawmills for the logging camps of Michigan, Ohio, Arkansas, and later, in the Pacific West; textile mills in New England and parts of the South. You flooded the land around a likely spot to make the millpond. You dammed the pond and let the water flow through canals as you needed it. You channeled the water to the big wheel. To this energized spot, where the wheel turned and activated the machines, you had to lure a work force and make sure it stayed. So started the mill towns of New England.

Mill towns were self-contained industrial communities. In the unsettled wilderness where streams were found, the entrepreneur had to set up factory villages with their own housing and supporting services. The first true mill town was Derby, Connecticut, which took root in 1803. Three years later Slatersville, Rhode Island, introduced what came to be known as the Rhode Island system. This meant that the mills were owned by a family or partnership, that the owners supervised the mills directly, and that children and families were the preferred work force. For workers, the owners provided modest family houses and tenements. In the alternative "Waltham system," mills were owned by joint-stock companies that might lease waterpower from an agency; the work force consisted of young unmarried women from New England farms, "spinsters" in that double sense of the word, who lived together in boardinghouses.

The company town at Saco, Maine, was founded in 1825 in a seven-story wooden factory building more than 200 feet long. It

Saco, Maine. Mill buildings along the Saco River. They are currently being adapted for new business and housing.

Mill buildings of the Amoskeag Manufacturing Company, Manchester, New Hampshire. Built on the Merrimack River, Amoskeag eventually developed into the largest textile complex in New England.

was the largest factory building of its time, but burnt down a few years later. Then Saco got going in earnest, under new management, the Boston Associates. This group of entrepreneurs probably qualifies as the country's first corporation. They controlled banking, insurance, a lot of rail mileage, and ten waterpower sites up and down New England; the one at Saco, by a 40-foot waterfall called Cataract Falls, was the best. It was near the tidewater, so raw materials could be easily shipped in and the finished products out. Along the east bank of the Saco River, and at Biddeford on the opposite bank under a rival company, whole towns grew up to serve the new order of the textile mills. These great monuments of the first industrial age—at Saco, at Lowell, at Amoskeag, and dozens of other places—would remake forever the look of the New England landscape.

The earliest mills were unattached buildings, small and compact, and they were carefully designed by "millwrights" in association with the manager. By the 1830s professional engineers—sometimes called "mill doctors"—specialized in this kind of work. The problems of mill design were standard. First, the machines had to be kept inside the mill as close as possible to the waterwheel for power transmission, because the shafts that transmitted the power would dissipate most of it if the distance from the wheel to the machine was too great. This meant tight, multistoried buildings right at the edge of the water. Then there was interior lighting to consider. Because mills relied largely on natural lighting, many peripheral windows were needed, and rooms narrow enough for daylight to penetrate effectively and uniformly. The tall, narrow mass of the standard mill also minimized the area necessary for the foundation—the most expensive feature of mill construction. Foundations had to be very deep for the building to withstand the vibrations of the machines, and digging them cost a lot of money.

From the big wheel tucked in the groundwork, shafts rose to several floors and then across their length to bring power to the bale breakers and spinning looms. As business grew, new mills were linked with the original building, each with its own wheel. In time great sweeps of brick framed the water's edge. At its peak, the Amoskeag plant on the Merrimack River in Manchester,

Female employees of the Royal Corset Company, Worcester, Massachusetts.

Workers in the spinning room of a New England textile mill, ca. 1890.

New Hampshire, alone encompased thirty mills which were joined together with great care as to their appearance. The bricks were meticulously matched in color to those of the earlier buildings. The millyard was left open at each end; it stretched out in a gentle curve, and tree-lined canals and railroad tracks ran its entire length. The buildings' solid walls of red brick, punctuated by archways and bridges, swept majestically for a whole mile on one side of the Merrimack and half a mile on the other.

Early mill towns were orderly, handsome places. At places like Lowell, the boardinghouses for the mill girls enclosed wide, regular, tree-lined streets. The young women stayed for an average of three years, and then went back to the family farm with their savings. The employers believed they were providing more than a job. The women were treated with solicitude. To make sure of a virtuous stay, they were constantly supervised. Church attendance was compulsory, and there were other social events after working hours. They attended lyceums and edited a literary magazine called *The Offering.* Working hours were long but not backbreaking. Most job routines were flexible; there was time to walk around and chat by the water fountain, or even to read or knit. In Rhode Island, on the other hand, child labor and crowded tenements had already gained notoriety.

By 1850 the farm girls had been pushed aside. Immigrant labor began to flood the mill town landscape. The Irish arrived first, brought in originally to dig the canals and build the factories. Then came Catholic families of French Canadians, and later mixed waves of Armenians and Poles, Swedes and Italians and Portuguese. Close to 900 mills were now operating with a ten-hour limit set by law for a day's work. Both the housing and the working environment soon deteriorated. In most places the employer refused to provide any housing, and so shantytowns and appalling crowding became endemic. But this was home now, so they stayed—and so did their children, born on the premises and indentured to the mills. The mill town schools impressed upon the children obedience and the values of their employer. For the adults there were few distractions. In time some companies promoted social and recreational activities through clubs, like Amoskeag's Textile Club. But the mill town routine was deadly. You

Young worker in a textile mill.

shuttled between your house and the spinning loom, day after day, from dawn to dusk and even later, in an endless hypnotic ritual.

A permanent and immobile factory class was now a reality, and the identity of workers in an industrial society, their rights and their relations with the employer, became the central issue that was to preoccupy working America for generations.

The Promise of Pullman

Paternalism did not disappear altogether; on the contrary, many employers were genuinely convinced they were the custodians of the workers' morals. They also believed human happiness was a business asset, that contented workers would be inclined to work hard. These proponents of what was called "industrial betterment" tried to prevent labor unrest by providing amenities like lunchrooms, bathhouses, clinics, and thrift clubs; they established benefit funds for the workers and launched profit-sharing plans.

So company towns continued to be planned and developed, even when location or necessity did not require it, as the means to control the lives of the workers and ensure their productivity— Pullman, for example, a company town a few miles southwest of downtown Chicago and well connected to it by rail. This was the most famous company town of them all. It was the brainchild of George Pullman, the sleeping car tycoon. The Pullman Palace Car Company started in Chicago until it moved in 1870 to an ampler site in Detroit. The decision to relocate once more, and to build an entire town, was taken in 1880.

By this time a manufacturer like Pullman could put his factory wherever he wanted to. In the 1880s steam power, which had been sparingly used until that time because of its expense, and then only in conjunction with waterpower, was broadly adopted. This meant that factories were liberated from restricted, remote stream sites, and the need to supply housing for the work force was no longer pressing. The advanced transportation networks worked marvels in shrinking distances, and Pullman's location was such that the workers could have lived in Chicago and got out to the factory fairly easily. A company town, then, was not an imperative; it was a matter of conviction and a calculated venture. On the face of it, an idealistic venture. How could he keep his workers "clean, contented, sober, educated, happy," Pullman wondered, if they went home from his factories to "crowded and unhealthy tenements, in miserable streets . . . subject to all the temptations and snares of a great city?"

Perhaps George Pullman had other things in mind. By taking workers away from the city, the company town isolated them from

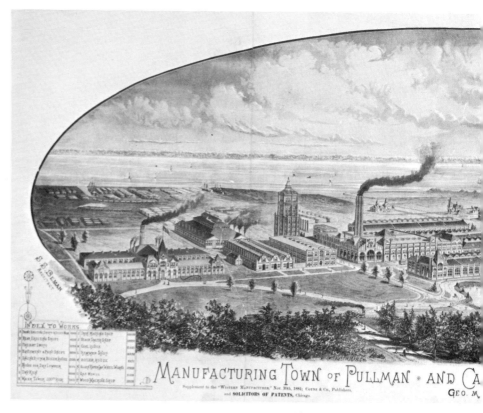

The town of Pullman, Illinois, 1881.

George Pullman, 1831–1897.

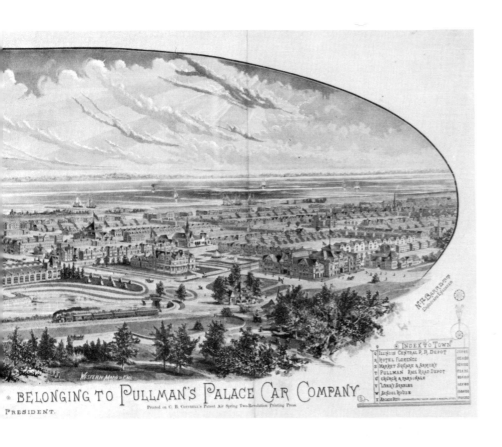

BELONGING TO PULLMAN'S PALACE CAR COMPANY

PRESIDENT.

Worker housing in Pullman, Illinois.

unions and alternative sources of employment, making them totally dependent on the company. Absenteeism and morning lateness were cut down. Workers spent their money in the company store, and the credit extended to them tied up their pay well into the future.

So George Pullman was investing in a good business proposition when he bought 4,000 acres next to Lake Calumet, hired a young architect from New York, laid out a grid town for some 8,000 inhabitants, and named it after himself. But Pullman was different from other company towns. It was plainly advertised as a business venture that was intended to make money. "We are landlord and employers. That is all there is of it," Pullman said. What is more remarkable, he believed that beauty improved the individual, and it was in the businessman's interest to provide for it. His town would therefore be aesthetically pleasing, planned and executed with care. The architect, Solon Spencer Beman, was asked to collaborate with a landscape designer, one Nathan Barrett—the first time in America that such a team planned and supervised the execution of an entire town, its houses, public buildings, industrial plants, and landscaping. In this sense the town of Pullman was like the sleeping car—functional and beautiful at the same time. And beauty was worth paying extra for— higher fares in the sleeping car, higher rents in town.

The arrangement of the town was quite calculated. An attractive boulevard, named after his daughter Florence, separated the industrial quarter from the community. To the south, in a parklike setting, were the company shops, a lumberyard, a gas works. The shops were grouped around a monumental water tower, and the office block was topped by another tall tower that held an illuminated clock. On the other side of the boulevard, facing the train station to create a striking first impression upon visitors, of whom there were thousands, stood a two-story hotel girdled by a broad veranda, the single nondenominational church, the Market Hall which contained stores, and first in the line of view, the huge glass and iron Arcade Building. This impressive block was Pullman's main street. On the ground level was a variety of shops, including a stationery store, a tailor, and a pharmacy; at the gallery level were meeting rooms, a library, and a theater. All the buildings in town were of brick manufactured on the site from clay dredged out of the lake. What was not used went back into the lake as fill for an artificial pleasure island. Pullman also had a band, choirs, schools, a park, and a six-acre greenhouse and tree nursery.

The residential streets were broad and had cobblestone gutters. Red and yellow brick rowhouses, for one to four families, lined the streets behind wooden sidewalks. They boasted skylights, gas, running water, and front and backyards. There were also boardinghouses for single men and ten "blockhouse" tenements with twelve to forty-eight flats in each. The houses ranged in site and comfort according to the worker's level. Beginners were assigned to tiny houses on Langley Avenue, nicknamed Incubator Row. Skilled craftsmen had bigger houses, and foremen more elaborate ones. At the top came detached or semidetached "boulevard" houses, with as many as ten rooms, for company managers and the town physician. More than one thousand of these Pullman houses survive.

Chicago was impressed. Employers across the country were impressed. Yet things didn't go according to plan. The workers who were supposed to be happy and quiescent were not. In 1883, within three years after moving in, they went out on strike for an eight-hour day. And when they went out again in 1894, the National Guard and federal troops were called in. Thirteen workers were shot dead. The strike was crushed—and with it one man's dream to create the ideal company town.

The truth is that Pullman was a stifling paradise. No property was ever for sale at Pullman; everyone had to rent from the company. So families were deprived of the American dream of homeownership, and this meant that the town missed its chance to ensure its stability. No drinking was permitted at Pullman. There were no pawnshops, no bordellos. There was no self-government—which made for restlessness. A company agent ran the town, and inspectors paid visits to make sure that the property was well taken care of, and that the occupants behaved themselves. And in the end, the way George Pullman treated his workers inside his plant was probably more important than the refined homes they walked back to every night.

Frederick W. Taylor, 1856–1915.

Taylorism and the Assembly Line

Pullman died three years after the strike of 1894, unrepentant and proud of his town to the end. In his will he left money for "a free school of manual training," which opened in 1915. Shortly after his death the company sold the town and left it to its own devices. Chicago swallowed it in its sprawl, and Pullman went into a slow decline which it has started reversing only within the last ten years.

The lesson of Pullman was not lost on other captains of industry. The answer to productivity, they realized, lay not in new ideas outside the factory but within it.

No one knew this better than Frederick Winslow Taylor. The scion of a well-to-do Philadelphia family, Taylor was a fanatically methodical man. He rejected college for the factory, starting as machinist in a small pump factory and then moving to the Midvale Steel Company in 1878, where he rose through the ranks to become chief engineer of the works.

A motion study of a worker assembling a braiding machine, ca. 1920.

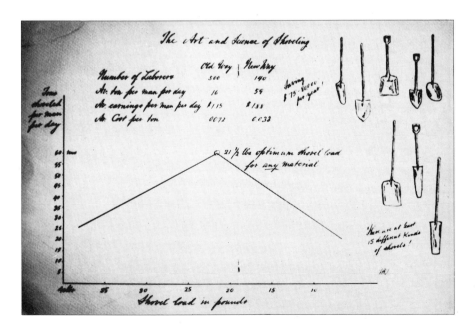

"The Art and Science of Shovelling," part of Frederick Taylor's demonstration of the optimal shovel load of 21.5 pounds.

He had a point to prove. Factory work was inefficient and wasteful, and he knew how to correct the archaic ways of the American workplace. To that end, he undertook a series of time-and-motion studies scientifically designed to establish the most efficient way in which each small operation could be performed. He set new production standards and insisted that, if they were rigorously enforced, "soldiering," or loafing on the job, would cease. He broke down lathe work into many small operations—"putting chain on . . . lifting work to shears . . . adjusting soda water . . . considering how to clamp"—and worked out a precise time frame for each one. He calculated that the optimum shovel load for any material was 21.5 pounds and prescribed the kind of shovel that would ensure this rate. Bethlehem Steel Works could claim that, by applying these findings, within a short time a single shoveler's work had increased from 16 to 59 tons per day. It was to be a survival of the fittest and the most obedient. "If a man won't do what is right, *make* him," Taylor said.

And what was the carrot? Not profit-sharing plans, or nice housing in the manner of Pullman, or uplifting leisure activities. It was hard work itself that brought about well-being and high morality. And the way to encourage hard work was through bonuses and wage increases. The employer wanted better and more work, and so would the worker if he were rewarded with the only thing that mattered to him—cash. Taylor promised that his theory, which he called "scientific management," would make "each workman's interest the same as that of his employers."

People listened. He became famous. He held court at Boxly, his eleven-acre estate on Philadelphia's Chestnut Hill, and by the time he died in 1915 Taylorism had spread beyond the factory, even beyond the workplace, as the new American gospel of efficiency. Feminists set out to apply scientific management to the running of the home, culminating reforms that had started with Catharine Beecher seventy years earlier. The house, as one feminist put it, was "part of a great factory for the production of citizens."

If Henry Ford knew of Taylor's work, he would not admit it. He too was thinking along the same lines when he entered the fledgling motorcar business in Detroit early in this century. By

Henry Ford, 1863–1947.

1908 he had perfected his Model T—and within the next two decades he would literally put America behind the wheel. Over 15 million tin lizzies rolled off his assembly line and out of his buildings.

Detroit at the turn of the century was a busy lake port and an important manufacturing center for marine engines. In nearby Flint, carriage manufacturers were first in the country in advanced assembly methods of production. The state had also a heavy concentration of bicycle manufacturers. So it was not altogether fortuitous that a new industry aiming to produce a better vehicle would stir in this choice spot on the Great Lakes waterway.

When Ford got started, the factory was still primarily an enclosed space designed without much attention to process. The typical arrangement of the industrial plant of the day would be a narrow, multistory building fronting on a street; narrow wings of similar design, branching off from this main stem, enclosed open courts. Sometimes these courts would be roofed over to provide additional sheltered space. Lean-to structures contained facilities like toilets.

With the general adoption of steam power in the 1880s, some exciting changes began to take place. For one thing, steam power had not only freed plants from their water-locked sites, it had also freed them from the restrictions imposed by the waterwheel. Plants could now spread out as single-story buildings, with the bulk of the shafting relegated to the basement. The new low massing avoided the vibrations characteristic of multistoried plants. Structurally safer near the ground, the buildings could also open up to the daylight with large windows and special roofs. The sawtooth roof was an English invention; here the tiered arrangement of windows in sawtooth shape, turned toward the north, provided maximum natural light from one direction. The sawtooth was a truss or a frame of beams and posts; the sash that held the glass was made of steel, and was designed to allow natural ventilation. The monitor roof doubled the light source. Here a continuous section at the top was raised to admit light from both sides.

Yet the machines were still closely tied to the steam engine, strapped to it with a cumbersome system of shafts and belts. The arrangement of the machines depended on the amount of power they needed, not on the efficient organization of tasks.

The revision of Thomas Edison's electrical systems in the late Eighties turned things around. With alternating current equipment and Nicola Tesla's polyphase electric motor, it was possible to apply electricity to industrial operations. When the new electric utility industry made cheap electricity available after 1905, the steam engine met its swift demise. The electric motor allowed power to be incorporated directly into each tool and machine, spelling the end of cumbersome shafting and belts. Machines could now be put anywhere to facilitate the operation, not just where belts and shafts could most easily reach them. The work on the plant floor no longer had to be arranged around the steam engine.

It was this flexibility Ford seized upon. Taylor had not been concerned with the reorganization of the factory as such, but only with the efficiency and speed of single tasks performed by single workers. Ford looked at the problem of efficiency more comprehensively. You could subdivide the assembly of automobiles into single, repetitive tasks, but you could go even further. You could keep the workers performing each one of these tasks in one designated station, have the appropriate parts and tools at the ready there, and then bring to it that unit of the automobile on which

Interior of a National Cash Register Company machine shop, 1898.

The moving assembly line in Ford Motor Company's Highland Park (Michigan) Plant. Model T's were moved by an endless chain conveyor, and wheels and radiators were brought to their proper stations by a gravity feed system.

the task was to be performed. This meant craneways, conveyors, and a highly coordinated linear organization—the moving assembly line. In turn a new kind of plant was required. Who was to design it?

At first Ford seemed unaware that his ideas had to find a new architectural resolution. "If you build me a building big enough and strong enough," he would say, "I can always use it." That was before he had met Albert Kahn. Born in Germany, Kahn emigrated with his family to Detroit in 1880 and joined an architectural firm specializing in Shingle Style houses. He was busily designing town and country houses, the story goes, when one day a client of his, Henry B. Joy, asked him to draw up plans for his factory, the Packard Motor Car Company. Kahn was launched.

By the time America entered the First World War, his office was able to take on the design of the government's newly developing aviation facilities. In the late Twenties even the Russians invited him to do a tractor factory for them, and his office eventually designed and built hundreds of plants there. By the late Thirties the Kahn office employed a staff of over six hundred and produced about twenty percent of all architect-designed industrial buildings in the country. Whenever possible, Kahn tried to house the entire plant in one building. Dispersed plants raised the cost (more exterior walls to be built), wasted good space in their intervening courts, and wasted heat.

Many of Kahn's buildings are masterpieces of understated, functional elegance. But Kahn made light of his achievement. "When I began," he recalled later in life, "the real architects would design only museums, cathedrals, capitols, monuments. The office boy was considered good enough to do factory buildings. I'm still that office boy designing factories. I have no dignity to be impaired." He was also fond of saying that "Architecture is 90 per cent business and 10 per cent art," which is the sort of thing that doubtless played well to his business-minded clientele.

Kahn first got together with Henry Ford on the Highland Park plant, which began operations in 1910. It was in a Detroit suburb, northwest of the city, and geared to the railroads that

Albert Kahn, 1869–1942.

reached it from the north. There, Kahn still worked within the old, tall factory mold which we see in the New England mills of the nineteenth century—but now with a big difference. Kahn's four-story building, except for ornamental brick bastions at the four corners, was made of steel, concrete, and glass—a brand new look, even a stylish one, for this hitherto unpampered building type. The skeleton frame allowed Kahn to use the whole wall for windows; and since the walls were no longer load-bearing, they could be punctured fearlessly. Today this is a common look. We see it in every industrial community in America. For 1910, it was indeed revolutionary.

Alongside the main building on Woodward Avenue, and for almost its entire length, ran a one-story machine shop with a sawtooth roof, where engines, transmissions, axles, and radiators were made. Between the two buildings extended a skylight-roofed craneway, with cranes that could deliver materials to both buildings through their side openings or transfer materials from one building to the other. Galleries on either side of the craneway enabled workers to unload the materials. The raw stuff was hoisted as near the roof as possible and then worked its way downward through chutes, conveyors, and tubes, until it became a finished article on the ground floor.

Walk into any heavy-industry factory today, and you'll be looking at the handiwork of a most unlikely conceptual partnership of three men. One was, of course, Henry Ford and that aggressive business savvy of his. Alongside him, Frederick Winslow Taylor who analyzed and codified labor efficiency. Above all, there was Albert Kahn whose brilliant sense of design responded to an unprecedented challenge of organization. What Kahn achieved at Highland Park would decide the look and behavior of the American factory for the next fifty years.

At the River Rouge Plant at Dearborn, Michigan, only a little more than a decade after Highland Park, Kahn laid out in full Ford's grand vision of the new American workplace. It was called River Rouge after the river of that name. It still stands, and runs, today. It is still, despite some neglect and loss of purpose, an astounding landscape of industry. At its height a huge industrial empire supported the operation of this sprawling behemoth, for

The original building at Highland Park, Michigan, by Albert Kahn, 1910, with later remodelings. Assembly of the Model T stopped in 1927, by which time most of Ford Motor Company's production had moved to the River Rouge Plant. The Highland Park Plant reopened during the Second World War for the production of tanks, bomber parts, and army vehicles. More recently the plant has been used for tractor manufacturing. A large part of the Highland Park property is now a National Historic Landmark.

Ford did not like to be dependent on anyone. Ford iron mines and sawmills in Northern Michigan, coal mines in Kentucky and West Virginia, glass plants in Pennsylvania and Minnesota, a rubber plantation named Fordlandia in Brazil—these supplied the raw materials. A small Ford-operated railroad system helped transport these raw materials. They were stored in huge bins south of the concrete-lined slip which locked into the river. Along the south edge of the bins ran the High Line, a concrete structure forty feet high whose flat top carried five railroad tracks.

On the other side of the High Line were the ovens where the coal was converted to coke for Rouge's own furnaces and foundry. The Open Hearth Building, with a capacity of ten furnaces, made steel which was processed in the adjacent mills and the Pressed Steel and Spring and Upset buildings. The foundry made the iron, brass, steel, and bronze castings used by Ford branch factories, which totaled thirty-five in the United States by 1925, with several more abroad, every one of them designed by Kahn's office.

Left. *Highland Park. In the center is the monitor roof which runs over the craneway.*

Right. *The craneway at Highland Park. It is 860 feet long and 57 feet wide.*

By then some 500,000 wage earners were dependent on Ford business for all or part of their livelihood.

So Ford did it by himself. He made his own steel and tires here, and put together the engines and the bodies. Then, from Kahn's great assembly buildings, he sent the finished tractors and Model A's out into the world. Yet Ford would learn, as had George Pullman before him, that grand designs do not always yield correspondingly grand results. Self-reliance on a grand scale could spawn its own problems. In River Rouge itself, for example, a strike or a shortage in one section of the plant might shut down the entire complex. Today, the wisdom of smaller, more manageable units, and of cooperation with others, is commonplace. For American industry the doctrine of self-sufficiency expired along with its greatest prophet.

The other lesson of the future had already been anticipated in the original choice of River Rouge as a site, indeed even of Highland Park before it. That lesson is that the modern, horizontally disposed factory needs to be in the open countryside, so that it can spread to suit its own purposes. Ford employees who began to drive to work in greater and greater numbers needed space to park their cars. Urban sites were too crowded, too precious: plenty of reasonably priced land was available in the suburbs. What is more, by moving out you avoided high municipal taxes.

So the flight of industry to the suburbs, a familiar story since 1950, started before the First World War. The concluding chapter is the industrial park of today. It is set up by a real estate operator or by chambers of commerce, municipalities, or railroad companies seeking to increase traffic and appreciate the value of their property. The industrialist benefits by having lots of elbow room, a site properly coordinated with highways and parking areas, plenty of warehousing, and protection against the depreciation that might be caused by undesirable development nearby.

The romance of the spectacular River Rouge, the evocative power of its mighty structures, should not obscure the human cost

Crossing conveyors at the River Rouge Plant, a photograph by Charles Sheeler, 1927. Sheeler, one of many artists in the early part of this century interested in machine forms and architectural themes, was commissioned in 1927 by the Ford Motor Company to document River Rouge as a creative interpretation of American technology. Late in 1927 he spent six weeks there, making photographs which emphasized the inherent geometry of the industrial forms.

this enterprise entailed. The assembly line meant dull and repetitive jobs, cramped, fixed positions. In Ford's heyday, every raise in pay brought a speeding up of the assembly line; so the worker was driven faster and faster in routinized operations. Profit-sharing and other seemingly decent gestures were accompanied by increased supervision of the private morals of the workers and their families. The Ford Sociology Department checked on how you spent your evenings, how you spent your earnings. Sending money to the Old Country or spending money "foolishly" might mean that you would forfeit profit-sharing; separation or divorce definitely did.

Design and Comfort in Office Architecture

The assembly-line factory is one great invention in the architecture of the American workplace. The office building is the other. If the factory is happy in the open countryside, with room to spread out and expand and generous docking and loading areas that dovetail into major transportation spines, the office building is quintessentially urban. Nothing is really made in these buildings. Working here are people who talk, who buy from each other, who write and draw, keep books, make decisions—decide, for example, what is to be made in factories. So the office building has to be in the thick of things, cheek by jowl with others like it. It also needs an urban skyline against which to make its own competitive statement, to take its own distinctive stance. And of course it has to get the most out of a very crowded, very valuable downtown spot. For all these reasons the office building has to be tall.

Tall office buildings were a phenomenon of the increasing specialization of the industrial city. Over the years the financial and administrative coordination of big business began to cluster in a handful of major cities, which raised the value of downtown land. In response, the office tower gained favor as a speculative rental property. In cities like Chicago and New York the lure of maximizing profit by going up unleashed a craze of tall buildings. These buildings were called skyscrapers, and the word skyline was first used at this time, the 1890s, to describe the new image of the downtown they created.

Historically, two limitations restricted building height. The first one had to do with vertical transportation; it was solved by the perfection of the elevator in the 1860s. The second involved the structural system. Steel, mass-produced by 1890, made possible a skeletal frame of columns and beams, much lighter than traditional masonry. The steel members supported their own weight, and that of the floors, and were thin enough to leave ample room for windows. The outer walls in this so-called skyscraper construction were simply a curtain of weatherproofing and ornament hung on the metal frame.

The remaining challenge was a visual one. How could an office building of ten stories and more be articulated so it would *look* tall—proud and soaring and of one piece? That challenge was an-

The Wainwright Building, St. Louis, 1890–91, Louis Sullivan and Dankmar Adler.

swered by an architect who lived and practiced in Chicago—Louis Sullivan. The design he created to sheathe the tall office building had a ring of finality about it. Vertical shafts of piers soared uninterrupted through the uniform office floors, to be capped with a mighty cornice. For a whole generation of Chicago architects this became the norm to emulate and play variations upon.

The interior of the early commercial towers was another matter. "Only in rare instances," Sullivan wrote, "does the plan or floor arrangement of the tall office building take on aesthetic value." The floors were divided into hundreds of small offices—private, walled-in cells, much like hotel rooms, for self-employed workers, agents, lawyers. Each office had a rolltop desk with a high back that had pigeonholes and drawers; you sat facing into the desk and getting light from the street if you had a street-front office, or from an inner court. And yet here, behind the splendid public presence of the skyscraper, a quiet revolution was playing itself out with little help from architects. As businesses got bigger, they wanted whole floors, and then entire office buildings to

Office interior of the New York Dramatic Mirror Company, 1899.

116

themselves. Internal flexibility became critical, and so did the supervision of hundreds of office employees. Taylorite efficiency swept through office management.

A man named W. H. Leffingwell started codifying matters. The cells were broken open, and a system of movable partitions installed (Sullivan himself had pioneered this system in his Wainwright Building in St. Louis)—or no partitions were used at all. There were to be no private offices for any but the highest ranks of office labor. Open floors made it easier to supervise the personnel, which by 1900 was once again almost exclusively female, as it had been earlier in the century in the textile mills of Lowell and Manchester. The rolltop desk was replaced by one that made it impossible to hide behind. Adjustable desks appeared, so that stenographers and typists could work standing or sitting. Office work was itself standardized in line with Taylor's experiments. Uniformity of appearance was stressed, and all the women were issued identical smocks. They were now arrayed in regimented rows facing in one direction, their routines fixed and unvarying, their deportment under constant scrutiny.

Then, in 1904, one architect, a pupil of Sullivan's, married the interior and exterior of the tall building into a unique office environment. Frank Lloyd Wright was already famous for his prairie houses in Chicago when he was asked to build one of them at Buffalo, New York, for Darwin D. Martin. Martin was a high-ranking executive of the Larkin Company, a nationwide mail-order firm which produced and distributed soaps. Shortly thereafter, Wright was also commissioned to design the Larkin administration building which was to accommodate the 1,800 corresponding secretaries, clerks, and executives of this flourishing family business.

This great building is no longer standing. It was torn down in 1950 to make room for a truck-storage garage. All that is left of it is a solitary pier at the edge of the site. But when the building went up in 1904, it was the first classic example of the open-plan office block. It was also prophetic of the future in sealing itself entirely from the outside and relying on its own ambience, its own environmental controls. In the originality of its vision, the magnificent spaciousness of its interior, it would be matched

Larkin Building, Buffalo, New York, 1904, Frank Lloyd Wright; interior of the central hall.

only by one other office building in the next three or four decades—Wright's own Johnson Wax Administration Building constructed in the 1930s.

Wright organized the Larkin Building around a glass-roofed central space that rose the entire height of the interior; he then wove horizontal office floors around this space. Stair towers at the four corners also held the equipment that purified and circulated air. On the fifth floor was a restaurant, and above this a conservatory, visible from the main floor some seventy feet below, with palms and tubs for aquatic plants. On either side of the conserva-

Johnson Wax Administration Building, Racine, Wisconsin, 1936–39; exterior.

The "Great Workroom" at the Johnson Wax Administration Building. Skylights fill the spaces between the ceiling disks atop the "lily pad" columns.

Office furniture, Johnson Wax Administration Building. Wright designed the chairs with three legs, as seen on the right, but they were considered a safety hazard and were recently remade in a four-legged form, left.

tory was a roof garden and a paved promenade, where the employees could take their exercise.

The entrance was on the side; you almost had to look for it and squeeze through it—to be released into this vast hall, lit from above and filled with rows of neat, orderly desks where uniformed women sat facing each other as if they were taking part in a solemn ceremony. To Wright and his Protestant clients, work and worship were kin, and in that sense the organ which the management installed in the upper gallery seems appropriate, as do Wright's inscriptions there—"Ask and it shall be given you, seek and ye shall find."

Thirty-two years later, in 1936, Wright designed the Johnson Wax Administration Building in Racine, Wisconsin; it opened in 1939. Like the Larkin Building, it too sealed itself entirely from the outside and created within one great single-room hollow, its own mechanically controlled ambience. You penetrate the fortress-like enclosure, and you are in what is called "the Great Workroom." No windows, no walls, no roof in the traditional sense—just an airy canopy and flowing space. Wright liked to quote Lao-tzu, the great Chinese poet who wrote five hundred years before Christ: "The reality of the building does not consist in the four walls and the roof but in the space within to be lived in." Wright, who was never known for modesty, would then add, "Lao-tzu said it, yes. But I built it."

To enclose the Great Workroom Wright used tall plant-like supports that are amazingly small at their base, sitting in nine-inch bronze holders, but that expand to four times their size at the top, twenty-four feet above the ground. The supports are capped by big, round discs of concrete, twenty feet in diameter, edged with glass tubing. Under these "lily-pad columns" the workers sit in Wright-designed chairs, at Wright-designed desks with swinging tills instead of drawers. The room was meant to be "as inspiring a place to work in," Wright said, "as any cathedral ever was to worship in."

But the future of the office tower did not follow Wright's lead. The skyscraper of Sullivan and his peers carried on as a type, first in period costume in the decades between the two world wars,

Skyscraper construction in Chicago.

Construction of a steel-framed skyscraper at the Schal Associates site, Randolph Street and Wacker Drive, Chicago, 1986.

Above, left. *Skyscrapers in Chicago. In the foreground, is the classical Wrigley Building by Graham, Anderson, Probst, and White, 1921. On the right stands the Tribune Tower of 1923–25 by Howells and Hood, with its elaborate Gothic details.*

Above, right. *Lever House, New York, 1952, by the firm of Skidmore, Owings & Merrill. This was the first of the glass-slab skyscrapers in New York and was to have a great influence on office tower design of the next two decades. It was declared a New York City landmark in 1982.*

then progressively in more abstract form, until it settled for the steel and glass transparencies of recent decades. Many of these towers stand because of audacious corporate patrons who caught the fever of image-making and were willing to pay a handsome price for it. Inside, neat stacks of open floors rose under banked fluorescent lights—streamlined, modish, monochromatic.

Trends and Portents

The factory of the last forty years has also been efficiently codified. It is a simple box on the outside—sealed, almost windowless, artificially lighted and air-conditioned within. What we are given is a steel frame building, one story high, with panel walls and a flat roof, usually a mezzanine for lavatories, and suspended walkways connecting them to locker rooms and cafeterias. Production area in the middle, offices up front, and shipping and storage at the back. Nothing much left to fret about architectually here, except prettifying the sheath with shiny materials like aluminum or reflective surfaces of one kind or another; aside from this, some attention might be lavished on the entrance lobby so it can impress visitors and intimidate workers into dressing better. The

The Foxboro Company Headquarters, Plymouth, Massachusetts, 1984. The company manufactures pneumatic and electronic instruments and computer systems.

The Foxboro Company; interior.

type is endlessly repeated regardless of the kind of product manufactured inside.

No doubt the modern factory building performs well. In the old factory, natural light, however plentiful within, was never satisfactory—it was either too bright or too dull, and it could never be spread evenly throughout. Uniform artificial lighting is free of such arbitrary changes. Moreover, an inward-turned environment, sealed against the outside, eliminates distractions. To the manufacturer, the ultimate objective of a good industrial plant is flow. Materials must move smoothly and with a minimum of human handling through the production line—starting at the dock, where they are unloaded and stored; through the various stages of processing; down the line to the storing of the finished product and its shipping. It's that simple.

But what is good for business is not always good for people. This is easy enough to see in hazardous jobs or tough workplaces. Workers are subjected to excessive heat at foundries; to excessive cold at meat-packing plants; to the noise and pollution of mines and construction sites. But in the sleek, tidy, smooth-running environment of the modern factory, or the modern office building for that matter, the damage, though less direct, is no less serious.

Socony-Mobil Oil Company office interior, 1950.

The efficient, hermetic world of the factory can be hard on people. Cut off from life outside, time can lose its sparkle. The uneventful sameness of place can cause tedium, disorientation. The flat lid of the ceiling presses down, human glances everywhere bounce off an opaque outer frame. In this even, rather cold light, it's not hard to feel small, somehow unconnected.

The onerous side of factory design has not been lost on the farsighted employer. At the Foxboro Company in Plymouth, Massachusetts, for example, a few adjustments have made an ameliorative difference in the workplace. The ceiling is bright and airy,

color has been added on doors and wall panels for warmth and orientation, the central space is inhabited by teams working together on one kind of product from start to finish in a spirit absent from the routinized procedures of the assembly line.

A parallel drive has been under way in the last fifteen years to make the office floor more hospitable. At its crux is the recognition of the employees' need for territoriality—for a workspace that carries in it some imprint of the worker. Not so long ago management in stylish skyscrapers decreed against adjusting blinds, bringing in personal property, or putting up family photographs—all in the name of preserving the purity of the architectural design. In these elegant buildings, the walls were all windows, but the windows did not open. The uniform artificial light had no connection to the individual work stations and the social space people might want to draw around themselves. And there was no privacy; the feeling of always being on display was hard to shake.

That purism is now over. Office landscaping is in. This means simply that the office floor is now more loosely organized—that systems of furniture are assembled independently of the exterior skin to create a variety of individuated stations. The rectilinear layout of desks has been abandoned; there are curved acoustical screens, potted trees. The message seems to be: I put in long hours in this place, I want to make myself at home when I'm here.

And there are other, more radical changes. The atrium, often greatly oversized, has opened up the core of the office building. Natural light is courted and used with dramatic effect. Even the

RepublicBank Center, Houston, 1983, Philip Johnson and John Burgee. To the left is Pennzoil Place, 1977, by the same architects.

A private office at the Union Carbide Corporation's World Headquarters, Danbury, Connecticut, 1984, Kevin Roche, John Dinkeloo and Associates. Employees choose their furnishings from thirty-two different selections.

outer shell pleats and postures in newfound freedom. The buildings look out onto trees and running water, and have operable louvers that control the sun. In fact, the change of mood is not in skyscraper design alone, but in the preferred landscape of the office buildings themselves.

There is a growing impulse nowadays to move out of the city and seek corporate peace in the countryside. Yet in abandoning its dense, metropolitan tower-forest, the office building is seeking more than country solitude, tree views, and the rush of brooks. It is also trying to break away from the immaculate anonymity of corporate order—the ambience of endless corridors and uniform fittings. Embedded in the broad, open frames of these new rural office buildings, full of sunlight and green, is something of the home, its privacy and comfort. The offices are small and individualized, the paths to them are broken up and suggest incident. The work areas are carved up in a relaxed and intimate way to create office neighborhoods.

Kevin Roche is the master designer of several of these self-absorbed corporate idylls. In the striking administrative head-

General Foods Corporate Offices, Rye, New York, 1983, Kevin Roche, John Dinkeloo and Associates. The building is sheathed in white horizontal aluminum siding with insulated glass windows to help conserve energy. The domed atrium in the center allows natural light into the surrounding work and circulation areas.

quarters for Union Carbide, in Danbury, Connecticut, he gives us an aluminum-clad, serpentine building a quarter-mile long, raised on exposed concrete columns. The building spans a saddle of land in a forested setting of almost 700 acres, which sheaths it from highways and subdivisions. You enter at either end via motor ramps and park right inside the building, within 150 feet of your office. The middle of the building is, in fact, one huge multilevel parking garage with access from nineteen lanes of roadway. From it splayed office "pods" branch out. The offices have windows that open, and you have your choice of office furnishings—traditional, "Scandinavian," or modern. All offices are the same size; there is to be no relating of status to office size and fittings. Carbide's previous home base was an elegant postwar skyscraper on Park

General Foods Corporate Offices, Rye, New York. Adjacent to the atrium is the small museum in the foreground. At the back is the interior "Main Street."

Avenue. Here, instead, in the open Connecticut countryside, the office tower, that monument to sublimated urban congestion, stretches out like a giant serpent basking in the sun, rejecting the energy and excitement of the big city. (See color section.)

By contrast, the General Foods headquarters in Rye, New York, is a formal palace block of two symmetrical wings on either side of a domed central rotunda that is penetrated by a roadway where the grand entrance would be. It is white and gleaming and reflected spectrally in a pool of water—a classical vision afloat in a

A supervisor at Memorex Corporation in Santa Clara, California, takes an air shower in a "bunny suit" before entering a "clean room." Because microscopic flecks of flaked skin, saliva, dust, and makeup can ruin computer semiconductors, manufacturers use hermetically sealed "clean rooms" in which the air is continually filtered to keep their work places dirt-free. Workers wear specially designed polyester "bunny suits" that protect the workplace from the millions of microscopic particles a person can shed each minute. All writing is done on polyester-coated paper with special ballpoint pens, since ordinary paper and pencils shed microscopic fibers.

suburban, residential setting. The rotunda holds a spectacular atrium, its dome lined with a mirror finish, with trees below encased in mirror-clad pots. Adjacent to the atrium, in a kind of abbreviated Main Street, there is an attempt to recall those low lively ambiences of the old downtown—the urban strip with the hardware store, the insurance man, the clothing store and coffee shop that never left us through all those decades of drama in the factory and the sky-scraping office.

It's not quite the same of course. In that ragged urban strip you have the chance of free association. You can talk to people not related to you through work; you can window-shop; or you can just sit around at lunch and watch it all happen. To work and yet to be in the midst of things—that was what Pullman lacked, and River Rouge. By evoking Main Street in the countrified office building, by offering workers the choice of several kinds of eating places, corporate America is trying to make amends.

Yet while we seem to be in the mood to end the long divorce between labor and life, a new technology stirs new anxieties in the American workplace. Daily, robots invade the routines of heavy industry. Computers overturn the working habits of warehouse and office. More than ever since the advent of the telephone, systems of communication make a mockery of building walls and spread a web of work far beyond their confines.

As yet the new technology has not radically transformed the architecture of working America. But it has reshaped work itself, as fundamentally as Taylorism and the assembly line had done earlier in the century. You will witness as much if you visit one of the high-tech firms of Silicon Valley and see—in "clean rooms" where air is filtered and cycled through ion neutralizers and temperature is strictly controlled—workers in polyester jumpsuits, hoods, face masks, and two layers of gloves concentrate on the tiny silicon chips that are the electronic brains of the Computer Age.

These strange inversions of work may still translate themselves into a new architectural order. Will we see large-scale commercial and industrial buildings become obsolete? Will the steady growth of white-collar industries—health, service, entertainment—fashion settings to rival those of the golden age of industry? Will textile mills and automobile plants come to share the landscape of memory with the Silicon Valleys of the future?

Whatever may lie ahead, the American workplace has left its lasting mark in the history of monumental architecture. The Wainwright and the Johnson Wax, the Amoskeag and River Rouge—these and others of their class we can properly recite, along with the pyramids, and the Gothic cathedrals, and the palaces of European autocracies, as benchmarks of excelling vision.

3

The American Street

Gessford Court is a pleasant little thoroughfare in Washington, D.C. It is something less than a proper street—more a leftover space, an afterthought. Not quite one block long and just thirty feet across, it has no sidewalks or trees to frame it. The parked cars obviously do not belong there. Small, nearly identical row-houses of brick sit directly on the passage, without any mediating zone between the public and the private domain.

Some effort has been made to soften that edge, but the miniature porches with black iron railings, the hedges and shrubs, are recent additions. They were not there when alleys like this one were carved out within strait-laced residential blocks in the late nineteenth century, and the flimsy houses were put up as money-making rentals for lowly newcomers to Washington. These darts in the urban fabric then teemed with families, most of them black, who used the pocket of space inside the block as an open-air room. Here they lived out of sight, with the solid wall of stately street-front houses as their only view. Most of the alleys are now aban-

Gessford Court, Washington, D.C. The houses date from ca. 1868.

doned. Some, like Gessford Court, have been carefully rehabilitated and are lived in mostly by young professionals.

We come out of this alley into a more familiar residential thoroughfare, the sort of tree-lined street with sidewalks and small frontyards that has been home to many of us. We spent many hours playing under the trees; we pedaled tricycles, or roller-skated on the bumpy pavement, and even sent a ball or a Frisbee to playmates across the way in defiance of the traffic, which is, in any case, slow and infrequent. At the corner of our block, there might be a grocery store where a street like ours crosses at right angles, and we can see, further down the road, other intersections of this predictable, reassuring residential grid.

Beyond the grid, the scale changes abruptly. A slashing diagonal runs headlong, against the grain of the blocks. Traffic is heavy and swift. A pedestrian here looks out of place. The street channel is far too wide to create a neighborhood. It sweeps single-mindedly into the distance and needs a landmark of some sort at the end to fix it there. The breadth and length of this impressive vista call to mind processions, parades, motorcades—it is at once a fast-paced traffic artery and a ceremonial way.

This is what Major Pierre L'Enfant intended when he drew up the plan of Washington, D.C., in 1791. He laid out a grand design of radial avenues over a close-grained grid of residential blocks. He wanted the avenues to swing between monumental terminal points; he wanted them, in his words, "to make the real distance less from place to place" and to provide a dramatic contrast with the general regularity and local beat of gridded neighborhoods.

Pennsylvania Avenue, Washington, D.C.

An interurban freeway, San Francisco, California.

At the edge of L'Enfant's expansive prospects, we leave Washington on a verdant parkway, from which pedestrian traffic is altogether banished; so are most commercial vehicles. There are no intersections at grade level, and access to the road is allowed only at a few points along the way. Our relation to flanking structures is remote now, and picturesque. The road moves gracefully through the landscape, married to the green and trees. Its broad, sinuous curves are beautifully expressive of the high-speed mobility for which the parkway is intended.

Not for long, however. The spatial dance will come to an end further out as speed becomes its own end. The conquering of distance across the vast land will favor the undeviating straight line. We will flow on a multilane band of concrete, isolated from large and small settlements on our path, not allowed to slow down or stop, bent on one thing only—making time. When we decide to peel off from the swiftly flowing river of cars, a few hours later, we will be hundreds of miles away from Washington, in Boston or Cleveland or Charlotte; and if we stay with this interstate net of freeways and keep on at that same speed, in a few days we will have reached the limits of our continental spread—the Florida coast, the banks of the Rio Grande, the Pacific shore.

From alley to superhighway—a rational, magnificently defined armature of conveyance and connection. In the history of American design, this is surely our finest national effort—and it took a long time to bring about. Always the road came first. Before there were houses, there had to be access; before there was political order, there had to be a pattern to inscribe it within; before there could be cities, a blueprint of streets had to be laid out on the unmarked land to promote occupation and ensconce public life. The road brought farmers to market, soldiers to the battlefield. The road served as a vessel of community and bonded us into one nation.

In view of this undeniable primacy of the road, it comes as a surprise to know that the creation of our local and national system, as we know it today, is rather a recent story. The federal and state governments did not get seriously involved in highway planning until only a hundred years ago. In the cities, until the end of the nineteenth century, the initiative for paving and lighting streets, or extending their reach, had to come from individuals. Public transportation lines were privately owned and operated. Progress was slow, intermittent, and of course motivated by profit. The physical condition of our streets and roads made travel tedious and city-living harsh; it kept rural America isolated and dependent.

But we pushed on. We strapped far-flung mines to shipping ports. We planted thousands of new town grids at the ends of the open road. We invented new means of transportation to move vast crowds of people and to shrink the extravagant distances of the continent. There is nothing haphazard about our network of urban and regional roadways. It is the outcome of premeditation, resolve, enterprise, and inventive genius.

Traveling on the Water

Before the railroads invaded America beginning around 1830, before the opening up of the West, long-distance travel was a slow and unpredictable adventure. The safest mode was river or coastal travel on a steamboat.

From the start, our rivers were our best highways. The French before us had managed a sweeping inland empire of widely spaced settlement clusters, from Canada to Louisiana, by plying the routes of the St. Lawrence and Mississippi in their flatboats and canoes. And when the steamboat was introduced in 1815, the impact was enormous. It was faster than earlier forms of water transport, and it could go upriver against the current, which canoes and small craft could not. The trip from Louisville to Pittsburgh took a month and a half by flatboat; a steamboat could cover the same distance in 64 hours.

River towns had a quality all their own. You first saw them from the dock at the river's edge. The busy strip along the waterfront was called Wharf or Front Street, sometimes simply First Street. This is where the railroad lines are going to run later on. From here a wide street cut through the center of town. The

A steamboat near Lake Canandaigua, New York, ca. 1870.

Cincinnati: The Public Landing, *a watercolor by John Caspar Wild, 1835.*

wharves, Front Street behind them, and the one or two busy streets leading to the market made up the true center of town. These were often the only public areas to be paved and regulated by the town authorities.

For life on Front Street the most anticipated event was the arrival of the steam packet. It was witnessed by crowds of town-folk who gathered at the wharf. The boat took away the produce of the surrounding countryside and carried it downstream to the few big river ports like Pittsburgh, St. Louis, and New Orleans—bustling centers of inland traffic and of commerce. Thousands of passengers and great quantities of cotton and wheat, pork and whiskey, much of this destined for the markets of Western Europe, passed through these ports. Their docks teemed with Mackinaw boats, keel boats, and steamboats, and Front Street was lined, along the town side, with warehouses and small businesses. In St. Louis a broad sandbar extended the street space to the water; the

A canal boat in tow on the Georgetown Level of the Chesapeake and Ohio Canal, Washington, D.C. The canal was originally built to connect Baltimore, Maryland, on the Chesapeake Bay with the Ohio River at Pittsburgh, Pennsylvania. In 1850, nearly twenty-five years after it was begun, it wound just over one hundred eighty-four miles to Cumberland, Maryland, but it never reached the waters of the Ohio.

boats were pulled up onto the sand, and a profusion of men, horses, and carts scurried about, unloading and loading the cargo.

By the 1820s canals were beginning to supplement and extend the great river highways. The canal boom began in New England around 1800; one of the earliest was the 27½-mile long Middlesex Canal, which connected Lowell and Boston by establishing an inland route between the Merrimack and Charles rivers. From New England, this novel transportation system spread west and south— in a decade or two it had reached to New York, Pennsylvania, Maryland, and the Carolinas. Canals often followed a river or a sizable stream, to take advantage of the easy gradient and the ready supply of water which could be fed into their channels by setting up dams at critical points. In fact, canals were at times no more than calm, dependable surrogates for rough or swampy waterways. Along their reaches, the more important canals spawned communities—from simple rows of houses built by the canal company for its workers, to full-fledged towns like Williamsport, Maryland; Frankford and Little Falls, New York, on the Erie Canal; and in Ohio, Middletown and Milan.

The basic design of the canal system was simple enough. There was the channel itself, a berm along one side which was made by heaping up the earth removed during the digging of the ditch, and a tow path on the other side for the draft animals, commonly mules or oxen, which pulled the boats. At intervals came the wooden locks, their V-shaped gates strapped by rope to windlasses, and the lock-keepers' houses with their vegetable gardens.

The canals were a spectacular engineering triumph for the young nation. They involved enormous efforts of digging, roadmaking for the towing teams, and the building of viaducts, tunnels, and even portage railways which carried the barges overland where necessary. Some of the viaducts, like the Canton Viaduct in Massachusetts, were truly monumental masonry structures. So were the aqueducts, of stone or wood, that carried the canal over rivers

Lockhouse Eight on the Chesapeake and Ohio Canal, 1830. This lock has an eight-foot lift. The total lift for the canal is just over six hundred feet.

Inclined planes on the Morris Canal, Newark, New Jersey. The canal ran from Newark to Phillipsburg, New Jersey, and was completed in 1831.

and streams. The channel itself had to be bridged at road crossings, either with structures high enough for boats to pass under, or with pivot-bridges that could be pushed aside by a moving boat and then returned automatically to their original position after the boat had passed through.

The Pennsylvania Main Line Canal that linked Pittsburgh to Philadelphia was a peculiar marvel. It flowed through a series of locks and aqueducts on its way to Johnstown. Then, as if by miracle, it crossed the slopes of the Alleghenies by means of inclined planes, along which the boats were pulled up mounted on rail cars. The cars were hitched to heavy hemp cables about six inches thick, and the cables to winding gears operated by stationary steam engines at the head of each plane. The rope frayed easily and was a constant hazard. It was John Roebling, the future designer of Brooklyn Bridge, who in 1841 invented a wire rope which was thinner, lighter, and stronger than hemp. A few years later he was manufacturing it in bulk.

The English novelist Charles Dickens made the trip on the Main Line Canal about this time—in 1842. He described how

occasionally the rails are laid upon the extreme verge of a giddy precipice; and looking down from the carriage window, the traveller gazes sheer down, without a stone or scrap of fence between, into the mountain depths below. . . . It was very pretty travelling thus at a rapid pace along the heights of the mountain in a keen wind, to look down into a valley full of light and softness; catching glimpses, through the tree-tops, of scattered cabins; children running to the doors; . . . terrified pigs scampering homewards; families sitting out in their rude gardens; . . . men in their shirtsleeves, looking on at their unfinished houses, planning out tomorrow's work; and we riding onward, high above them, like a whirlwind.

The whole amazing journey, from Pittsburgh to Philadelphia, took three and a half days.

Town and Country

To make the same trip from Pittsburgh to Philadelphia overland, you could spend two tiring weeks or more on the road, depending on the season—and then only if you could afford to take the Pennsylvania Turnpike. Without canals, inland travel anywhere was slow and rough. Country roads were littered with rocks and stumps, mired in mud in the rainy season and a blizzard of dust when dry.

The Colonial legacy was primitive. Many Indian paths had continued in use, and were widened only intermittently. New roads reflected the needs of towns. In New England, for example, roads and highways linked a town to its mills which cut wood and ground grain. Annual pilgrimages to the big towns on the coast, where livestock would be sold, called for broad roads, as much as 160 feet wide, fit for the movement of large herds and for wagon-turning. All this was the responsibility of township authorities.

The best roads by far, after the War of the American Revolution, were the turnpikes of the East Coast, toll roads sponsored

Tollgate house, 1833, on the National (Cumberland) Road, now U.S. 40, in La Vale, Maryland.

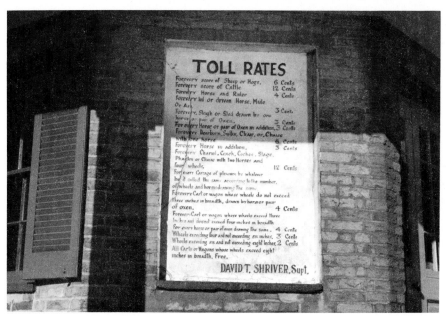

TOLL RATES

For every score of Sheep or Hogs, 6 Cents
For every score of Cattle 12 Cents
For every Horse and Rider 4 Cents
For every led or driven Horse, Mule Or Ass, 3 Cents
For every Sleigh or Sled drawn by one horse or pair of Oxen, 3 Cents
For every Horse or pair of Oxen in addition, 3 Cents
For every Dearborn, Sulky, Chair, or Chaise with one horse, 6 Cents
For every Horse in addition, 3 Cents
For every Chariot, Coach, Coachee, Stage Phaeton or Chaise with two horses and four wheels, 12 Cents
For every Carriage of pleasure by whatever name it called the same according to the number of wheels and horses drawing the same.
For every Cart or wagon whose wheels do not exceed three inches in breadth, drawn by horse or pair of oxen, 4 Cents
For every Cart or wagon whose wheels exceed three Inches and do not exceed four inches in breadth For every horse or pair of oxen drawing the same. 4 Cents
Wheels exceeding four and not exceeding six inches, 3 Cents
Wheels exceeding six and not exceeding eight inches 2 Cents
All Carts or Wagons whose wheels exceed eight inches in breadth. Free.

DAVID T. SHRIVER, Supt.

Toll rates on the National Road.

erratically and run for profit by private companies of investors which were often financial failures. The word turnpike refers to a hinged bar positioned across the road to facilitate the collection of tolls. It is related to "turnstile"—an early device intended to keep horse traffic away from footpaths.

Turnpike building started in New England and spread westward. By the 1860s these toll roads were the lifeline of the remote mining camps along the Rockies, from Montana to New Mexico. They were usually about twenty feet wide, bordered by grassy slopes. They were paved with gravel, or with logs laid perpendicular to the roadway. One of the earliest was the Philadelphia & Lancaster Turnpike Road, built in the 1790s, which cut through Pennsylvania to get to Lancaster. At the time, Lancaster was the nation's largest city not on navigable water, and a prosperous inland market center for the extremely productive farms of the region. The turnpike was surfaced with limestone, an extraordinary refinement for the time.

A demanding large-scale design, toll roads were referred to as "artificial roads," to distinguish them from trails, which were thought to be just "there." Today, as we speed along sleek, hard-surfaced public highways, we give little thought to this extensive, if helter skelter, early system of private roads, but the evidence for it is still there if you look around. A tollgate house near Cumberland, Maryland, for example, was one of many built fifteen miles apart along a highway corresponding to the old U.S. Route 40. Back then, in the early nineteenth century, this was called the National Road or the National Pike, and it was, incidentally, the only toll road to be built with government funds. At the time, the constitutionality of federal involvement in public works was bitterly challenged, and the road quickly reverted to the jurisdiction of the states through which it ran. Not until this century, a hundred years later, would the government reassert its leadership in the planning of highways.

The National Road had iron mile posts and iron gates along its path, and it crossed waters on handsome stone bridges. From the time it was opened to the public in 1818 until the arrival of railroads, the National Road was the main link between East and West, connecting Cumberland with Wheeling, West Virginia. Eventually it was carried as far as Illinois. The road followed earlier paths cut through the wilderness during George Washington's and Braddock's campaigns against the French, and these in turn had taken advantage of old Indian trails—Nemacolin's Path, which led from the upper Potomac to the vicinity of Pittsburgh, and its continuation, the Great Trail, which followed the north bank of

Wilson Bridge over the Conococheague Creek, west of Hagerstown, Maryland. This bridge was built in 1819 as a step in extending the National Road westward to the Ohio River backcountry.

the Ohio, ending near Detroit. Indeed, the role of the military in road-making was central from the start. Turnpike construction relied on the experience of military engineers from abroad, like Captain Claudius Crozet, a French artillery officer under Napoleon Bonaparte, who became state engineer for Virginia and was responsible for the Northwestern Turnpike, the predecessor of U.S. Route 50.

In the river-rich American landscape, overland roads had to negotiate frequent hurdles. You can still find standing many of the bridges built by the toll road companies—the stone bridges of the National Road, like the single-span Little Crossings bridge of 1813 over the Castleman River in Maryland; the skewed "S" bridges built at an angle to the flow of the stream; and those peculiarly American covered bridges whose wooden roof and siding protected the ingenious truss systems that stabilized their frames from the ravages of weather and, incidentally, shielded crossing animals—cattle, horses, or sheep—so they would not shy at the rushing water below. Their origin can be traced to New England; we know the names of several of the early designers—people like Timothy Palmer, who built the first covered bridge on record, the Schuylkill Permanent Bridge in Philadelphia, in 1804; Theodore Burr; Ithiel Town and William Howe, both famous for the trusses they patented; Colonel Long; Squire Whipple—all natives of New England. Dickens describes heading into a covered bridge nearly a mile long, on the way to Harrisburg, and rumbling "heavily on, filling the bridge with hollow noises."

A covered bridge over the Upper Ammonoosuc River in Stark, New Hampshire. The roof overhangs to shelter pedestrian walks on either side. The church was built in 1853, one year after the bridge was completed.

The Eagle Inn and a Conestoga wagon, in a painting by Ourand, ca. 1840.

It was profoundly dark; perplexed, with great beams crossing and recrossing it at every possible angle; and through the broad chinks and crevices of the floor the rapid river gleamed, far down below, like a legion of eyes.

And these roads were well traveled, despite the cost. All day long herds of cattle and sheep, riders on horses and mules, and handsome Conestoga wagons in the colors of the Republic—upper body red, the canvas white, underbody blue—would pour down the roadway. There were good inns at intervals with well-stocked livery stables, and wagonhouses where the rather clannish wagoneers stayed. Some of these inns and taverns gave life to small towns, usually a string of houses on two sides of the toll road. These towns were known as "road ranches."

To arrive in a major city after such arduous progress through the countryside was to experience an entirely different spatial order. Contrary to the prevailing norm in Europe, American cities had no defensive walls around them, no imposing city gates through which to enter. You knew you were there when the overgrown and underbuilt countryside met a denser settlement, and the winding country roads came up against a formal network of streets, commonly a grid. Regular geometric layouts characterized urban existence by 1800. "Curved lines, you know," said Daniel Drake of Cincinnati in 1794, "symbolize the country, straight lines the city."

The simplest way to survey land and divide it for settlement was to use a grid system. It served as an expeditious pattern for fast colonization, and so was uniformly applied to new towns. When the old established towns set about to dispose of their public land, which came quite early, they gridded it for efficient sale. In 1811 the city corporation of New York imposed a mechanistic grid on Manhattan, with no provision for open space or public squares, and quickly finished the job of transferring ownership of the island to private hands. The commissioners' report asserted "that a city is to be composed principally of the inhabitations of men, and that strait-sided and right-angled houses are the most cheap to build and the most convenient to live in." As for open spaces "for the benefit of fresh air, and consequent preservation of health," nature had blessed the Island of Manhattan with plenty of sea air, so there was no need to make provision through planning.

Savannah's grid was exceptional in a number of ways. It was, first of all, the center of something like a regional plan, with a carefully thought out transition from the thickly forested countryside to the town proper. The land was cleared for an outer zone of farming lots. Further in came garden lots of five acres each; then, "a Common round the Town for convenience of Air," as one contemporary put it; and finally the town itself along the Savannah River. The grid of streets was aired by open squares, one for each of six neighborhood units called "wards." A ward had forty house lots to the north and south of a square, and fronting the square on the east and west sides were public buildings of one sort or another, like churches and stores.

The planner of this remarkable scheme was, most probably, James Oglethorpe. He had served in the English army and under Prince Eugene of Savoy in northern Italy. Back home, he was elected to the House of Commons in 1722, and there he interested himself in prison reform, especially the plight of those turned in by their creditors. George II named him a trustee for Establish-

James Oglethorpe, 1696–1785.

Savannah, Georgia, in 1734. This view from the north shows the first four wards and squares of the city.

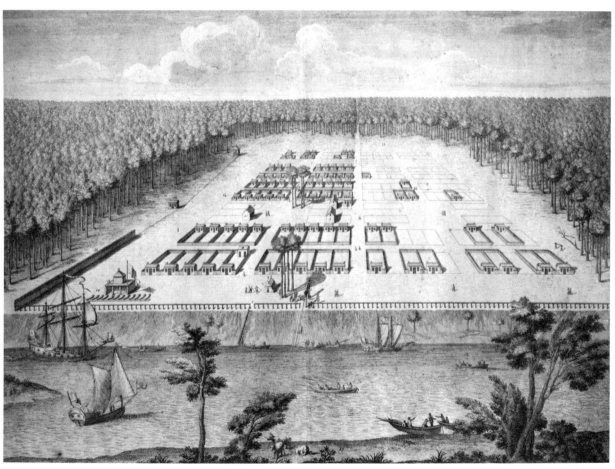

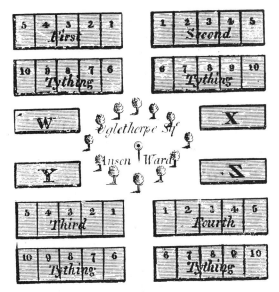

A detail of the John McKinnon map of Savannah, 1820. On the east and west sides of the square are the "Trust" lots for public buildings (W, X, Y, Z) and, to the north and south, the four Tything lots, each with ten private house lots.

Bird's-eye view of Savannah in 1871. By 1855, the city had been extended from the original six squares of 1734 to twenty-four. The area of the original settlement is shown in the center foreground at the river's edge.

ing the Colony of Georgia, putting him in charge of planning and building towns in the new colony. In November of 1732 Oglethorpe sailed out of Depford with 114 persons, most of them indigent families of artisans and shopkeepers from London with no farming experience whatever. He chose the site of Savannah himself, marked out the town and the common, and supervised the clearing. He laid out the streets and wards, and named them. Then, in a formal ceremony marred, we learn, by too much drinking, he assigned town, garden, and farm lots to freeholders.

Oglethorpe's distinctive town plan is proof that grids can be much more than dull blueprints of land division. And it held its own for more than a hundred years. As the town grew, it added wards with the same arrangement around open squares. Long before tree-lined streets were cultivated systematically in American cities, Savannah had planted its squares and main streets with shade trees. Beyond the busy riverfront with its stores and cotton warehouses, the town was green. The streets were broad and sandy. Among the densely gridded towns of America, the city stood out as a picture of gracious urbanity, and does still.

Oglethorpe was undoubtedly inspired by the contemporary residential squares of London. Yet another model lay closer still. Philadelphia's grid had been famous since the day in 1682 when William Penn determined the plat that called for streets "uniform down to the water from the country bounds." Penn's plan provided spacious lots with plenty of room for gardens and orchards, and five squares intended as recreational grounds—the ancestors of our urban parks. The squares, however, were soon neglected, becoming dumps or cemeteries. Overcrowding began to put pressure on Penn's dream of a "green country town, which will never be burnt and always be wholesome." In a short time, the generous city blocks were cut up by additional streets, mostly narrow alleys.

Street design entered a new phase when small townhouses, based on the London model, made their appearance along these narrow lanes. Blocks of several attached houses now framed the street into a closed space, giving it a premeditated look. The detached house on its own plot of land, always the preferred American residence, tends to work against the concept of the street as

Rowhouses in Savannah. By the mid-nineteenth century, Savannah had interspersed single-family houses with rowhouses in the manner of Baltimore and Philadelphia.

a well-defined volume and a corridor of movement. The independent house masses, set back from the street plane and not always holding to the same line, tend to diffuse the purpose of the street, to blur its visual clarity. We know of some early attempts to enforce regularity. We looked at Williamsburg's prescriptions for holding to a common street line when we discussed its houses in the opening chapter. In Penn's Philadelphia the intention to have uniform spacing of buildings along the streets, and so to underscore the regularity of the checkerboard town plan, was made clear. Penn wrote:

[L]et the houses built be in a line, or upon a line, as much as may be. . . . Let every house be placed, if the person pleases, in the middle of its plat, as to the breadth way of it.

Yet these attempts at regularity were special cases. By and large the appearance of streets was a matter of private initiative. Boston, for example, periodically empowered individuals to open new streets at their own cost; they realized a profit by selling the adjacent lots and left the pattern of occupation up to the new owners. Something of this laissez-faire attitude is suggested in the description of early Colonial settlement forms in the north by the president of Yale University, Timothy Dwight.

A town in the language of New England, denotes a collection of houses. . . . A Street is the way, on which such a collection of houses is built; but does not at all include the fact, that the way is paved. . . . Nor is it intended that the houses are contiguous, or even very near to each other.

In fast-growing cities like Philadelphia, Boston, and Baltimore, the fashion of attached townhouses forced the issue of street design. It gave the street the kind of enclosure and direction it had not insisted on before. With this began the practice, just before 1800, of retaining architects to design whole streets. Earliest were Charles Bulfinch's rows for Boston and Robert Mills's (the designer of the Washington Monument and the U.S. Treasury Building) for Philadelphia and Baltimore. Generally, the relation of the houses to the street channel was studied. The rows were brought close to the edge of the lots, and between them and the street channel an intermediary space was created in the form of a sidewalk. These sidewalks defined a pedestrian island separate from the increasingly crowded traffic of the street. The rowhouses

Street scenes of the Five Points Area of New York in 1827 (details of a lithograph from Valentine's Manual, *1855).*

related to this intermediary in a number of ways: directly, by means of decorous doorways lined up at the street level; or with stairs or stoops that led up to a landing well above the sidewalk, leaving space below for a basement unit, or for servants' quarters in the richer rows.

The new arrangement intensified the public aspect of the street—its use as a stage of activity and chance encounters—which had been established from the beginning. A Boston observer in 1650 wrote: "The streets are full of Girles and Boies sporting up and downe." This public life was especially lively in administrative capitals, like Williamsburg and Annapolis, and in port towns with their shops, the crowds arriving on boats, the bustle of the wharfs, and those corner taverns which put up visitors, distributed mail, and served as social centers for neighborhoods.

The condition of early American streets was somewhat less than ideal. As a rule they were unpaved. Mud was always a big problem during rainy weather. Refuse and garbage clogged the roadway, and in all parts of the country scavenger animals were encouraged to roam town streets at will and devour what they could. Hogs were most common, but Charleston promoted turkey buzzards, and other Southern towns placed their faith in goats and geese. Dickens describes encountering "two portly sows . . . and half a dozen gentlemen hogs" on New York's fashionable Broadway as they headed homeward after a day's scavenging was done. And some years earlier another English traveler, the redoubtable Mrs. Trollope, writes of getting used to them in Cincinnati.

In truth the pigs are constantly seen doing Herculean service . . . through every quarter of the city; and though it is not very agreeable to live surrounded by herds of these unsavoury animals, it is well they are so numerous, and so active in their capacity as scavengers, for without them the streets would soon be choked up with all sorts of substances in every stage of decomposition.

Meantime abutters encroached upon the public space. Shop owners sent wooden awnings over the sidewalks, spilling out their wares as they still do on some of our livelier streets. Cellar entrances pushed out. In Lexington, Kentucky, there were ordinances against hog pens and other enclosures set up within the

Street traffic in 1883 on Broadway at Park Row, New York.

public ways, and Cleveland limited to three feet the distance that huge wooden replicas of boots and saddles advertising shoemakers and saddlers could project over the street. Repeatedly, legislation tried to curb galloping horses and speeding carriages. By 1830 the horse-drawn omnibus had joined coaches, carts, and carriages, causing massive traffic jams in the busy part of town.

The Tracking of America

While the center of town was a knot of activity, outside the city you could move freely and fast. For now a new kind of vehicle was making its way along a new kind of road. Beginning as early as 1830, trains had started rumbling through the countryside. It was hard to predict their impact at first—but not for long. Spurred on by huge grants of public land, railroad companies cut a hungry path through the continent, starting deep in the heart of great Eastern cities and pushing out along the suburbs they both served and created, into farmland and the mountain wilderness beyond.

The path had its own design, its own ecology. The iron rails, crossed by wooden ties and ballasted by sand or crushed stone, were flanked by strips of land that formed the right-of-way. The limits of this right-of-way were marked off by stone walls and rail fences, later on with barbed wire, which were meant to keep live-stock out. On the other side began the tidy order of the fields; inside were trapped wildflowers and weeds.

The tracks ran alongside canals and rivers, aggressively challenging their long service, but also shot off into uncharted terrain changing old patterns of human occupation overnight. Trains rushed over mountains and across plains in a frenzy that would finally spend itself, late in the century, against the shores of the Pacific. "Railroad iron is a magician's rod," Emerson wrote, "in its power to evoke the sleeping energies of land and water." By 1870, 50,000 miles of track had been laid, "enough," as one geographer wrote, "to girdle the earth twice." Miles of track were punctuated by coal piles on one side of them and ashes on the other—vivid monuments to the prodigious consumption of energy.

Favored as major railroad junctions, a handful of cities like

Chicago, Kansas City, and Seattle would witness spectacular booms. The old established cities, too, felt the transforming power of the iron horse. Railroad terminals were their gateways now. Freight yards and railroad lines usurped their cemeteries and parks and harbors, cut them off from their waterfront, pushed into the urban core as deeply as they could. The trains were kept back from playing havoc with our cities even further because of the smoke and the noise and the high speed, and people's abiding fear of explosions.

In the countryside there was no resistance. The tracks could be laid down fast and, unlike canals, they could go anywhere. In their wake, the big railroad companies planted towns at will, since

Railroad tracks across the central Illinois countryside.

their placement need no longer be bound by the paths of river commerce, or other natural routes of trade. There were far too many of these overnight railroad towns to populate adequately, as companies competed fiercely to open up new tracts ever westward.

Often the towns were identical in plan: a grid of streets, with an industrial axis along one edge, where the depot, the water-tower, and the roadmaster's house were placed, along with a ware-house or grain elevator for storing shipments the rails were bring-ing in. Around the depot, as if to civilize the sprawl of coal sheds, oil tanks, and lumberyards, the companies would provide a track-side park with a bandstand. The towns were rarely large enough to jump the tracks; when they did, low-income families, mostly blacks or migrant laborers, would live on the other or "wrong" side of the tracks. Towns of only several blocks were common. As soon as the station stop was announced and the town was plotted, the company would build a hotel, the warehouse or grain elevator, and a house for their agent. Free lots and a cash subsidy would then be offered to congregations to entice them into building churches. Schools would also get free lots, usually on the outskirts of town.

Greed was the real power behind the locomotive, and the name of the game was land speculation. Land offices in New York or Boston were busy selling "choice" lots in unborn paper towns out West while buyers were anxious to sell them right back for profit. A lot could change hands several times during the day. For the gullible few who bought in earnest, sight unseen, and boarded the trains with all their belongings for a new life in a new town, the reality at the other end would prove a bitter shock indeed. What they usually found was a patch of wilderness, remote from any semblance of urbanity, where the town was supposed to be.

Empty railbeds or abandoned tracks in the open countryside, in places like Patoka, Illinois, and Hazel, Minnesota, tell the story of those railroad towns that did get going. One day a hundred years ago gleaming tracks carried a load of hardy settlers and put them down in these spots. Their hopes were high. The promoters' bombastic words rang in their ears. But the crowds never fol-lowed, the network of links never took shape, the towns' tiny grids never fleshed out into real cities. And when trucks replaced

The settlement of Bunker Hill, Missouri, on the Kansas Pacific Railway, ca. 1880.

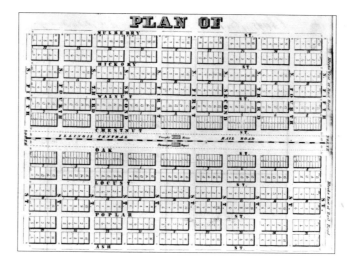

The standard town plat of the Illinois Central Associates, ca. 1855.

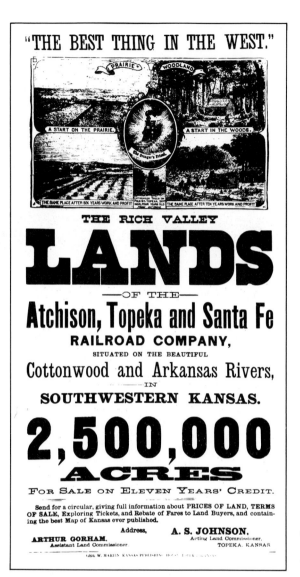

Land advertisement for the Atchison, Topeka and Sante Fe Railroad Company.

freight trains in the Twenties, the little settlements were deprived of their very birthright.

Then the depots were sold and moved, parks and bandstands disappeared. Eventually the tracks themselves were ripped out and removed. Today you can see sad remnants of this precarious chain of planted towns as you drive along the lines of the Illinois Central south of Chicago, or the Northern Pacific through Minnesota's Red River Valley: a lone grain elevator by the tracks; a

Main Street of a Texas town, 1939.

dense clump of mature trees; a smattering of houses unevenly distributed in a faint grid of streets, the empty lots which went unclaimed for years now serving adjoining homes as gardens or garages.

Main Street/Elm Street

The one indispensable element of these fledgling towns, the one that has survived as a fundamental American institution, was Main Street.

Main Street, of course, is much more than a place name to Americans. It is a state of mind, a set of values. It is what has defined the heartland of the nation for generations. The general appearance of Main Street is easily conjured. In railroad towns it ran parallel to the industrial axis along the tracks or, less often, at right angles to it. It was usually not more than two or three blocks long, wider than the rest of the town's streets, and open to farmland at either end. The business premises usually were on the ground floor, but tall "false fronts" advertised the owners' wish to get the most value out of their lot by going two stories high when they could. These upper stories, if they were ever built, were rented out to professional people like physicians and lawyers, or to groups as meeting rooms; the exterior sides were used for advertising. Until that time the false front gave the establishment prestige and dignity, and it masked the gable ends of single-story shops to provide a proper flat-topped street front like that of the urbane row buildings of Philadelphia.

Orange, Texas, May 1943.

"Main Street," Disneyland, Anaheim, California.

Main Street actually preceded the railroad and would live to survive it. In the farmland of the South, it probably started with the crossroads general store and the nucleus around this store that supplied the services farmers needed. The stores of road ranches along turnpikes may be another early model of Main Street. West of the Appalachians where town plats were surveyed before there were any farms, Main Street probably imitated densely built fragments of Eastern cities, especially the Pennsylvania towns intended as farm service centers, as a wishful shorthand of prosperity.

Along Main Street, farmers would find the stores with city-linked supplies and city luxuries, the barbershop, the offices of the local lawyer, and the local newspaper. On Saturdays farmers rode into town, put up their teams at the livery stables, picked up their mail, and patronized the saloon. Main Street was where the Fourth of July parade was held, and later on it was where the young people would kill time at the drugstore and the movie theater, and cruise around on weekend nights. And small-town life is still there on Main Street, even if it seems caught in a time warp. Friday nights, there is high school football; Saturdays, all day, farmers come to town for business and socializing; Sundays,

The "Main Street" of a California shopping mall.

church in the morning, TV football afterward. You find the Civil War monument in front of the railroad station, the corner bank, and J.C. Penney's and "Monkey" Ward—if they have not already retired to the shopping mall.

It was always something of a myth, the simple insular life of Main Street, U.S.A., easygoing and genuine—the sentimental setting of Rod Serling's *Twilight Zone* and Andy Hardy movies, where decency and common sense always ruled. So, like all myths, it could be challenged sometimes, and even disowned. On Main Street novelists like Sherwood Anderson and Sinclair Lewis could find ignorance and bigotry and closed-mindedness. Still, Main Street remains one of the central landscapes of American life. It has even been enjoying something of a comeback recently, and we have also been finding ways to enshrine and reinterpret it.

At Disneyland it has been given trees and sidewalks and harmonious Victorian street fronts. At either end there is no farmland openness but focal monuments—the railroad station and Sleeping Beauty's castle. An equally sanitized and disembodied replica of Main Street, one for present-day suburbs, has taken shape

"Elm Street, U.S.A."—Bay Street, Alameda, California.

in shopping malls, where the scale and proportions of the facades along the linear strip are carefully controlled. Excluded are bars and second-hand stores, and the kind of people who would patronize them, and instead of bustle and dirt and traffic, we are presented with tasteful landscaping and Muzak.

The real Main Street in most towns was a gritty, discordant sight. Buildings were rough-hewn and clashed with one another in their styles. Some lots remained vacant, overgrown with goldenrod and ragweed. The gap-toothed prospect was ambitiously wide, "so that there is no escape from gales or the grim sweep of land," Sinclair Lewis wrote, "[and] the breadth which would be majestic in an avenue of palaces makes the low shabby shops creeping down the typical Main Street the more mean by comparison." Today, in the era of the automobile, that breadth has served Main Street well, for it provides plenty of parking and there is no need to widen it. At its time, however, it had a scale of expectations unfulfilled.

The pendant to Main Street was Elm Street. The practice of lining street channels with uniform rows of trees had early precedents. Philadelphia and Savannah were the first cities to use trees in this way in the eighteenth century. Then in 1803, on orders from President Jefferson, Pennsylvania Avenue in Washington was planted with double rows of poplars from the White House to the Capitol. In New Haven ten years later, James Hillhouse, who owned vast tracts in the northern part of town, organized a private campaign to plant elms on all major streets and the Green—and this started a national trend. By mid-century tree-lined streets were a common sight. Broader streets would even run a row down the center. New England favored elms and maples; the rest of the East Coast went in for poplars and the fast-growing ailanthus, called the Tree of Heaven by its admirers and Stink Tree by others.

Medical arguments were soon buttressing the aesthetic grace of tree-lined streets. Cholera epidemics, for example, were attributed to a lack of sufficient electricity in the air resulting from urban congestion. "If cities must exist," a physician wrote in 1849, "let many and large spaces be devoted to parks, and let all the streets on each side of the way be lined with trees, with two or

Trees lining Pennsylvania Avenue, Washington, D.C., in watercolor of 1824 by Charles Burton. In the background is the U.S. Capitol as it was reconstructed after being burned by the British in 1814.

Drexel Boulevard, Chicago, Illinois, in 1893. The boulevard was described in 1887 as "ornamented with trees, shrubbery, grass plots, plants of many kinds, beds and borders of flowers, and other attractive features as make it the favorite equestrian resort." A mixture of two- and three-story houses and apartments lined each side.

three trees to every building, so that the people may be supplied with electricity and oxygen from Nature's own laboratory."

At the end of the century, Elm Street took on a French look. The Parisian boulevard came to the edge of town. Exclusive residential streets, some of them private, had been around earlier. We have the famous example of Louisburg Square on Boston's Beacon Hill from the 1830s and 1840s, with gates at two ends and an oval garden in the middle protected by a beautiful cast-iron fence. The model for this was the English residential square. The elegant residential street in the second half of the century was inspired instead by the new boulevards of Paris, especially in the rising towns of the Midwest, where it shaped up as an urban monument to the new super-rich, the American millionaires, a confraternity of more than 4,000 by 1890. For the first time in our urban history, the street hosted a show of conspicuous grandeur, as the house became an accessory to a contest of wealth. Cleveland had its Euclid Avenue, known also as Prosperity Street and Millionaire's Row; St. Paul had the graciously curving Summit Avenue; Milwaukee had its Prospect Avenue; and Chicago's 200-foot wide Drexel Boulevard was laid out in conscious imitation of the Avenue de l'Imperatrice in Paris.

Of course the differences were as telling as the surface likeness. The Paris avenues were framed by cliffs of uniformly designed apartment blocks; in America the private mansions on residential avenues came in a variety of fancy styles. And the active mix of commerce and residence in Paris—the sidewalk life of cafes and high-life shopping—had no place on Prosperity Street or Drexel Boulevard.

Lighting now enhanced these and other principal streets in the city. Gaslight had been used for street illumination since 1818, when it was first tried in Baltimore. But for a long time gas lamps hung only on important buildings and stayed lit only until midnight—and not at all during the full moon. The arrival of electric power changed all that. Arc-lamps came first, and then incandescent tungsten-filament electric lamps. They hung from tall wooden

Night lighting on State Street, Chicago, during the dedication of the World's Columbian Exposition, 1893.

171

Broadway from Maiden Lane, New York, in the 1880s.

posts and were owned by the private sector. New York had thirty-two competing utility companies that ran six lines of posts down Broadway, which was now called the Great White Way. With central power stations beginning to operate in the 1880s (the first in Edison's Menlo Park, New Jersey), lighting could be utilized for commercial purposes. Shops now stayed open late; night entertainment flourished. A new life seized the streets after dark.

Soon the lamps were being grouped into ornamental clusters, set on ornamental posts. These handsome iron, pressed metal, or concrete posts also supported street signs, flower bowls, alarm boxes for police and fire. A red globe was often used to signal a street hazard to drivers—the precursor of our traffic lights. For a multicolored night of signs and flashes we would have to wait until 1923 when the neon tube was perfected.

With electricity, a more far-reaching reorganization of the city would be under way. This side of the story has to do with urban transportation.

Above Ground and Underground—The Streetscape Expands

Just before the Civil War, the horse-drawn streetcar challenged, with great success, the slower omnibus, for thirty years the common means of public transportation. The advantage of the streetcar was that it moved on rails, so it could go faster. Cities were soon rushing to offer streetcar companies franchises, which generally required them to lay the rails at their own expense, and to pave the street within their tracks and for several feet outside.

Until about 1880 over one-half of all paved streets in the country used gravel, or else crushed stone on a surface graded for proper drainage, a roadway called macadam after its Scottish inventor. With the arrival of the steam roller and the mechanical stone crusher in the 1860s, macadam became widespread. Cobblestones—oval stones worn smooth by water action on beaches or river bottoms—were common on both the East and West and in the Ohio and Mississippi river valleys where stones were available. They were laid end up in a foundation of wet sand. These early pavements provided a good foothold for horses, but were exceedingly difficult to clean. Granite was better; it was the best heavy-duty stone, durable and easy to maintain, but it was expensive. New York used these expensive paving blocks first, most extensively, because its large volume of traffic could justify the expense, and because it had direct access to granite quarries.

A few other methods of paving existed, none very satisfactory. Wood had been widely used since Colonial times. Early turnpikes sometimes resorted to whole logs. These so-called "corduroy roads" were usually a short-term expedient against recurrent mud. They still exist in the New Jersey Pine Barrens and are used when harvesting Atlantic white cedar to facilitate the hauling out of lumber. The turnpikes of the 1850s tried plank paving to make them-

*Street paving on Compton Avenue,
St. Louis, 1906.*

selves more competitive in the wake of the railroad's popularity,
and in the suburbs plank roads were in use until the end of the
century. To this day, you can trace the run of one plank road
between San Diego, California, and Yuma, Arizona, though not
much is left of the wood. Just before the Civil War, Samuel Nicolson, a construction engineer for a plank road company, patented a pavement of treated square wood blocks, coated with tar
to prevent decay, and nailed to a plank base. The Nicolson pavement became all the rage in cities like his hometown of Boston,
New York, and Washington, D.C., but it proved disastrous in a
very short time. The blocks were foul-smelling because they
absorbed street liquids when dry, and secreted them back in

humid weather, along with preservatives; laid too tight, the pavement popped open when moisture expanded the blocks. The Upper Midwest preferred round cedar blocks grouted with gravel and tar.

The streetcar, when it entered the scene, presented a thorny problem for street design. The tracks needed a smooth, strong surface, the area in between a yielding but steady surface for the horses. Stone or even iron wheelways, though expensive, were much in favor. As for the middle, the best solution by far came with the perfection of asphalt, a flexible mass of stone and sand on a concrete foundation. It was smooth and quiet and easy to main-

Laying streetcar tracks in New York, 1897.

New York street scene of the 1890s.

tain. From 1885 onward, it began to replace gravel, macadam, cobblestone, and granite as an all-purpose, modern street surface.

With the coming of electricity, horsepower could be retired altogether. Trolleys and electrified street rails took over decisively in the 1890s. Of course there were consequences for the appearance of the street. The trolley's overhead wire joined the telegraph and telephone wires that had been hoisted above the street a little earlier. These wires were held up by poles that cluttered the street banks.

Some changes went deeper. City streets until this time had been vital public spaces for their neighborhoods. You could visit or gossip or argue with neighbors, and children could play stickball or tag there. Often the streets were their only playground. Streets were open-air markets, too, with pushcart vendors peddling their wares from door to door and shops spilling out onto the sidewalks. The abutters had control over the kind of street they wanted. It was they who decided when and how their streets would be paved. With the appearance of streetcar companies, this control eroded. The slow process of deterioration set in as streets became primarily traffic arteries moving people through the city and out into the mushrooming suburbs.

In the suburbs you went to live away from street life, which is to say away from public life. You removed yourself from the workaday world, from that mixed environment of home and business, of rich and poor. There was no open-air selling, and neither the physical tumult nor the pageantry that are companion energies of the traditional urban street. The suburb aspired to be close to nature—which meant lawns and leafy trees, and in some in-

Streetcars crossing the Bogye Falaya River, Covington, Louisiana.

stances, winding streets intentionally different from the ubiquitous right angle of the urban grid. The curve, once a trait of the country road and a symbol of rusticity, signified the privilege of suburban withdrawal.

Picturesque, curvilinear streets found little favor in the less affluent suburbs or in the layout of new towns. The pattern was hard to apply, and in the context of the fast-buck speculative market, it was also wasteful; too many odd-shaped lots were left. When Frederick Law Olmsted, the great planner of parks and picturesque suburbs, submitted a sophisticated curvilinear design for the new town of Tacoma, Washington, a design that exploited the eventful topography of the site, the client, Northern Pacific, turned it down derisively.

It was the most fantastic plat of a town that was ever seen [a contemporary wrote]. There wasn't a straight line, a right angle or a corner lot. The blocks were shaped like melons, pears, and sweet potatoes. One block, shaped like a banana, was 3,000 feet in length and had 250 plots. It was a pretty fair park plan, but condemned itself for a town.

If the sensible grid carried the day in the new subdivisions outside of town, often with complete disregard for the terrain, the notion of an alternative way of life free of urban restrictions was permanently established by the second half of the nineteenth century. In a purportedly healthy and virtuous suburban setting, people retreated from the traditional role of the citizen as a social being and opted for a private environment which, unlike the inner city where they worked, could be shaped and controlled by them alone. This quiet retreat was theirs to enjoy because of regular streetcar service—and then something even faster.

After the Civil War, a new offensive from the private transit companies was launched when New York introduced the elevated train—the "El" for short. Other big cities followed suit—Boston, Chicago, Kansas City. Darkness descended on Manhattan's Ninth and Sixth avenues and all along Chicago's Loop. Noise and dirt assailed the pedestrians below. They felt the vibration of passing trains and could plainly see the oil and hot ashes spewn by their locomotives. Even after the lines were electrified, the El thoroughly shattered the conventions of street life. The abutters re-

Elevated railway over Wabash Avenue, Chicago, Illinois.

belled. In New York they sued repeatedly, until the courts ruled against the companies and affirmed the legal right of abutters to "light, air and access." That was the last hurrah for community control of urban streets. Soon suburban clout and the bureaucracy of municipal engineers would win the day and take over for good.

Before the end of this eventful century, the urban street saw a final transformation. Speed on public conveyances in the downtowns escalated sharply when the cable car was put to use in San Francisco and about fifteen other cities, among them Chicago, Kansas City, Cincinnati, and Seattle. This mode of transportation also dispensed with horses. Instead, the cars were moved using an underground cable controlled from a cable house. A device which grappled the continuously moving cable passed from the cars through a slot run down the middle of the streetcar tracks, pulling the cars in a kind of towing operation.

In cities like Boston and New York, the subway too now came into its own. With electric power, trains could run in tunnels

The network of cables, piers, and pipes under a present-day city street, as recreated in a drawing by David Macaulay.

without being plagued by the gas, smoke, and dirt spewed out by steam locomotives. So the street which had usurped space above the pavement with the El now sank underground as well. Subway stations made large holes in the street surface. It must have been startling, at first, to see crowds of people emerge from these holes at intervals and mingle with the street traffic.

Indeed, the ground beneath the street was developing a most extraordinary configuration of its own, accessible through manholes from which steam shot out now and then. To make room for these underground tunnels, millions of tons of soil and rock would be removed through the years. Buildings, increasingly taller and more massive in the downtown, sought a firm grip in the subsoil with long tentacles of piers and friction or bearing piles. Their waste, once disposed of in open sewers at the street level, was now carried in individual underground pipes that fed into large laterals, which in turn connected to mains; as sewage systems became more sophisticated, huge pipes called "interceptors" would be added to move the growing volume of effluent to treatment plants. The water supply had an elaborate pipe network of its own, where it was kept under constant pressure and fed into plumbing systems and fire hydrants. Electricity moved through heavy cables enclosed in pressurized pipes, and in time telephone wires also moved underground to join other utilities, like natural gas used in heating and cooking. Below all this underground mesh capacious storm drains made of brick carried away the rushing waters of flash rains and melting snow that would otherwise flood basements and subways.

To some it was an exciting time. There were urban prospects, sensations, experiences to be had which were unparalleled in the memory of the townspeople. In a novel published in 1890, William Dean Howells' *A Hazard of New Fortunes,* there is a glowing description of an El ride at nighttime on New York's Third Avenue. Mrs. March professes to love "the fleeting intimacy . . . formed with people in second and third floor interiors, while all the usual street life went on underneath." Looking out of the El into the homes of people along the avenue, Mr. March finds the sight more riveting than theater: "a family party of workfolk at a late tea, some of the men in their shirt sleeves; a woman sewing by a lamp; a mother laying her child in its cradle; a man with his head fallen on his hands upon a table; a girl and her lover leaning over the window-sill together." At Forty-second Street, standing at the bridge that crossed the tracks of Grand Central Station, they

looked up and down the long stretch of the Elevated to north and south. The track that found and lost itself a thousand times in the flare and tremor of the innumerable lights; the moony sheen of the electrics mixing with the reddish points and blots of gas far and near; the architectural shapes of houses and churches and towers, rescued by the obscurity from all that was ignoble in them; and the coming and going of the trains marking the stations with vivider or fainter plumes of flame-shot steam—formed an incomparable perspective.

To others, no amount of romanticizing could do away with the chaos and ugliness and noise of the new urban scene. For them 1893 was to be a memorable year.

The City Beautiful

Eighteen ninety-three was the year of the World's Columbian Exposition. The occasion was the 400th anniversary of Columbus' discovery of America, and the nation, with its dreadful Civil War behind it and its territorial expansion at an end, was in a mood to celebrate. Chicago, the capital of the Midwest, was selected by Congress in 1888 as the site of the fair. The city was itself an amazing exhibit of the nation's energies. "Those who come here will wonder how," one visitor wrote, "in less than fifty years, in less than a man's lifetime, it has been possible to transform a swamp, producing only a sort of wild onion, into a powerful and flourishing city." Chicago worked hard for five years. In the undeveloped marshes of the South Side, a network of lagoons was created and on it floated a white vision of harmonious Classical buildings, all holding to an even cornice line, fortified with lofty sculptures and floodlighted at night. The fair was promptly nicknamed the White City.

During the preceding decade a grass roots movement of tidying

The World's Columbian Exposition of 1893, Chicago.

up had begun to spread across the land. In this mood of self-improvement, citizens' groups went to work to save their waterfronts from the ravage of railroad tracks. Olmsted and others endowed several cities, Buffalo and Minneapolis for example, with lush park systems tied together with beautifully landscaped boulevards. Improvement societies, in city and small town alike, set their sights more modestly on projects of street-paving, tree-planting, and the artistic design of lampposts.

Unlike this piecemeal beautifying, the Chicago World's Fair was a dream come true: an entire city, problem-free and pure, cut from one cloth, subject to some superior order. To the millions who came there, the lovely scene reflected in the still waters, at once monumental and ethereal, seemed to promise a brilliant future for urban America. This was the start of the so-called City Beautiful Movement. Its premise was that overall plans like that of the Fair would bring order to the disquieting jungle of American towns, an order based on uniformity, on the Classical style in public architecture, on reverence for natural beauty. Its guiding spirit was a Chicago architect and entrepreneur, Daniel H. Burnham.

Daniel H. Burnham, 1846–1912. This portrait was painted by Anders Zorn in 1899.

Burnham's office had played a leading part in the development of the Chicago skyscraper during the Eighties. Now his energies were directed toward the disorder of the cities, the jumble of buildings that "sadly disturbs our peacefulness and destroys that repose within us that is the true basis of all contentment." He toured the magnificently planned cities of Europe—Rome, Paris, Versailles, Vienna—in preparation for his first major planning assignment—the improvement of the nation's capital in accordance with the Senate Parks Commission Plan (1901–2) nurtured by Senator James McMillan.

L'Enfant's grand scheme for Washington had fallen on bad times and looked ragged and unfinished. Burnham's provisions for its recovery were the first opportunity he had since the Chicago Fair to apply the City Beautiful principles to an actual city. His design removed the railroad yards that had invaded the Mall, carpeting this space with grass and flanking it with rows of elm trees. Lined with public galleries and museums on either side, the mall controlled an axis extending beyond the Washington Monument, to the Potomac's banks, where a memorial to President Lincoln would be set and a bridge would go across to Arlington

Proposal for the improvement of Washington, D.C., 1902, from the Report of the Senate Committee on the District of Columbia. Senator James McMillan, Chairman of the Committee, appointed Daniel Burnham in 1901 to head a commission to create a plan for the development of the entire park system in the District of Columbia. The final drawings were prepared under the supervision of the other commission members, the architect Charles McKim, the young landscape architect Frederick Law Olmsted, Jr., and the sculptor Augustus Saint-Gaudens.

National Cemetery. Boulevards and parks would encircle the city, and a monumental railway terminal, Union Station, would be built northeast of the Capitol.

Burnham followed with other grand plans—for Cleveland and San Francisco, for Manila and Baguio in the Philippines. But he lavished his prodigious talents as visionary planner and organizer on his native Chicago. He fired up the business community with this magnificent vision, which his renderers depicted with great brilliance on large panels. Over a vast area within a sixty-mile radius from the center, where the endlessly sprawling grid left its thin plat on the prairie and was cut off from its lakefront by streams of railroad tracks, Burnham now swung his forceful lines. He embraced the region in a generous chain of outer parks. He rid the lakefront of steel and greened it. He carved a spacious inner harbor framed by causeways that stretched a mile out into the lake and served as breakwaters for the fierce Chicago winds. Then he galvanized the relentless checkerboard with sweeping diagonals, much as L'Enfant had done on paper for Washington one hundred years earlier. Within the Loop, these breathtaking avenues converged on a monumental civic center, at the intersection of Halsted and Congress, and the city hall itself was transfixed by a dome as tall as a three-story building, which would have been a towering landmark for this flat, featureless prairie scene.

Burnham's magisterial civic center was never built. But the type it represented—a monumental core symmetrically disposed around a mall, with administrative and cultural buildings all part of a uniform Classical design—did materialize in Cleveland and San Francisco, and fragments of City Beautiful schemes can be

Davies Symphony Hall, San Francisco, as seen from the west steps of City Hall. The hall was designed by the firm of Skidmore, Owings & Merrill and opened in 1980. On the right is the War Memorial Opera House, 1932.

seen in many cities and towns across the country—in Berkeley, California; in Duluth, Minnesota; in Springfield, Massachusetts. Some are still being completed. In Washington, the Lincoln Memorial was not inaugurated until 1922; the National Gallery of Art, not until 1941. A new symphony hall in San Francisco has just filled out the mall of the civic center, some sixty years after the fact. "Make no little plans," Burnham is quoted as saying; "they have no magic to stir men's blood. Make big plans, aim high in hope and work, remembering that a noble, logical diagram once recorded will never die."

He was right. The City Beautiful plans had no legal force. They were not buttressed by any fundamental change in land ownership or administrative control. In a democratic society, they could not be imposed from above. Cities had to secure the championship of their industrial and business leaders and persuade the citizenry to vote for huge bonds. It is all the more remarkable— a measure of the appeal the City Beautiful dream exerted on the national imagination—that we are left with such a splendid urban legacy from the blueprints of those distant years.

This uplifting, imperial urbanism did not address the core problems of the cities—congestion and poverty and overburdened services—nor did it affect more than a tiny fraction of their physical fabric. But the invention of a single artifact in those same years of the Chicago World's Fair—the automobile—would lead to the total restructuring of our cities, our road network, our whole way of life, far beyond anything imagined by Burnham and his colleagues.

The Automobile

Actually, the lobby for better roads had started well before the advent of the automobile.

When the nation was being swept up in the glories of City Beautiful, rural communication remained primitive. Railroad lines connected towns, but did little for the countryside. The section lines of the National Survey, which determined the strict checkerboard of townships a century earlier, were badly obscured, if

Members of the Philadelphia and Germantown bicycling clubs riding on Belmont Avenue, Philadelphia, in 1879.

they were ever uniformly visible. Most of them never became roads. The farmer's overwhelming concern was to get to market, and farm-to-market roads took the easiest bend or crossing. These crude dirt roads were not graded and had no side ditches. They were not good enough for mail carriers, and cream being delivered to towns could turn to butter on the way from too much shaking. Road maintenance fell to unskilled local labor, because the road tax in most states could be paid by putting in a day's labor on county routes, and many individuals took the option of working away their tax obligation.

Just before the Chicago Fair, pressure began to mount from various quarters to improve the rural network. Granges and other farm organizations lobbied to advance the lot of their constituencies. "Get the farmer out of the mud," was the trumpet call. The federal program of Rural Free Delivery (RFD), initiated in 1891, linked home delivery of mail to the local care of roads. If farmers did not fix their roads, they would have to go once a week, as before, to the nearest general store or post office to collect their mail. In the meantime, the League of American Wheelmen raised its voice on behalf of several million Americans who were discovering the pleasures of a new contraption—the bicycle.

All this pressure paid off. The states set up their own highway

Early motoring on a Colorado road.

departments, and under their professional supervision, section roads were straightened, graded, and paved. For the first time, the Survey lines became visible on a grand scale. Farms on either side of roads contributed half of the rights-of-way, up to fifty feet on their boundaries, to make the section roads. And the government at long last recognized its responsibility to promote a national system of highways by passing the Federal Highway Act of 1916.

The government had taken on road-building only once in the past—and then not for long—when in the opening decades of the nineteenth century it undertook to build the National Pike across several states from Maryland to Illinois. Thomas Jefferson at the time enunciated the need for a national road network, "commensurate with the majesty of the country," which would guarantee the unity of his agrarian republic. "New channels of communication will be opened between the States," he wrote in his Message of 2 December 1806, "the lines of separation will disappear, their interests will be identified, and their union cemented by new and indestructible ties." Now, one hundred years later, the government would finally embrace the cause of providing coast-to-coast communication.

The first fully paved road across the country, grandly named the Lincoln Highway, set out to connect New York and San Francisco a few years before the act of 1916. It would be another ten years before this road would be completed as a true cross-country highway, now called U.S. Route 30, and by then the Motor Age had moved well beyond its dawn. Hard smooth asphalt surfaces were scoring the land. Automobiles, and bicycles too, were well served by these roads, which responded nicely to the suction of the rapidly turning wheel; they required no new kind of paving. Driving opened up worlds of virgin countryside unknown to railroads. The freedom from railroad tracks, from timetables, from depot hotels, was a thrilling emancipation. You could now go anywhere and see everything. Railroad travellers had 300,000 miles of fixed lines along which they were channeled by the companies. Motorists now had three million miles of road, even if sections were still dirt and pocked by mudholes, and they could choose their path as they wished. There was a great sense of adventure, of camaraderie.

Americans had always thought of the open road as freedom, opportunity, self-realization. Walt Whitman's "Song of the Open Road" expressed it best in 1856 when he saw himself

> loos'd of limits and imaginary lines,
> Going where I list, my own master total and absolute,
> Listening to others, considering well what they say,
> Pausing, searching, receiving, contemplating,
> Gently, but with undeniable will, divesting myself of the holds
>   that would hold me.

Freedom was here as never before. And it was transforming the countryside along with the Americans who raced through it. Whitman's "long brown path" would in time become a long grey ribbon. A whole new roadside environment would take shape—from the first free campgrounds and pay camps, to motor courts in Mission, wigwam, or Colonial styles, offering separate cabins and most hotel comforts, and a variety of services like restaurants and gas stations.

The Shady Grove roadside motel, Lyons, Georgia, in 1940.

We know now only too well how far that commercialization of the roadside was to be carried over the next few decades. In 1926, there were an estimated 2,000 cabin camps for cars, mostly in the West and Southwest, especially California. By 1935, 16,000 "motels" cropped up in the country, and by 1940, they totaled 20,000. The number would reach 60,000 by 1960.

The installment of the car culture was not without tension. At the start, well-to-do cityfolk owned cars and drove them in the country as if it were their private preserve. Farmers resented these leisure-mongering tourists, and it was only when Ford made the Model T, which fit the farmer's need and pocketbook, that rural America accepted the car.

Until the Thirties motoring trips by country-folk were short. Cars were used to go to town, for family visits, and Sunday drives—but not for work, where the horse was still on duty. This separation of work and entertainment held fast until tractors replaced the horse. Meanwhile, shopping became more and more centralized. Goods and services once supplied from farms or villages, or available in the block or two of Main Street, moved to regional town centers. Rural space was thus reorganized. The car changed the landscape of the small town too. Barns, liveries, blacksmiths, and harness shops gave way to auto dealers, garages, gas stations, and parking lots. In the end, Main Street spilled out at both ends onto the strip development along the highway.

If the car promoted tourism and gave the farmers the gift of movement, it also enabled the poor to go where the work was. Migrant workers were beneficiaries of the Motor Age; for them and their families a car was more than a vehicle: it was also where they lived. In *Grapes of Wrath,* John Steinbeck wrote of the predominantly white and native-born migrant workers who had made "the highway . . . their home and movement their means of expression."

Modern highways also meant new towns—and the expansion of old ones. The Florida boom of the Twenties, when dozens of cities were laid out in a repeat of the overnight towns of the previous century along railroad lines, was spurred on by the automobile and its road system. Only this time around the settlers were not farm-minded pioneers. They came down from the big cities to find balmy winters and untroubled retirement days—a rosy picture that developers held up to them. The tropical climate of Florida, the closeness of New York and Washington, and Coolidge prosperity were allies of the new contraption in turning the summer and autumn of 1925 into a frenzy of land speculation. In Miami, Frederick Lewis Allen wrote in *Only Yesterday,* "motor-busses roared down Flagler Street, carrying 'prospects' on free trips to watch dredges and steam-shovels converting the outlying mangrove swamps and the sandbars of the Bay of Biscayne into gorgeous Venetian cities for the American home-makers and pleasure-seekers of the future." The coast from Palm Beach southward, and the surrounds of West Coast towns like Tampa and Sarasota, were being staked out into fifty-foot lots. New towns like Coral Gables and Miami Beach were fast taking form; whole subdivisions were sold out within a day. Only the ferocious hurricanes of 1926 were able to sober the developers and buyers and bring the fever under control.

This is also the beginning of a new age of suburbs—car suburbs. Their biggest day was yet to come—in the decade or so after the Second World War—but the novelty was already apparent. These suburbs would no longer be bound by the fixed distances set by the reach of train or trolley; nor would they be restrained in spread by how far a suburbanite could walk to get home from the station. The floodgates opened, and the countryside was swept by far-reaching waves of suburban sprawl. Cities spilled out and touched other cities in a prelude to the age of the megalopolis, the great urban regions of East and West.

The network of all-weather roads mushroomed during the Depression, when New Deal programs of the Roosevelt Administration to relieve unemployment set highway construction as a top priority. The nation now witnessed for the first time the engineering marvels of superhighways and clover-leaf intersections (the first in New Jersey in 1928), of spectacular long-span bridges and vehicular tunnels.

The first federal highway was U.S. Route 1 along the East Coast. When it was completed in 1938, it ran for 2,500 miles from Fort Kent, Maine, to Key West, Florida, and linked fourteen states. Route 1 was actually earmarked in 1925 as a result of the new Federal Highway Act, whose purpose was to unify the rapidly growing system of roads, and it soon became synonymous with vacation trips to Florida. Route 1 is truly piecemeal, incorporating the Main Streets of small towns and stretches of downtown streets as it passes through main cities. It crosses the Hudson River on the George Washington Bridge, goes past the Jefferson Memorial in Washington D.C., and skirts the great Okefenokee Swamp which straddles the Georgia-Florida border.

The first *limited-access* superhighway, one that was to set the pattern for things to come, was the Pennsylvania Turnpike. Its challenge was to cross the mighty Alleghenies. A hundred years earlier, this had been the challenge of a historic predecessor, the Pennsylvania Main Line Canal. The Pennsylvania Railroad had followed the canal twenty years later and had hooked up, at least in the beginning, to the original inclined-plane system that carried Dickens on his Main Line run in 1842. Then came the abortive, half-finished South Pennsylvania Railroad which tunneled its way through the mountains. Abandoned tunnels and the partially graded right-of-way of the South Penn were repossessed by the Pennsylvania Turnpike to run the 160 miles from Middlesex, near

A cloverleaf intersection near Chicago, Illinois.

U.S. 40 in Maryland.

*Architecture of the car culture—
Herberts, on Fairfax Avenue,
Beverly Hills, Los Angeles, by Wayne
McAllister, 1936. This drive-in's
circular design with radial parking
made all customers equally
accessible to the carhops and central
kitchen; its neon pylon helped attract
passing motorists.*

*Interior of a Biff's restaurant in
Southern California, ca. 1950,
Douglas Honnold, architect. At Biff's
customers had an unimpeded view
of the kitchen area where their food
was prepared and of their parked
cars in which they had arrived.*

Carlisle, 16 miles west of Harrisburg, to Irwin in Westmoreland County, 21 miles east of Pittsburgh.

The four-lane (two through the tunnels), all-weather, toll highway was opened to traffic on October 1, 1940—and it was a smashing success. There were no traffic lights, no intersections, no steep hills or sharp curves. There was no speed limit. A support system, including service stations and a chain of Howard Johnson's restaurants, made it possible to stay on the highway until the very end. It was called "the magic motorway."

From that time forward, Americans set out to fuse their lives and their cars. They learned to eat, court, and even worship behind the steering wheel. The car brought about an indigenous twentieth-century culture, whose roadside landmarks were motels, drive-in movie theaters, road houses, chain restaurants, and the brassy, untameable strip which drained the vigor of an upstaged Main Street.

Just as the Pennsylvania Turnpike opened a new era in motoring, so did Howard Johnson's mark a new era in public dining. If the turnpike prefigured the great Interstate system, so Howard Johnson's was the forebear of Stuckey's and McDonald's in the standardization of roadside food—national chains with their familiar logos which created what Daniel Boorstin has called a "consumption community." This automotive society had grown immensely. In the boom years of the Twenties, car ownership had expanded from under 7 million in 1919 to over 23 million in 1929. The road began to be identified in the 1930s with national unity. Motoring was described as a family experience. At a time during the Depression when many worried about family dissolution, the automobile vacation came to be seen as a means of "togetherness," and motoring was advertised as a way to save the family. This bent toward family fun spurred a demand for home-like accommodations—informal, domestic, deliberately old-fashioned. Driving was also generally applauded as a democratic experience. Fast food, the same everywhere, served in informal, comfortable settings, was perfect for these sentiments.

By 1930 three kinds of roadside eateries were visible. Tea-rooms, set in old farmhouses, renovated taverns, and other "historic" buildings, catered to the prohibitionist, pro-family crowd—

Howard Johnson's Motor Lodge and
Restaurant, Milwaukee, Wisconsin,
1965.

ruffled curtains, candlelit interiors, toney, a bit pretentious. The hot-dog, barbeque, fried chicken, or ice cream stands were low-class, egalitarian, dispensing no frills fare. And finally the diner, which had started as a working-class "nickel lunch" in the late nineteenth century, was mass-produced by 1930 in the hands of a few large companies, with standardized, professional kitchens. Diners appealed to all classes and were in that sense truly democratic. But they had the wrong connotations, those of the railroad era, and they lacked the kind of rural-historic image sought after at the time.

Howard Johnson combined all three roadside themes. His restaurants had the tearoom's homeyness, the diner's democracy and efficiency, the stand's fast-fried formula. On the Pennsylvania Turnpike, since he had a monopoly, Johnson let the restaurants follow the style of local Colonial stone architecture. But out on the national roads, to become competitive, he settled for the familiar New England town hall/church image, with the stucco walls, a bright orange steeple, green shutters and overhanging eaves; inside you had New England prints, paneled walls, neo-Colonial furniture. Riding on success, in 1954 Howard Johnson diversified and started to attach motels to his restaurants. In line with a trend that had started in the Forties, when major motel chains like Quality Courts and TraveLodge went into business, Howard Johnson motels squeezed out many independent, family-run roadside inns. When the federal Interstate highway program was launched in 1956, the big hotel chains like Sheraton and Hilton also got into the act and started grabbing prime sites and key interchanges and exits.

A Story Without End

The National System of Interstate and Defense Highways, as the 1956 program was named, had as its goal the completion of 41,000 miles of superroads connecting ninety percent of all cities with a population of over 50,000. The funding was to be derived from a gasoline tax. These funds accumulated at a staggering rate and by law could be used on nothing other than the building of highways. A tremendous national effort now got under way. In the Sixties some 90,000 people per year in the path of new highways were being evicted. Park land, creek beds, and black ghettoes were the most vulnerable, because they were the cheapest to acquire.

In 1967 when President Lyndon Johnson tried to divert some of the gas tax, called the Highway Trust Fund, to other programs, he was soundly defeated. The highways had unbeatable support. Their lobby consisted of a powerful alliance of truckers, builders, automobile companies, building materials companies, oil companies. The Fund still sits and accumulates; it cannot be diverted to systems of public transportation, and it remains to be seen whether some of the money can even be used for the upkeep of aging bridges and old stretches of highway.

The great Interstate web did indeed shrink our continental distances; it brought us all closer to one another. But it also dried up the old long-distance highways and isolated travelers from the

It winds_____ from Chi - ca - go to L. A.,__
miles all the way.__ Get your

life of the country. The open roads of lore were reduced to lack-luster carriers of local traffic. U.S. Route 1 was bypassed by Interstate 95; its straighter stretches save travelers hundreds of miles, and a lot of time that would have been spent going through towns and villages. Many of these settlements and roadside stops are now

An abandoned gas station on U.S. 40, seventeen miles west of Cumberland, Maryland. The newer, bigger Interstate 70 now siphons off most of the through traffic in this area. This stretch of U.S. 40 was originally part of the National Road.

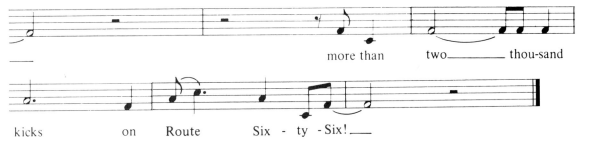

more than two_____ thou-sand

kicks on Route Six - ty - Six! ____

ailing; some are dead. All along Route 1 you can now see abandoned gas stations and stores, old billboards, rusting gas pumps. Route 66, the 2,200-mile highway stretching from Chicago to Santa Monica, California, immortalized in songs and novels and on television, has suffered a more ignominious fate. The American Association of State Highway and Transportation Officials recently voted to decertify it and remove its signs.

Cities too were forced by the highway system to decline and decay. Some hooked up to this national flow at great cost to their built fabric. Old towns which had adjusted to railroads and then to the El had to adjust once again to a vehicular invasion of unparalleled scope. This is the story many of us have seen unfold and that others accept as a matter of course. Why rehearse the fever of widening streets, the loss of sidewalks, the chopping down of trees, the stop lights, parking meters, and one-ways, the elevated freeways that violate street culture more brutishly than the old El, the open-air parking lots that take up as much as fifty percent of downtown land and rend urban fabric far worse than the railroad yards of yesterday?

The evils of the car make an easy target. But when their recitation is over, we still have to recall what automobiles have done to open up the range of opportunity for millions of job-seekers; to bring backroad folk out of their isolation; to speed and ease travel. Every period in the past had its share of ugliness and woe along with its vitality. Rush-hour traffic jams today are no worse than the crush in the days of the omnibus. The filth and mud of unpaved streets a hundred years ago were as noxious as the present mindless paving over of our cities that denies us green and turns the pedestrian into an endangered species.

Design is the tool that, skillfully used, sorts out the messes we make of our physical world, or at least keeps them within bounds. Through good design, we are learning to regiment the road of the Motor Age. Interspersed in all the dreary landscape of developer tracts, urban freeways, and parking lots, we have lodged thoughtfully planned units of housing and engineering marvels as beautiful as the very best road designs of the past. Our freeways at their finest can stage spectacular displays of high-speed motion through space—especially at night. On a different scale and with a different agenda, some communities in the recent past have found ways to strike a better balance between drivers and pedestrians. In the old center districts, pedestrian malls have attempted to bring back, not very successfully as it happens, some of the social excitement of the traditional street. Diverters have been set up in urban residential neighborhoods to cut down on traffic and make streets safe for children. A handful of garden suburbs have experimented with keeping through-traffic to the perimeter of super-blocks that form neighborhood units, or facing the houses away from the street toward interior grassy parks with strictly pedestrian walkways.

The street at all times is a field of conflict between private rights and the public good. For those of us who live on it, the street is our frontyard; but we have to share it with neighbors and total strangers, with passing or resting vehicles. A thousand restrictions, agreements, understandings regulate this shifting balance between the wishes of the abutters and the needs of the townfolk at large. Zoning keeps businesses away from the street; social pressure or price keeps away classes of people we do not care to have as neighbors. The law tells us when and where to do things and what things we cannot do—where to cross, which way to drive on the street, where to park our vehicle and for how long.

We learn to live with all of this. When the balance tips against us, we move if we can. The street shifts and adjusts: stylish blocks go seedy; back alleys are gentrified; what was a busy throughway turns somnolent, or else the reverse happens. Buildings grow taller, denser, brighter, or more subdued: the scale and shape of the public space changes.

So the beautiful street is an evanescent thing. It comes in many

Street signs, San Francisco.

forms, both modest and fancy, and is short-lived in any one. It is made of buildings and trees and textures and people, and all are caught in a flux of change. We must know how to see beauty in this broad variety, to catch it at its bloom, to find it again in the same street under a different guise. We must learn how to read streets, because the nation's life is inscribed in their changing face.

Pedestrians and rush-hour traffic in downtown San Francisco.

The story of the American street is a story without end. Today the total length of our streets and roads nationwide comes close to four million miles—that is better than one mile of road for every square mile of land. And still we build and still we change.

In the realm of design, the final measure of success is not in numbers, not in shapes. It is in the rituals our designs play host to—which means in us. We are the ones who fill buildings and roads with life, and so give value to these abstractions of architects and engineers. In the ways we use what is designed and built, in the demands we make and the changes we bring about, we are all designers of America. On all of us falls the blame for what is ugly in our surroundings, what is inhumane and derelict. To all of us belongs the credit for the beauty we fashion and the love, the excitement, the grace we allow it to contain.

203

4

The Public Realm

Boston Common is one of the earliest public places in America. For over three hundred years it has remained an open space—and that is no easy feat in the heart of a thriving city, where land is gold and progress virulent. The Bostonians' open-air living room has survived intact from the seventeenth century—when cows grazed there, and the local militia exercised, and "the Gallants a little before Sun-set walk with their Marmalet Madams," as an English visitor wrote in 1663, "till the nine a clock Bell rings them home to their respective habitations." And so it continued, free of encroachments, a common ground for pleasure and civic use, where all could come and go as they pleased and encounters were easy and unrehearsed.

In time, buildings surrounded the Common—churches with their graveyards, shops, elegant houses along Beacon Hill. The Massachusetts State House, one of the first capitols to go up after Independence, sat on an eminence on the Beacon Hill side, with an imposing set of stairs descending toward the Common. Mon-

Boston Common and the Public Garden. In the foreground is the Back Bay area of the city, built from the 1850s through the 1880s over filled land. The boulevard with the parkway down the middle is Commonwealth Avenue (also see figure page 19). It runs up to the Public Garden, which was designed by George F. Meacham in 1860. Beyond the Garden is the Common; it dates from 1634, four years after the settlement of the town. The Army and Navy Monument, erected in 1877, can be seen just beyond the treeless part of the Common, and near the upper left is the domed State House.

uments cropped up, to honor publicly what Boston thought worth honoring—a Civil War memorial, for example, to Colonel Robert Shaw and his regiment of black soldiers from Massachusetts, or on a central knoll, the Army and Navy monument topped by the "Genius of America." When department stores came of age in the 1880s, Filene's, one of the best, turned one side toward the Common, only one block away from it, and the other toward the central business district.

At the far side of the Common, toward Arlington Street, on land reclaimed from the mud of the Back Bay in the mid-nineteenth century, a lovely Public Garden was installed. The great landscape artist Frederick Law Olmsted made this the starting

The Massachusetts State House, designed by Charles Bulfinch in 1795. The town purchased this land for the state from John Hancock's heirs, who had a house nearby.

Robert Gould Shaw Memorial, by Augustus Saint-Gaudens, with a stone frame designed by Charles McKim. The work was commissioned by the state of Massachusetts in 1884 and was completed in 1897.

point of a beautiful park system he called the Emerald Necklace. The Public Garden is all the things the Common is not—small, fenced in, manicured. It has a choice variety of trees, properly labeled, formal flower beds that change with the seasons, a shallow lake shaded by willows, swan boats. It was meant for the more genteel Bostonian, and to this day it is preferred by people who disapprove of loud radios, winos, and running dogs.

Boston Common represents the public face of America. Every town, however small, designs into its fabric a stage of this sort. We seem to need more from life than just food, shelter, work, and entertainment. Beyond self, beyond family and neighborhood, there exists a public realm which holds our pride as a people. We need public places to enjoy the unplanned intimacy of civil society and to celebrate that sense of belonging to a broad community—a community with a shared record of accomplishment. We expect public buildings to express the dignity of our institutions. We choose to make monumental gestures that commemorate our heroes and mark the passage of our history.

Early Public Spaces

The public open space was there at the beginning, from the first European towns planted on this continent.

In the middle of their gridded pueblos, the Spanish invariably left a large plaza, one longer than it was wide and surrounded by porticoes where goods were sold. The administrative palace and other public buildings fronted the plaza, and so very often did the main church. But the center belonged to the people, for their fiestas and the customary evening stroll or *corso,* a time of socializing, flirting, showing off. The ghost of one such plaza survives in Santa Fe, New Mexico, where you can still see street merchants set up their stalls in the portico of the Governor's Palace. It was twice the present size originally, extending eastward to the present cathedral. The landscaping and paving are later refinements. A military chapel on the south side of the plaza related to one of its original uses—military exercises.

French towns were on rivers, and the town square, which dou-

The plaza and Governor's Palace in Santa Fe.

209

Jackson Square, New Orleans. In the foreground is St. Louis Cathedral, rebuilt in its present form in 1850. Immediately to its right is the Cabildo, built to house the city government in 1795–99. It was here, on the second floor, that the United States took possession of the Louisiana Territory in 1803. The rowbuildings along the right side of the square are townhouses built in 1850. Between Jackson Square and the Mississippi is Washington Artillery Park.

bled as a parade ground here too, overlooked the waterfront. The buildings that defined the square usually included a barracks and a hospital. In New Orleans, the capital of the French province of Louisiana, a brick church stood on the inland side of the square, and the quay along the river had a gravel walk planted with orange trees. The square, miraculously, lives still—a charmed, evocative public place, full of shade and pungent odors. There is a later church on that axis now, and the framing buildings span the French, the Spanish, and the early American eras of the city. In the middle is Andrew Jackson poised on his horse. This statue and the landscaping, which turned the square into an urban garden in the 1850s, are American contributions.

Americans, that side of them that derives from the English at least, were never very comfortable with an empty public place. They liked it filled with something, preferably some sort of public building that would provide a good excuse for wanting to be there.

Take the New England common. At first, it was neither an open green nor the grazing ground for local livestock. Boston Common seems to have been an exception. Ordinarily, a common was much too small to sustain more than a few animals. Besides, there was no green on it at all. In the early morning, townsmen on their way to fields at the edge of town led their cattle to the "close" in this open, central area where a herdsman waited to lead them to graze in the common pastures. At dusk the returning men collected their animals and herded them home.

The real reason for the common was the meetinghouse—a religious center and town hall in one. When land was first allocated in a new town, a large plot was set aside for this most important building of community life. Once the meetinghouse was up, and the graveyard fenced in with a neat stone wall, other buildings gathered around. There was the nooning house, for example, where in winter months the parishioners could find shelter and heat during breaks in the long, cold services of the Sabbath. The tavern was just as good for this purpose, at least for the less scrupulous. It also served as temporary courthouse, and later, when regular stagecoach service was established, as a stage stop—often marked by a huge inn sign that dwarfed everything around it except the meetinghouse. A blacksmith shop did well on the common, and so did bootmakers and hatters. There might also be a magazine for the storage of powder, horsesheds for the parishioners, or a schoolhouse.

Otherwise, the common was an unsightly, rutted piece of barren land, riddled with stumps and stones. The town's militia used it for its quarterly training, and its other public uses were reflected in its furnishings: the hay scale, the bulletin board, the well, the whipping post. To turn this stern Puritan civic center into the town green we now admire, the monopoly of the Congregational church on town life had first to be broken. Then Baptists, Methodists, and others could stand their own churches on the common and civilizing improvements could begin.

In New Haven we have a classic example of this transformation. After the War of 1812, the city cleared its common, then called the Market Place, of its old buildings and roads, moved the graveyard, and in the middle, where the old meetinghouse had

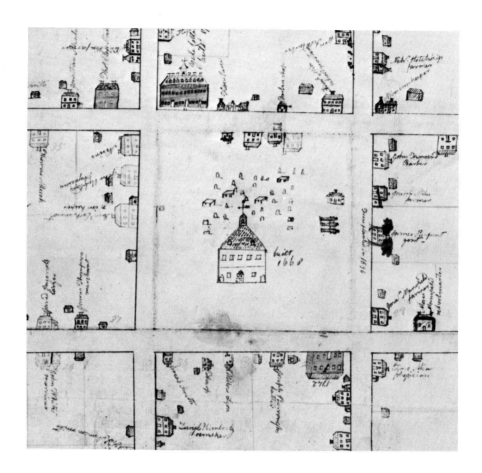

Plan of New Haven, Connecticut, 1748; detail showing the Meetinghouse and its graveyard.

stood unchallenged, made provision for three churches—two of them for the Congregationalists and one for Episcopalians. Planned spaces were also allotted to the Methodists and Baptists at two corners of the common, now called the Green. The Methodists actually did put up a church, but the Proprietors of the Green, now full of civic pride, found the building too crude for such a public stage. They bought the Methodists out and moved them off the Green, across the street. The Baptists never took advantage of their allotted site, but chose instead to make their stand in the less formal Wooster Square nearby. North of the three new churches on the Green rose the new state house, in temple form, replacing an older building, which now seemed to spoil the symmetry. Yale's Brick Row faced the state house across College Street, and on the

New Haven Green in 1831. The church on the left is Trinity Church by Ithiel Town, 1814. In the background near this church are buildings of Yale University, and just to the right the Greek Revival State House, 1831, also by Town. Farther along to the right is the First Congregational Church, 1815, built by Town from mail-order plans from the Boston architect Asher Benjamin. In its crypt are remains of the Old Colonial Burying Ground over which the church was in part built. The church at the far right is the United Congregational Church, 1815, a design by Ebenezer Johnson built by David Hoadley.

opposite, Church Street side, the town hall went up. As a finishing touch, the area was fenced in and edged with elms. When the elms matured this place became one of the most celebrated public squares in America.

By the middle of the nineteenth century, in the new railroad towns of the Midwest and the South, the New England green had found its counterpart in the courthouse square. It was the central feature of towns that served as county seats, and it represents as authentic a piece of American urbanism as Main Street. The courthouse stood in the middle of the one-block square, on a slight rise, surrounded by trees. In the treeless tallgrass prairie, this leafy oasis was a statement of survival and permanence. The townfolk spoke of it proudly as the "park" or the "grove." The jail and a clerk's fireproof office might be at the corners of the square. For the rest, it was small, local retail businesses, a hotel, and a restaurant or cafe where the businessmen ate their lunch. Board roofs projecting from the fronts of these establishments furnished shade, and plank seats between the roof supports made it easy to spend time there.

Farmers from the surrounding countryside stopped in regularly to take care of legal and tax matters. In the courthouse were kept land grants and commercial debt-bonds, and so the building would have to be solid, made of stone. To William Faulkner's eyes the courthouse at Jefferson, Mississippi, was "the center, the focus, the hub; sitting looming in the center of the county's circumference . . . protector of the weak, judiciate and curb of the passions and lusts, repository and guardian of the aspirations and hopes."

On the grounds there was room for the weekly market and sometimes the county fair. Here statue-soldiers on pedestals memorialized past wars. In the South none was more sacred than the Confederate monument to the Civil War: Johnny Reb holding a

Courthouse Square, Carrolton, Illinois.

214

Confederate Monument and Courthouse, Laurens, South Carolina.

rifle at parade rest, or else with arms folded, or carrying a flag or bugle, most often facing north whence the invasion came. And always an inscription, like this one at Lumberton, North Carolina.

> This marble minstrel's voiceless stone
> In deathless song shall tell
> When many a vanished age hath flown
> the story how they fell.
>
> On fame's eternal camping ground
> Their silent tents are spread,
> And glory guards with solemn round
> The bivouac of the dead.

So a public, urban place like the courthouse square, in these old days, was the setting where all sorts of people came together informally, where collective civic rituals like markets and parades took place, and where the prevalent values and beliefs of the community were made manifest. The institutional building—courthouse or public library or town hall—dominated. The space was well bounded and its scale intimate; it took its shape from the street pattern. It had many uses, some of them unplanned. But the urban square was above all political territory. Within its confines, people knew their place and found strength in their local tradition. The space held them, gave them identity. It is where they learned to live together.

Parks and Cemeteries

The urban park came later and was a different sort of public place. It was anti-city, to begin with, both in form and intent. What it offered visually was an invented romantic landscape, with no relation whatever to the city's street pattern. The sense was of a pleasure ground, a place of quiet and passive enjoyment. The park would set people free from the structured order of the town, free from its organized but also volatile behavior, its tensions. At the same time, the park would provide a neutral setting where the rich and poor could come together as equals. Alexis de Tocqueville, for one, believed that parks were a necessary instrument of democracy because they neutralized the strains of class consciousness built up within the cities.

So ran the rhetoric. But this outward look of innocent escapism and fraternal equality couched a more serious purpose. It had to do with the imposition of moral order where it was thought most wanting—among the urban poor. The creators and administrators of parks were gentlemen-idealists; in origin they were native-stock Americans, "Yankees." They viewed the park, from the very beginning, as an uplifting experience, a means to improve the social behavior of the citizenry—which really came down to making sure that the working classes, the immigrant labor of Yankee-owned businesses, behaved like their betters, the cultured upper crust. This is how Andrew Jackson Downing, for example, put it in 1848:

You may take my word for it, [parks] will be better preachers of temperance than temperance societies, better refiners of national morals than dancing schools and better promoters of general good-feeling than any lectures on the philosophy of happiness.

Frederick Law Olmsted thought of the park in the same way. His name more than any other was to govern the philosophy and design of America's parks for the first fifty years of their history. Olmsted's attitude was moralizing from the start. Yes, the purpose of the park was to allow urban folk to enjoy an unadulterated rural experience. But what he really intended to do with his park designs was to wean the working classes away from their ethnic neighborhoods, away from the adventures of city streets, and to make proper Americans out of them.

By training, Olmsted was neither an engineer nor a landscape architect—the two preeminent skills called into use to transform and embellish large tracts of land into carefree "nature." In fact, landscape architecture did not as yet exist as a profession in this country. When he won the competition for the design of Central Park in New York in 1858, Olmsted had behind him the rudiments of surveying, which he learned from an engineer to whom he was apprenticed briefly at age fifteen, some experience at clerking and seafaring, and ten years or so of farming in Connecticut and Staten Island.

Parks were unknown in America at the time, and in Europe, where parks had always been the preserves of noblemen and royalty, publicly owned parks were just beginning to take shape. Birkenhead Park outside Liverpool was Olmsted's immediate model; the example of the informal style of the English landscape garden formed the background of his thinking. At home, besides the newly fashionable Gothic cottages of Downing and his peers sitting in their picturesquely landscaped suburban lots, the only precedent was the rural cemetery.

In Colonial days people were buried in the churchyard, or in graveyards in the center of town. Burial was the right of every church member; you did not have to pay to get a plot. The graves had headstones with symbolic carvings and instructive inscriptions—reminders of the virtues of the deceased and the fearsome-

The Doctor Palsgrave Wellington gravestone, 1715, Massachusetts.

ness of death. These unlandscaped, fully visible churchyards in the center of town were a kind of collective monument that stressed the oneness of the living and the dead.

By 1800 most churchyards were crowded and neglected. Graves, and the stones of their occupants, were commonly reused. The need for larger and more sanitary burial grounds became evident, and one model cemetery was, in fact, planned as early as 1796— the New Burying Ground in New Haven, Connecticut, just north of the town, conceived by James Hillhouse. It was laid out as a regular grid and planted with Lombardy poplars and yews. This rational scheme did not catch on, however. Only after 1850 did the idea of a formal layout, with family plots delimited by iron railings and later on by curbstones, take over. By then the cemetery was a specialized, isolated place, removed from the urban scene. It gave one more proof of that nineteenth-century tendency for family, church, and community to drift apart—a tendency also evinced in the separation of workplace and dwelling and the eventual exit to the suburbs, where the family became a world unto itself.

These planned cemeteries were nondenominational, and you had to pay to be buried. Death here was nothing to be dreaded; it was the way to reunite with your loved ones and with God.

The death's head of the Colonial headstone gave way to the neo-classical willow and urn, and the metaphor of the rose on a broken stem. Private, and not collective, commemoration was the ruling order, and cemeteries became showplaces for fancy family monuments. In time, these cities of the dead would reproduce the structure of real cities, with their fashionable and unfashionable neighborhoods, their main streets and alleys, their suburban sprawl and segregation of blacks.

But prior to this institutionalization of burial, in the 1830s death was given an alternate setting—a romantically conceived garden, more for the living than for the dead, with serpentine carriage avenues, graveled footpaths, and statues of patriotic figures. The original inspiration was probably French. The Père-Lachaise cemetery in Paris, designed in 1815, may have started the trend. The first rural cemetery in America was Mount Auburn in Cambridge, Massachusetts, which opened in 1835; in quick order followed Laurel Hill in Philadelphia in 1836, Brooklyn's Greenwood, which was called "The Garden City of the Dead," and others in Baltimore, Lowell, St. Louis. The new cemeteries were, in fact, the first instances in America of public or semi-public gardens associated with cities. They were part cemetery, part experimental garden. At Mount Auburn the carriage avenues carried names of trees and the footpaths, names of flowers. The arrangement insisted on being democratic and nondenominational. Lot owners were allowed to design and decorate their own tombs, and the mood of these rural cemeteries was pastoral, a view of death culled from ancient Greek and Roman authors. City folk flocked to these peaceful, nostalgic gardens to spend the day among the flowers and the trees.

So from the rural cemeteries of America, and the eighteenth-century aristocratic tradition of English landscape design, our municipal parks drew their inspiration. But this is to put it too simply. What became Central Park was a huge piece of uninviting open land north of Fifty-ninth Street, between Fifth and Eighth avenues—some two and a half miles in one direction and half a mile in the other. Much of it was treeless swamp, large boulders pushed out of a thin hard soil. In other words, the park was a massive public works project, one which presented acute technical

Lafayette Cemetery, New Orleans, 1833. Because graves dug into the swampy New Orleans soil would quickly fill with water, above-surface burial practices were developed. Gridded cemetery plans like this one were more common in New Orleans than in the rest of the United States, where the example of New Haven's New Burying Ground, now called Grove Street Cemetery, laid out by James Hillhouse in 1796, did not catch on.

Facing page. *Mount Auburn Cemetery, Cambridge, Massachusetts, 1835. Nathaniel Dearborn, one of the cemetery's founders, wrote of it: "Hill and glen salute the eye at almost every stopping point, and the ever varying forms of mausoleums, temples, and obelisks, from the most splendid production of the sculptoring art, to the neat and simple pyramid, claim attention in every direction. The grounds are mostly overshadowed by foliage of large forest trees, the whole combining to affiliate the spot, as a suitable place for the living to visit and there ponder on the ever changing state of man's mortality." (See also color section for a period view of the cemetery.)*

Frederick Law Olmsted, 1822–1903.

and political difficulties. The transformation was nothing short of magical, and the precedent of Central Park forever changed the look of American cities.

Olmsted and his gifted partner Calvert Vaux left the rocky, semi-wild northern section much as they found it, highlighting the terrain with cascades and plantings of evergreens. The southern half they laced with groves, small boating ponds, meadows, and they skirted these with open walks. They arranged the gently curving pedestrian walks, bridle paths, and carriage roads in such a manner that there were no intersections at grade with cross-town traffic, which was kept out of sight in four roads below park level. All these intersections were handled with graceful stone bridges at various heights that served as underpasses and overpasses.

Olmsted was uncompromising on the issue of built structures within his parks. There were to be no monuments, no decorations; the urban square was the proper place for such "townlike things," as his disciple the educational leader Charles Eliot put it.

The site of New York's Central Park before its development.

The Grand Drive, Central Park, New York, *a Currier and Ives lithograph of 1869. The building in the distance was the arsenal built in 1848, before the park was begun, to house the National Guard. It served briefly as the Museum of Natural History and is now the headquarters of the Parks Department.*

Central Park today.

*The revised and extended layout of Central Park in a plan of 1873.
In the middle are the Croton Aqueduct reservoirs, endpoints of
the Croton Water System that brought water into the city across
the High Bridge, shown on page 305.*

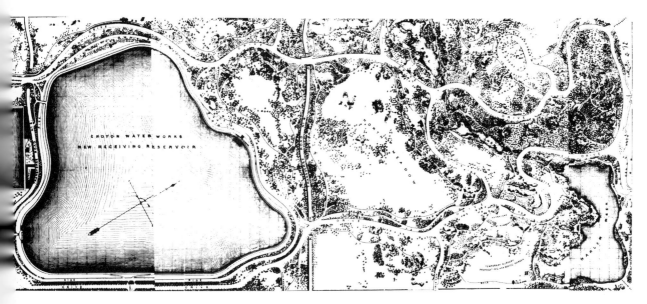

It took a long time for all this to take shape. And it was a bitter struggle. The beautifully composed picture became the battlefield for two contending social factions: on one side, the cultured, cosmopolitan elite of Olmsted's peers who saw the park as a pristine work of art, a soothing middle landscape between raw nature and the unseemly entanglement of the city; on the other, ward politicians to whom parks were vacant land that could be filled with job-producing structures. And there was the related conflict of use. To the reformers, the park was where the classes could rub shoulders; it was the ideal place for cultural enlightenment. In time, rejecting Olmsted's purism on the subject, educational institutions like museums and conservatories, aquariums, observatories, and zoos were ensconced within the park's bounds, their purpose to combine instruction with pleasure. The working classes, on the other hand, were far more interested in a sturdy playground, a place to have a good time.

These conflicts were never resolved. It is in the nature of public places to act as fields of interaction and to change character in the process of mediating social behavior. The working classes insisted on, and got, their own playgrounds, distinct from the refined pleasure-garden of the middle class. After 1900 the urban park itself responded to their pressures. A new type of park that stressed organized activity gained currency. This was an accessible lot of ten to forty acres, ringed by shrubbery, with a straightforward layout and a dominant indoor plant called the field house, which had an assembly hall, club rooms, and gymnasiums. No meadows or undulating paths, no attempt to block the views of the city round about. Now there were shorter work weeks, longer vacations, early retirement. All this was creating what came to be known as "leisure time"; and it was best if it could be filled in an orderly way. So throughout the land came a sudden profusion of municipal beaches, stadiums, tennis courts, picnic areas, and public playgrounds.

But Olmsted's vision held its own. During his long career, he managed to give substance to twenty urban parks of his particular brand, and to go far beyond, toward a notion of the city as a landscape at large. He preached tirelessly that each city should be aired with a whole constellation of parks, linked together in an integrated system. Connectors would be green boulevards and parkways. Boulevards were broad and straight, with landscaped medians, and were meant to be bordered by elegant houses behind dense rows of trees. These were often run diagonally across the street grid. Later on cars would find these expansive connectors a godsend for fast, unencumbered travel and would change their intended character as tranquil, idyllic stretches, suitable for pedestrians and slow coaches, into dangerously paced fast-traffic lanes. But parkways, once out in the suburbs, moved in gentle curves along natural contours, looking out on broad expanses of landscape. Commercial traffic was allowed, but only at the far sides of the roadways.

Olmsted started it all with the magnificent Emerald Necklace in Boston, a loosely strung system of pleasure drives, ponds, and parks that followed the city's suburban edge along the grassy marshland of the Muddy River. He laid out six other park systems before his death, and his disciples added others—George Kessler in Kansas City and Cincinnati, and Horace W. S. Cleveland in Minneapolis where a chain of lakes was incorporated into a continuous greenbelt.

The American Renaissance

The boulevards and parkways used stately public buildings as focal points. In the time between the Civil War and the Chicago Fair the scale of our public buildings had steadily escalated. This was true for traditional institutions, like government agencies, libraries, and museums, and for more modern structures, chief among them railway terminals and department stores. By the end of the century a spectacular monumentality had seized our cities, which made prewar courthouses, state capitols, and colleges look almost residential by comparison. Size was not all. There were sheathings of lavish materials, sculptural ornament and stained-glass windows, painted friezes and showy furnishings. Something had changed. America's vision of itself was not what it had been.

Nothing shows this escalation of public splendor more clearly than the nation's state houses. Like the later skyscraper, the state

Virginia State Capitol, Richmond, designed by Thomas Jefferson. This view shows the building shortly after its completion in 1798. The small structure to the right is a bell tower.

capitol was a uniquely American building type, and it struggled from the start to achieve a degree of monumental dignity and a suitable symbolic image. Jefferson's design for Virginia, interpreted in white stucco on an eminence in Richmond, resurrected an ancient Roman temple. Bulfinch's grandly domed State House for Massachusetts, overlooking Boston Common, took a contemporary English governmental building, Somerset House in London, for its model. But neither of these early capitols set a trend. What became the accepted formula was a building with balancing chambers on either side of a domed rotunda, and a portico up front. The obvious inspiration for this was the U.S. Capitol which was started in 1792, was burnt down by the British in 1814, and was revived along the same lines almost immediately.

Whatever their look, these early capitols were fairly modest structures. The walls and columns on the outside were usually of brick or wood, covered with a coat of stucco which was scored to imitate masonry blocks. The scale of the interior spaces was almost intimate; the furnishings, plain. The senate and house chambers were small rooms crowded with wooden desks. Flags and portraits of statesmen hung on the walls. A gallery for the public ran along one side just across from the speaker's dais. The

Saloon of the Virginia State Capitol, as reconstructed in 1909. The statue of George Washington was done by the French sculptor Jean-Antoine Houdon in 1788–92.

airy, bright rotunda, or saloon, might hold a statue of George Washington, not much bigger than an ordinary human, elevated on a pedestal and accented by the dome above.

In the decade or two before the Civil War, we see a rise in the level of rich effects. On occasion, real stone is used outside—Kentucky marble or the granite of Maine and New Hampshire—and marbling and graining inside. Even so, the workings of government are still accessible, direct, in these relaxed surroundings. Filing by these well-worn offices in a historic building like the old Illinois state house today, with their spitoons and cast-iron stoves, we can hear the echo of eloquent orations and sense a raw ingenuousness in the rituals of caucusing and favor-trading.

Yet after the Civil War, and especially from about 1885 onward, architecture and bureaucracy combine to distance us from this homey feel of the democratic process. Government is encumbered with the mechanisms of taxation, the pension system, land grants, and transportation. The capitol bulges outward and up; offices and corridors and stairs multiply infectiously. Along with

Interior of the old Illinois State Capitol, Springfield, 1837–54, designed by John F. Rague.

its spreading size, pomp increases. A bright Classical mantle of stone drapes the imposing bulk, over which towers some version of the great dome by Thomas U. Walter that completed the U.S. Capitol in the closing years of the Civil War. Foreign materials—marbles from Italy, tiles from Liverpool—contribute to a dazzling surface opulence, and a whole new repertoire of monumental imagery is carved and painted in every prominent corner.

Until this time, public art was uncommon in America and limited in scale and subject. National imagery centered on George Washington and a handful of symbols like the eagle and the flag. Two of the earliest civic monuments to be designed, both of them by Robert Mills, were in honor of Washington. One was begun in 1815 in a landscaped setting in Baltimore—a shaft of white marble with a statue at the top. The other, of course, was the Washington Monument in the nation's capital. Mills described it as a "grand circular colonnaded building . . . from which springs an obelisk shaft." In the original design of 1833 a tomb for the president was to be at the base of the obelisk, surrounded by statues of the heroes of the Revolutionary War. But when the monument was finally completed twenty years after the Civil War, nothing remained of the original design save the Egyptian obelisk—a stark, stripped accent on the great axis of the Mall.

Monument means "to bring to mind." And the nation in the later nineteenth century was in a mood to remember. The Civil War had created a new mythology of heroism, a mythology of noble leaders and foot soldiers. There was pride in the resurgence of a united nation; and for the unvictorious side there was the gallant sacrifice of the Lost Cause. Meanwhile, the Philadelphia Centennial celebration of 1876 had broadcast our maturity and

Illinois State Capitol, Springfield, 1868–88, by John C. Cochrane and Alfred H. Piquenard.

Minnesota State Capitol, St. Paul,
1896–1905, by Cass Gilbert.

Robert Mills's design of 1833 for the Washington Monument.

Minnesota the Granary of the World, 1904, by Edwin H. Blashfield. This is one of two murals in the Senate Chamber of the Minnesota State Capitol.

forced us to ask who we were and where we had been. So we started to look backward to our beginnings; and, at the same time, we started to commemorate the feats and actors of the Civil War, the bitter national conflict that reaffirmed the strength of our institutions and launched our ambition to cut a dashing figure in the world.

All this we could now do in the grand manner. Since the 1860s American artists had been studying painting and sculpture in European academies—in Dusseldorf and Munich, in the Hague and in the premier art school of all, the Ecole des Beaux-Arts in Paris. They came back armed with sophisticated techniques and a style that stressed historical pageantry and the rhetoric of allegory. These they applied to native themes. So in the capitols, along the

The Minute Man, *1871–75, by Daniel Chester French. The work was commissioned in preparation for the Centennial by the City of Concord, Massachusetts, which wanted an appropriate symbol of its past.*

Soldiers' and Sailors' Memorial Arch, 1889–92, on Brooklyn's Grand Army Plaza. John M. Duncan and McKim, Mead & White were the architects. The top sculpture, Quadriga, *1898, and the pedestal sculptures,* Army *and* Navy, *1901, are by Frederick MacMonnies. Inside the arch are bas reliefs—*Lincoln, *1895, by Thomas Eakins and* Grant, *also 1895, by William O'Donovan. The arch is the principal entrance to Frederick Law Olmsted's Prospect Park.*

walls and in the vaults, in fresco, mosaic, or low relief, you found epic friezes of local history: pioneer life in Illinois or *Minnesota, Granary of the World;* Classical figures representing abstract principles of law or government—Justice, Peace, Equality; and appropriately draped personifications of continents and nations that connected us to universal history.

At the same time, our public places were peopled with monumental sculpture. In Springfield, Massachusetts, a full-bodied statue called *The Puritan,* by the best of our sculptors, Augustus Saint-Gaudens, was raised in 1881, and near Boston, Concord got Daniel Chester French's *Minute Man,* a fitting memorial to that town's past. Civil War monuments sprang up everywhere—equestrian statues of Lee and Sherman, reliefs of battles and marching regiments. All were mounted onto finely proportioned architectural frames, fixed with studied care in urban open spaces—at the entrance to parks, in public squares, as terminal markers of avenues and landscaped vistas. A triumphal arch in honor of our soldiers and sailors went up in Brooklyn's Grand Army Plaza. In Richmond, Virginia, the equestrian statue of Robert E. Lee rose on a tremendous pedestal in the middle of a square, at the head of Monument Avenue—a grand boulevard lined with statues of other Confederate heroes. (See color section.)

Most dramatic of all was the Statue of Liberty, a gift from France, dedicated on a foggy October afternoon in 1886. It was the work of the Alsatian sculptor, Auguste Bartholdi, and stood poised on a massive base in the Doric mode designed by Paris-trained Richard Morris Hunt. The site could hardly have been more masterful. *Liberty Enlightening the World,* to use her formal name, towered over Bedloe's Island at the entrance to New York Harbor, greeting ships that steamed into The Narrows at the end of their long transatlantic voyage. At the time, nothing matched the grandeur of this colossal statue except perhaps the obelisk of the Washington Monument.

This new worldliness, which aimed to put us on a par with Europe, came at a price. The rich harvest of allusions in our public art left most viewers far behind. Unable to absorb the erudite references that kindled the artist's work, they settled for an overall look or some plain, straightforward message to attach to it. The Statue of Liberty they knew simply as the crowned lady who ushered oppressed people from abroad into the New World. Her learned pedigree—stretching back to the ancient goddess of Liberty, to her Christian reincarnations as Faith and Truth, and later to the heroine of the Romantic era who banished ignorance and beamed enlightenment—all this would be beyond most visitors to Bedloe's Island.

A similar distancing was taking place between our daily rituals and their aggrandizement through architecture. Reading, shopping, traveling were now being ensconced in luxurious settings, far grander than the functions themselves called for.

A visit to a public library, for example, had been a simple business until the Eighties. The building was small, without show even when dignified, and books were stored in alcoves, arranged around a central reading room. The idea of a free public library itself ranks as a great American institution. It originated in the 1830s (Peterboro, New Hampshire, is said to be the first), and it was meant to make knowledge broadly accessible and to encourage reading. But by the end of the century, the central libraries of

Liberty Enlightening the World, *1886,*
Frédéric-Auguste Bartholdi. The huge
copper-clad statue stands a hundred
fifty-one feet high. The arm holding
the torch measures forty-two feet
and has a diameter of twelve feet.

Boston Public Library, 1887–95, by McKim, Mead & White. This facade detail shows the entrance on Copley Square. Flanking the arched doorways are statues by Bela Pratt—Science, on the left gazing at a globe, and Art *on the right with painter's palette in hand. The relief panels over the doors were executed by Augustus Saint-Gaudens.*

Staircase, Boston Public Library.

many large cities were so monumental, so ornate, that they tended to intimidate the average user and discourage casual visits.

The Boston Public Library on Copley Square was the earliest of this resplendent breed. You climbed marble stairs and entered through fine iron gates—these enclosed within three spacious Roman arches and flanked by statues of seated women in classical garb, personifying Science and Art. Inside rose a grand staircase more appropriate, perhaps, to the great opera houses of Europe than to a library. At the top, the main reading room was a great vaulted hall that occupied the entire front of the building. Around an arcaded courtyard were rooms faced in rich marbles and decorated with sculpture and murals, where rare books and drawings were on display. This was indeed "a palace for the people," as the trustees had specified it would be. But it is also arguable that this cultural facility became so magnificent that it alienated the very people it sought to serve. And besides, in the opinion of some librarians, it did not function well as a library at all.

The enjoyment of art, once a domestic pleasure of wealthy Americans and their friends, was also elevated to a public spectacle. Great private collections were opened to the people by be-

Bates Hall, Boston Public Library, as it appeared when the library opened in 1895. This was the library's main reading room.

quest or grant, and most were housed in monumental buildings. Cities raised their own civic monuments to art, in the manner of the European palace-museums like the Louvre. Boston had its Museum of Fine Arts, Chicago its Art Institute. New York's Metropolitan Museum of Art gave its Fifth Avenue side a resplendent frontispiece of Roman imperial grandeur. Symphony halls and opera houses, and even small theaters like the Century in New York, smothered their frames with ornament.

The New Public Domain

The new tendency to design and build for show as much as for utility was not confined to institutions of government and culture. Metropolitan railroad stations now sat ponderously in the modestly scaled old townscapes. They were built of fine materials on a colossal scale and, in contrast to the older stations which tended to be picturesque, polychrome sheds with tall towers rendered in

Union Station, Washington, D.C., 1907, by Daniel Burnham.

romantic styles, had uniformly white exteriors using a narrow range of Classical forms. Inside, the concourses were vast and vaulted like Roman bathing halls. The facades were opened up with deep Roman arches, or else screened by long, impressive colonnades. At the same time, the three- or four-story office buildings of earlier decades were growing into spectacular towers which, while still retaining the archaic floor plan partitioned into rows of small cubicles, were clothed in embroidered skins and topped with fanciful ornate crowns. And, finally, shopping areas in the old downtowns and along Main Street were being preempted by yet another palace for the people—this one a palace of consumption known as a department store.

Macy's, Marshall Field's, Wanamaker's, Jordan Marsh, Lord & Taylor—between 1880 and 1910 these stores became the true centers of our cities. Here was a creation that was genuinely popular, more so certainly than museums or public libraries, and openly expressive of the excitement and vigor of urban life. The scale, the variety, the luxury were mesmerizing. In one, block-size architectural envelope there might be as much as forty acres, or one million square feet, of floor space. The block would commonly have a rotunda with a leaded glass skylight on the ground floor and, above this, galleries opening onto a central courtyard. On display you could find everything being produced in the factories of America, from ready-made clothing to furniture and appliances, attractively designed and packaged. Much of it was novel, unfamiliar, astonishing. You were introduced to new cosmetics and medicines, to typewriters and fountain pens, to kitchen gadgets of all sorts, and you were made to feel that you could not do without them. And while you were entrapped in this wondrous showcase of the nation's horn of plenty, you could also make use of lavish lounges and rest rooms, restaurants, beauty salons and nurseries.

Department stores were large retail shops in the center of town and were revolutionary in a number of ways. First, they were accessible to everyone; they had none of the exclusivity of fine stores or the low-grade populism of markets, even though some department stores were considered smarter than others. They had a fixed-price policy, which dispensed with the customary rituals

Macy's in the 1880s: a view from the
Fourteenth Street staircase.

Rowland H. Macy, 1822–1877.

Macy's New York: the Fine Art, China, and Silver Room, 1880s.

Left page. *Macy's humble beginnings: the twenty-foot-wide store opened in 1858 at Sixth Avenue and Fourteenth Street.*

Left. *Macy's Herald Square store in New York today. This store opened in 1902, and through a series of additions in the 1920s and 1930s, grew to encompass an entire city block. It is now the world's largest store, with over two million square feet of floor space.*

of bargaining. They advertised extensively in newspapers, and they offered services like charge accounts and free delivery. They combined the traditional features of public-minded architecture, the grand staircase for example, with modern materials and conveniences. It was for a department store, A. T. Stewart's in New York, that the largest iron building of its day was erected in 1862. Cast-iron made for a light structure, with slender supports that opened up the floors. In conjunction with the new large sheets of plate glass, it turned conventional windows into show windows and conventional floors into airy, spacious display areas. And it was in a department store, the Haughwout Department Store on Broadway, that the elevator found its first regular use.

Most of these consumers' palaces began modestly and expanded incrementally. The first Macy's was a fancy dry goods store on New York's Sixth Avenue, near Fourteenth Street. It opened in 1858 and sold ribbons, embroideries, feathers, hosiery, and gloves. R. H. Macy was a young unsuccessful merchant when he arrived in New York that year after a string of retail ventures that did not make it—two in Boston, one in California catering to the gold rush forty-niners, and the last in Haverhill, Massachusetts, which ended in bankruptcy. This time was different. The store on Sixth Avenue prospered. Macy bought another store at the back in 1866, and so he continued, annexing neighboring property until, at the time of his death in 1877, his business occupied the ground area of eleven stores with separate departments for drugs and toilet goods, glassware, silver and china, home furnishings, luggage, toys and musical instruments. In the 1880s a new facade unified the look of this collection of buildings, and in 1902 Macy's Herald Square opened on Broadway at Thirty-fourth Street— a nine-story building with thirty-three hydraulic elevators and four escalators that could move 40,000 customers every hour; there was even a pneumatic tube system that could shoot sales checks and cash from one part of the store to another.

The change brought about through this imperial monumentality of American cities was two-pronged. First, railroad stations, department stores, and office towers set up a colossal public domain that overwhelmed the once dominant scale of churches and government buildings. Over time, government and religion had ceased to be focuses of real power anyway. The church no longer anchored whole communities in the way a meetinghouse, say, ruled the New England town. Government turned progressively more impersonal as an institution and seemed perennially subject to corruption; by the end of the century, it spread out licentiously and impressed many as an imposition rather than a moral force.

Traditionally steeples and domes punctuated the skyline of American cities. The domes which rose over government buildings were a feature of the nineteenth century. But they were preempted in the 1890s by libraries and campus buildings. What happened is that the same monumental dress covered a whole range of buildings, banks as well as state capitols, clubs and apartment houses as well as town halls; the same puffed up scale might prevail in the business district and upper-class residential avenues beyond. It was hard in this grand unity of the monumental townscape to assign symbolic priorities among individual institutions.

The steeple of Boston's Park Street Church, 1809, by Peter Branner, and behind it the office tower of 1 Beacon Street, 1972, by Skidmore, Owings & Merrill.

When the architecture of government could not stand out in a landscape of skyscrapers and department stores, it often had to be satisfied with providing office space for proliferating bureaucracies rather than attempting to project the authority and purpose of our political structure.

Church steeples had always been omnipresent—thick clusters of them in the big cities. By 1830 Philadelphia had ninety-six churches and New York one hundred. The churches played host to many sects, and were mostly plain beneath their aspiring towers. The centrality of Europe's cathedral towns had no place in a country that had said "no" in the end to an official state religion, and had made God at home in neighborhood communities. But faith compromised something of its public force when the temples of commerce began to overwhelm the landscape of God.

And there was a second aspect to this new monumentality. Now the public domain was not really public in the traditional sense. Once, in our past, collective activity had centered on, and been represented by, a genuinely communal pattern. The market, the wharf, places of assembly, courthouses and town halls—these were paid for by us and, in a fundamental sense, belonged to us. This was not true of banks and skyscrapers and department stores, not even of railroad stations. The new monuments were monuments to private interest. We basked in their splendor through the courtesy of companies who courted our business but could not speak for us collectively, as a civic society.

The more our public architecture celebrated the private sector, the weaker grew our sense of being a distinct and whole community. All along we ourselves assisted in this dilution of a public presence by refusing to behave as a public—that is, as a body of people with a clear political and social identity. During the last decades of the nineteenth century and into the twentieth, a broad coalition of reformers, educators, and politicians worked hard to mold us into a homogeneous society. But we tended to fragment. Ethnicity pulled us apart; sects, class, special interests pulled us apart.

So what civil and political cohesion we could not attain we directed into consumption and recreation. We became a buying public, a traveling public, a playing public. True public spaces, like streets and squares, lost some of their liveliness to the department stores, stadiums, bathing houses, and beaches. True public spaces declined because we chose to separate human life into isolated functions and assign to each one its own physical setting. We sequestered the family inside the house, and moved the house away from the workplace. We forced a split in our environment between the intensely built-up downtown and the unaccented spread of residential suburbs. There, the family turned itself into a microcosm of society, staging its own rituals of communion and leisure. Downtown, life ebbed after working hours, leaving public spaces to the homeless, the restless, and the rough. And this was so for both the old urban squares and the more recent Classical plazas of the period between the 1880s and 1920s, with their fancy stone floors, formal plantings, and grandiloquent monuments.

Preservation and Progress

What little remained in our core cities of that lively mixture of big buildings and modest-scaled ones, of starchy commercial blocks and promiscuous neighborhoods, would come under attack after the Second World War. The steady flight into the suburbs had long condemned the older center-city districts to decay. And a new American policy was now launched with the Housing Act of 1949—urban renewal. Its premise was that the deteriorating city fabric must be removed, the rot taken out, and in its place modern buildings put up that would look nice and would bring in moneyed clients to revitalize the downtown. In practice, this amounted to an often indiscriminate destruction of old, fine-grained neighborhoods and the setting up of tall corporate towers in the space radically cleared of buildings that had once been marked with the character of age and use.

It was about this time that modern architecture was going through a phase that denied tradition. Architects had no use for the familiar historical styles or storytelling decoration, no use for the slow accretion of buildings through time, the intimacies of a waterfront street or a partially enclosed urban square. The shiny towers they put up stayed clear of one another. Space flowed around and even under them, but rarely came to rest in pockets that might invite passers-by to stay a while and relax. As a trade-off for some bending of the rules in their favor, corporate clients would make room for a public plaza on their lot, in the shadow of their gleaming skyscrapers. But life would rarely find a perch in these unsheltered wastes transfixed with sleek, uncommunicative monuments of abstract art.

The buildings around us, singly and in combination, are the most pregnant monuments we have. They tell us who we are, what we have been through, what we have prized or allowed. That is the tangible record of our existence as a people. With each building we pull down, we erase a bit of that record, and so, bit by bit, deny ourselves the comfort of tradition, the sustaining pride of a collective past. As one of John Steinbeck's characters put it, "How will we know it's us without our past?"

In the last one hundred years of our history, we Americans have been enthusiastic destroyers. We are an impatient nation, committed to moving forward, convinced of the inevitability of obsolescence. We would much rather replace than reuse, rebuild from the ground up than try to repair. We assume that the process of tearing down what we have in order to make room for something more up-to-date, more efficient, more profitable brooks no argument. New York has been in existence as a city for three hundred and fifty years, but what is there left of the seventeenth century or the eighteenth, what is left of the nineteenth century but some scraps of much altered brownstones and a public building or two? And we have already been at work on the twentieth century.

With us, it seems, the only hope for a community to hold on to some of its old buildings, to some of its original flavor, is to be bypassed by the forces of progress, to be caught, as we like to say quaintly, "in a time warp." This is rare in a fast-paced civilization like ours, and may not last anyway, since conditions that affect the integrity of our built environment are always subject to sudden change. So we have two options if we are to "know it's us." We can create replicas of what is gone; or, more courageous, we can set limits to the pace and scope of our destruction. We have exercised them both.

The replicas began with Williamsburg. That was in the late Twenties. Until then historic preservation in America had been strictly an amateur game played by historical societies and genealogical groups. More often than not, it aimed no further than to save an occasional building associated with a famous person. To say the motivating urge was nationalist sentiment is to be imprecise. What was being preserved through these architectural relics was "the American way," and the preservers came from the older patrician elite—as represented by groups like the Daughters of the American Revolution, the Colonial Dames, the Society for the Preservation of New England Antiquities—and the middle class which embraced their ideals. Those who sought preservation feared the tempestuous ascendance of new money on the one hand, the industrial magnates and financiers too busy amassing fortunes to respect the niceties of tradition, and the crude immigrant working class, untutored in the values of their adopted country, on the other.

Williamsburg was different. For one thing, its patron was one of the feared newly rich. And it aimed at the preservation of a total setting. Thanks to the vision of the local minister Dr. W.A.R. Goodwin and the funds of John D. Rockefeller, Williamsburg set out to recreate an entire community where you could experience the look and life of preindustrial America. A past social order was being brought back all at once, not, however, in its unadulterated real form, but in a carefully edited version which, like the corporate world familiar to its patron, would be planned, clearly organized, free of messy or unpleasant detail.

Williamsburg would have to be frozen in time in a particular era, and so the eighteenth century was selected. The 1790s was seen as the cutoff date. Over a span of several decades, all structures that were of later vintage were taken down—seven hundred and twenty buildings in all. The surviving Colonial buildings were restored to some appropriate phase in their construction history; more than three hundred others were rebuilt from the foundation up, with great patience and as accurately as contemporary historical scholarship could ensure. The streets and houses were filled with people in period costume reenacting for the benefit of visitors the routines of Colonial life.

A costumed guide demonstrates colonial trades for visitors at Williamsburg.

The net effect was to celebrate the planter elite of Virginia, shown in the best possible light, and to present their way of life as the cradle of Americanism. "As the work has progressed," Rockefeller explained in 1937, "I have come to feel that perhaps an even greater value [than the preservation of the beauty and charm of the old buildings and gardens] is the lesson that it teaches of the patriotism, high purpose, and unselfish devotion of our forefathers to the common good." At the time of the Second World War, Williamsburg was well on its way to becoming the central shrine of the American faith. Troops were brought in for inspirational visits. After the war, it acted as a semi-official branch of the State Department and the U.S. Information Agency, working closely with the Defense Department's Information and Education Program. "Democracy workshops" were held; "Student Burgesses" discussed the nature of Freedom; foreign dignitaries visiting America made a first stop here for ceremonies enriched with period trappings before heading for Washington. It is not surprising, perhaps, that slavery was not discovered in Colonial Williamsburg until the Seventies.

Yet for most of its millions of visitors Williamsburg was an extensive outdoor museum—and it was fun. It started a national trend. Whereas Williamsburg resurrected a real place with scrupulous fidelity as far as its ideological program allowed, elsewhere actual sites, where there may or may not have been any historic buildings, were fleshed out with facile reproductions, in order to evoke a colorful ambience of the past. At Mystic, Connecticut, the remnants of the existing town were bloated in this way to complete the picture of an early New England seaport. At Plymouth, Massachusetts, a pioneer or pilgrim village was built up from scratch.

There were also total fabrications—mock-authentic environments staged at the whim of some wealthy patron, on a site that had more to do with that person than with our history. Stephen C. Clark, a businessman and art collector, sponsored a crossroads settlement at Cooperstown, New York, which was his summer home. It was a collection of old buildings brought to the site and arranged into an early nineteenth-century village. Albert Wells, a wealthy businessman, did the same at Old Sturbridge Village in Massachusetts, where the architectural antiques, which included an old mill and a general store, were grouped around a green or common in the manner of New England towns of the period from 1790 to 1840.

But it was Henry Ford who had the last word. He wanted no historian to tell him what to recollect, no architect to tell him how to stage his mythical past. "History is more or less bunk," he announced at first; then he started qualifying it with "as it is taught in school." What we could best learn from were the things that people used. So Ford launched a massive hunt for thousands of artifacts and had them brought to Dearborn, Michigan. These were exhibited at his own outdoor museum, Greenfield Village, along with a random collection of old buildings which were taken down, transported to Dearborn, and meticulously reconstructed. There was a European precedent: the open-air museum, where old buildings were assembled to illustrate the environment and life of peasants and craftspeople. The one in Stockholm, called Skansen, which opened in 1891, was probably the first. Other well-known examples are Frilandsmuseet near Copenhagen and Seurasaari in Helsinki.

Ford shopped in New England and the Deep South. He set up a Swiss chalet, an English Tudor shop, a Michigan inn, an Illinois courthouse where Lincoln practiced law, slave cabins and small factories. He tried to buy Philadelphia's Independence Hall, and when he failed, he had a replica built to serve as the entrance to his museum. In reality, the selection was not all that random. Ford wanted to honor common folk, the denizens of our rural republic. And he wanted to commemorate his own personal history, the history of the self-made man of invention, which is why he brought in Orville Wright's bicycle shop and faithfully reconstructed Edison's Menlo Park laboratory. What he thought it all amounted to was a record of the development of American industry, from the earliest days to the present.

In the Fifties, outdoor museums like Williamsburg and Greenfield Village begat the theme park. It started with Disneyland in 1955, and soon a flood of these fabricated sites could be found throughout the country—Worlds of Fun in Kansas City; Kings Island in Ohio; Storyland in Glenn, New Hampshire; Busch Gardens in Tampa, Florida; Opryland outside of Nashville.

The idea was the same. You arranged the show around themes like a mining town or a country fair, and you coordinated everything—music, architecture, employee's clothing, landscaping—to conjure up a complete experience. But you did not need to hunt for authentic old buildings anymore. It was all make-believe. In one park, you would combine several historical and international settings, without any attention to a strict logic of time and place. There could even be an area called fantasyland, which stood free of time and place and had no adherence to reality at all. Outside, the park put up a plain front, but the huge car lot gave it away—these far-flung Shangrilas were a big success. Inside, essences were served up. "Yankee Harbor" would have in it just enough by way of architecture and accessories to evoke a New England fishing village of the nineteenth century; "Hometown Square," rural

Orville Wright's bicycle shop at Greenfield Village in Dearborn, Michigan.

America of the 1920s; "Yukon Territory," the Klondike during the gold rush. This is how we experience the world on television, through the arbitrary switch of channels. And so it is fair to consider theme parks, as a student of them put it, "the meeting ground between the automobile culture and the television culture."

But this harmless, and instructive, fun cannot stand in for our living traditions, those continuities of culture and of memory that determine what it is to be an American. Preservation, the genuine, anxious effort to hold on to our past, must be staged in real cities; and in the actual, lived in, and forever evolving countryside.

The past we have in common has two faces—the Old World and Old America.

We are a nation of immigrants. We have a longing to stay in touch with our roots. "Most Americans," Kevin Lynch said, "go

"Yukon Territory" at the Great America park in Santa Clara, California.

away from home to Europe to feel at home in time." That is our ancestral memory, and we try to stay in touch with it through simple and subtle means. We use old European place names. Our very architecture for three centuries has echoed *their* architecture. Our towns are full of Parthenon banks and Roman terminals, of belltowers like St. Mark's and domes like the Invalides. This pervasive emblazoning of our ancestral memory is more to the point than the sprinkle of pastiche—the leaning tower of Pisa at Niles, Illinois, or the full-scale Parthenon in Nashville, or the Stonehenge in Maryhill, Washington, or London Bridge, the real thing, brought over and reassembled in the Arizona desert, which requires artificial aging because the clean dry air strips the ancient stones of their lovable grime.

The Old World is where we came from. But we have been on this Continent for a long time. We scored the land with forts and battlefields. Our heroes and statesmen were born in native houses, did weighty things in native buildings, died in some specific setting of this vast domesticated continent. There are ways of life we have left behind. This is the second face of our common past. And it too is embedded in the fabric of real places, in old town and country patterns. Here in these real, continuing places we must seek our lifeblood: here we must find our collective identity.

This search requires a long-term general commitment to our built inheritance. It impels us to maintain a thoughtful balance

Disneyland, in Anaheim, California, as it appears from the air. In the center is "Main Street," which is also shown on page 166.

A preserved part of old Charleston, South Carolina.

between conservation and progress. To achieve this balance, we have to go beyond the sparing of some arbitrary sample of "significant" buildings from the wrecker's dynamite. We have to think in terms of whole environments. The ultimate course of action must be to regulate the heartless course of progress—to take charge of our own evanescence.

Until recently we have been unwilling to embark officially on such an adventure. In this country the right to do with your property as you wish is considered sacrosanct, and society is loathe to interfere with that right. But the case for a wise policy of conservation is easily derailed when it comes up against expedience or profit. Against the currents of the marketplace, old districts have few defenses. The community must, at some point, decide to interfere. But how?

Fifty years ago, Charleston showed us the way. This South Carolina town had been the center of a plantation aristocracy for generations. Families stayed there even after the Civil War, and their wealth stayed with them. Nobody moved to the suburbs. The oldest parts of town, full of beautiful houses, were sheltered between two rivers on a natural harbor. They were bypassed by modern highways. And Charlestonians liked it that way. To make sure there was no rash change, the town passed a preservation zoning ordinance, set up an official board of architectural review, and started a revolving fund to buy and restore vulnerable old buildings that came up for sale.

That was in 1931. Five years later, New Orleans had the Louisiana constitution amended to legitimize the Vieux Carré Commission. The commission was given broad police powers to protect the environment of this historic French quarter of New Orleans, including the power to exempt old buildings from local taxation. A few other scattered communities took similar measures—Natchez, Newport, Annapolis, Monterey. The states meanwhile acted only fitfully, and without plan, to preserve this and that. The federal government moved to ensure the protection of the historic areas within the national park system, and in 1949 President Truman signed the charter of the National Trust for Historic Preservation

Plaque on St. John's Church in Washington, D.C., marking it as a Registered National Historic Landmark. The plaques are made by private companies for building owners who wish to purchase them for buildings on the National Register.

which was empowered to accept on behalf of the nation gifts of historic property. But that was all.

The turning point was the late Sixties. The decade was racked with discontent. Abroad, a nasty war seethed on. Leaders at home proved duplicitous. Our cities went into convulsions. Rallies and demonstrations became endemic. Crowds, roused by some common cause, poured into the streets and open spaces of America. There were young people and old, black people and white, poor people and those comfortably well off. Public life turned political, and so public places were reinvested with civil purpose. In the general anxiety of self-examination, the policy of urban renewal, too, began to raise doubts. Was the gutting of our inner cities really for the good of the people? Were the benefits of corporate towers and their immaculate plaza really so clear-cut? Where had the displaced poor been put? Was demolition the only way to cure ailing urban environments?

This ferment strengthened the hand of preservationists. A national act was passed in 1966 that provided for the establishment of historic preservation offices in every state. They were to draw up long-range plans and conduct field surveys, on the basis of which they would be able to save buildings with matching funds from the federal government. The act also provided for an inventory of historic property—the National Register of Historic Places—and committed the government to create incentives and offer grants for the preservation of such property. Today there are about 25,000 properties of national, state, and local significance on the National Register, and everyday more buildings and districts are designated as landmarks. These properties cannot be demolished or altered substantially.

The law now is firmly on the side of preservation. As early as 1954, the Supreme Court upheld "the right of cities to be beautiful" *(Berman* v. *Parker)*. "The concept of the public welfare is broad and inclusive," the Justices wrote. "It is within the power of the legislature to determine that the community should be beautiful as well as healthy, spacious as well as clean, well balanced as well as carefully patrolled." In practice, this ruling upset the general perception that, except where some dire public need or hazard could be demonstrated, nobody could restrict owners in

A 1960s political demonstration in Washington, D.C.

the use or disposition of their property. Now you can be told that what you own is a bit of America's cultural heritage to which you must act as custodian.

Have we already gone too far? Yes, say some critics. In the hands of urban reformers, preservation can now turn into a tool with which to force changes in the social structure. In New York City to date, for example, about fifty districts have been given landmark status; these contain some 20,000 buildings. The effort here has been to preserve modest as well as distinguished neighborhoods, to show where the average person lived in years past, as well as the architecture-conscious upper class. And that is commendable. But this vast reservoir of real estate involves the city's powerful Landmark Preservation Commission in matters of land use. The Commission is able to freeze development in valuable zones like the Upper East Side, without having to concern itself with the economic effects of its decisions. This is what its critics say.

The Return of Public Life

Charges of overzealousness to one side, this fresh respect for old age has breathed new life into our cities. Preservation has helped. So has the realization that blight is reversible without massive urban surgery, that decaying building stock can be rehabilitated, slowly, a little at a time. Once again, the government stepped in. The Department of Housing and Urban Development started a program of Community Development Block Grants to revive old neighborhoods. The inner city witnessed a gradual return of the middle class from the suburbs. Old rowhouses were gentrified. Cafes and restaurants opened in once derelict urban stretches, and at night strollers could be seen along piers and restored main streets. The old town squares livened up. It seemed that America was going public once again.

To take advantage of this gregarious mood, business-minded developers have cooked up new schemes for the downtown. They looked at the suburban shopping mall, which had proved popular since the Fifties as the only public gathering place of those thinly spread dormitory communities, and decided to replicate it in the city. But the sealed, isolated nature of most of these malls, with their shopfronts turning inward to face planned courts, does not suit the casual interaction characteristic of downtown street activity.

Something of the same inhibition applies to the trend in corporate buildings of the Seventies to internalize the underused open-air plazas of the previous decade. You have to brave the smartly polished revolving doors, the metallic lobbies with their uniformed guards, before you can experience the New York atriums of IBM, Ford, or Trump Tower. These inner courts are often exciting places—cagelike, lighted dramatically, and staged with intimate corners and interdependent levels that encourage people-watching. But there is something too controlled, even too secure,

Above, left. *Old Post Office Building on Pennsylvania Avenue between Eleven and Twelfth streets N.W., Washington, D.C., 1891–99, Willoughby J. Edbrooke, supervising architect. In the 1930s the building blocked completion of the Federal Triangle plan, and by the 1960s it was slated for demolition. During the following decade, however, admirers rallied to its defense, and it was marked for refurbishment and reuse.*

Above, right. *Enclosed courtyard of the Old Post Office Building as it appears today. The interior was redesigned by Arthur Cotton Moore and reopened in 1983.*

about them. They are, in the end, not *our* spaces: we are guests who came in from the street and are expected to behave. The safe retreat, the glitter of high technology, the cleanliness we are offered fail in the end to inspire that spontaneous, and always unpredictable, mingling that goes on in open-air pockets of living public places.

Such places are usually in the heart of things, well connected to the street system. In them, a working relationship between boundary buildings and open space takes place—a constant com-

Interior of the Atrium of the IBM Building in New York, 1982, by Edward Larrabee Barnes.

ing and going of people with different errands and diversions in mind, a constant shifting of the human landscape, a mixture of indolence and scurrying industry. Lately we have rediscovered the knack to create this kind of magic out of old cloth. We appropriate a big old urban scrap that has lain neglected or defunct, fill it with shops and eating places, let indoor activity spill over casually to the outside.

The master of this wizardry is James Wilson Rouse. He founded a large company of real-estate development and management based in Columbia, Maryland, the prime objective of which is to revitalize urban backwaters. To Rouse, the inner city is "a warm and human place, with diversity of choice, full of festival and delight." And he has a proved way of bringing this about. His firm creates what he calls "festival marketplaces," busy crowded centers that combine commerce, leisure, and showmanship. Sometimes they begin with what is there. Rouse made his name with the Faneuil Hall development in Boston, an old area along the city dock where three grand market buildings of granite were built in the 1820s—and survived. The Rouse Company stripped them of their accretions and impurities, along with the active but inelegant market they housed, filling them with shops and eateries where buyers and goods are thrown together in an open, festive atmosphere.

Sometimes the old is removed altogether, but remembered fondly and judiciously. That is what happened in Harborplace, Baltimore. Not long ago the area was a decaying waterfront— wharves, old warehouses, railroad yards. Rouse built two new waterside pavilions that hark back to the low, long wharf buildings on the site, and evoke at the same time the traditional harbor architecture of shed-like buildings—warehouses, ferry terminals, yacht clubs. The pavilions are simple structures of concrete beams and columns, open on both sides, toward the city and toward the water, where the three-masted frigate SS *Constellation,* commissioned by the young nation in 1797, is permanently moored. These transparent walls allow the people to see through the buildings and to pour in and out of them without inhibition. The pavilions have shed-like roofs of green aluminum that will fit in with the proposed lush park intended to engulf Harborplace.

And it works. There is the harbor to look at—that ancient waterfront scene of boats and birds. There is the open sequence of shops and restaurants on a generous ledge above the quay. And then, the cascade of stairs from the ledge down to the water which makes an adventure out of a stroll, blurring the difference between those who are there with a purpose and those who are simply there.

The means of this popular setting are clinically calculated of course. The Rouse Company interviews hundreds of businesses before it selects a handful as tenants; some businesses it invents. This occupancy is almost literally "designed" in terms of sight and smell. Institutional businesses are avoided. There are no department stores, and only a small fraction of chain-store outlets. Shopping mall fare—indoor fountains, plastic plants, and Muzak—is also excluded. And the lowlife pleasures of buying T-shirts and playing pinball machines and electronic games have no place in the tasteful world of fun and shopping that is being promoted. Rules about the conduct and the look of each of the business premises are strict. The use of certain materials like brick, simulated stone or wood, or textured paint is forbidden, and you must have the Rouse approval for all details having to do with flooring, lighting, counters, and signs.

Harborplace, Baltimore, Maryland, by the Rouse Company. The complex opened in 1980. The tall building is I. M. Pei's Maryland World Trade Center of 1977.

So the spontaneity is deceptive. And for some at least, urban centers like Faneuil Hall Market, Harborplace, or New York's Roused up South Street Seaport, a five-minute walk from Wall Street, are celebrations of the trendy superficiality of our time. They speak, as one reviewer of the Faneuil Hall project put it, "of the transformation of our society; of crafts, of franchise, of aspiring good taste and of our absorption with our own superfluous pleasures."

How To Remember

If we have demonstrated an aptitude for recapturing public life, if we have learned to preserve what we once built, we still find it difficult to assert ourselves through commemoration. There is nothing in the American environment today that could compare to Mount Auburn or Richmond's Monument Avenue. Our cemeteries are lawns, with no headstones, no monuments—just small bronze markers and containers for cut or plastic flowers. And at a more communal scale, we have not been able to revive our national predilection for setting up monuments and memorials. For all the glory and the sorrow of the last twenty years—the Moon Walk, Vietnam, the assassination of the Kennedy brothers and Dr. King, the Bicentennial—we have not been responding with new ideas to that trend to fill corporate plazas with mute markers that have no message to impart but their own abstraction. Why?

Public monuments must derive their authority from some unified vision—or its presumption. There are times in our history when a national mood of pride or hope sustains a confident language of public art. The years just after Independence were one such period; the declarative monumentality of the so-called American Renaissance, from the 1880s to the Great War, was the fruit of another. But there are also spells of self-doubt and ambiguity. We in these last decades of the twentieth century are familiar with them. We have to ask: Can the public realm be designed with clarity and force when the national purpose is itself in search of definition?

If monuments are meant to speak for the whole of society, if their function is to advertise common cultural ideals, it is no won-

Left. *St. Louis, Missouri, at the end of the nineteenth century. The dome in the center is that of the Old Courthouse of 1862.*

Below. *The St. Louis waterfront today, with Eero Saarinen's Memorial Arch, 1965. Visible to the left of the arch is the steeple of the Old Cathedral, 1834.*

der the last twenty years have not been rich in public art. Many of us have grown incurably cynical about great national agendas, about the methods of forging a national consensus or promoting national ideals. We are leery of the coercive orders of the Right or Left that are brutally mounted abroad in the name of national unity; we are leery of personality cults.

That cynicism stands in the way of commemorative expression. Since the Second World War there have been few national monuments we can point to. The best of these honor distant, and therefore uncontroversial, causes. One such monument is the splendid stainless-steel Memorial Arch in St. Louis, designed by one of our most brilliant architects, the late Eero Saarinen. Originally it was called the Jefferson National Expansion Memorial, intended to celebrate Jefferson's purchase of Louisiana and the subsequent opening of the West.

Today the Arch would probably not go up, at least not where it stands at present. Our value system is more conditional now.

Exterior of the Lincoln Memorial as seen across the reflecting pool. The memorial completes the axis of the Mall, which runs from the U.S. Capitol through the Washington Monument, as shown on page 186.

We would worry about the cultural cost, we would weigh alternatives. To make room for the Arch, some forty city blocks of original commercial waterfront had to be razed. All that is left now is the Old St. Louis Cathedral, the Old Rock House of 1819, linked to the early fur trade years of St. Louis, and the domed Court House of 1862. Yet here was a historic district of exceptional interest, with dozens of nineteenth-century warehouses. Allowed to live, and properly restored, it would have been a different sort of monument to the role of St. Louis as gateway to the West, but one that was as worthy as Saarinen's Arch and, though less spectacular, possibly more fitting. That alternative would appeal to us in these post-modern, history-affirming days.

So today, even when we want to remember, it is no longer a simple task to decide how we should remember. Take a more recent instance than the Arch. The U.S. Congress agreed in 1955 to establish the Franklin Delano Roosevelt Memorial Commission. To this day there is no Roosevelt Memorial. A competition was held in 1961. The site was to be West Potomac Park in Washington, D.C., stretching from the Lincoln to the Jefferson Memorial. In the old days we would know what to do. We knew when we wanted to honor another great president, Abraham Lincoln. Over life size and towering above us on a majestic throne, he is magnificently encased in a Classical temple raised up above a reflecting pool. His words are inscribed on the temple walls, those ringing words of private torment and official righteousness that can still stir strong emotions after more than a hundred years. His were the ultimate, terrible decisions. He alone is enshrined in honor: no one else shares this place with him, not his generals and ministers, not his soldiers.

In the Sixties we were not so sure. The traditional monumentality of the Lincoln Memorial was suspect; abstract monumentality, which was trying to replace it, did not communicate. The advisory committee for the Roosevelt Memorial competition reflected this uncertainty. It asked for "a less dominant form than the Lincoln, Jefferson, and Washington monuments." Then it

Lincoln Memorial, Washington, D.C., 1922, Henry Bacon, architect. The sculpture is by Daniel Chester French and the murals are by Jules Guerin.

Vietnam War Memorial, Washington, D.C., 1983, designed by Maya Ying Lin. The memorial stands on the Mall between the Washington Monument and the Lincoln Memorial. (See also color section.)

waffled further: "The site is an integral part of an extensive park system, and the memorial should enhance the park value of the area."

The winning design was an open group of smooth, contoured slabs of concrete set in the landscape, through which the visitor would freely move. There was no familiar architectural imagery of columns and cornices, no physical likeness of President Roosevelt—only his words inscribed on the slabs. The Federal Commission of Fine Arts rejected the design. It was not "harmonious" with the three adjacent memorials, they said; it was "lacking in repose, an essential element in memorial art."

The confusion is still with us. The latest monument to be proposed for the Mall in Washington, surely the most hallowed stage of our national life, has reopened the debate of what is and is not appropriate as a collective tribute to momentous events in our history. To complicate matters, this particular monument was for an event that few of us felt good about and many considered a tragic mistake—the Vietnam War.

Once again, there was a competition. The winner was Maya Ying Lin, an undergraduate then studying architecture at Yale. This time the winning design was built—with money raised by the veterans themselves. And a most remarkable design it is too, free of all the obvious conventions. It does not preach. It is stark— stripped of coded imagery. Nothing is heroic about it. The Vietnam War, like the Civil War before it, was a horrendously divi-

Vietnam War Memorial.

Frederick Hart's sculpture of three American servicemen, dedicated in 1984, was erected near one end of Maya Ying Lin's abstract Vietnam War Memorial.

sive adventure for the nation: only in this instance there is no hero of destiny like Lincoln to deify in the aftermath. Destiny is in the fallen—the more than 58,000 casualties whose names are inscribed on two triangular walls of black granite that meet under a gentle slope of the Mall lawn. They are listed in the order in which they died; the roster starts with one of the long columns in the middle and ends, back in the middle, with the circle of death finally closed. The veterans themselves had insisted that their memorial be contemplative and free of any political rhetoric. And that is what it is. We walk down toward that subterranean angle where the two shining black slabs come together: our reflection mingles with the names, we are conspirators, the sadness is on both sides.

But to some veterans at least, the black wall was too much like a memorial to defeat. They wanted to strike a balance. They had another monument put up just a little way off, something more conventional, more direct, perhaps less painful. It is a somber group of three American soldiers in fatigues, holding their automatic weapons. Sculptor Frederick Hart's men look a little lost, or just plain tired; too knowing in any case to strike brave poses.

The style of the two Vietnam memorials is obviously at odds. But the spirit of the memorials is much the same. The message of both is that in the tragic history of the War nothing could be found to celebrate, no national virtue to extol. It would appear, then, that when the sentiment is felt deeply enough the style of expressing is of small account.

What matters, in the end, is the need to remember. We do it with monuments like those on the Mall which distill our entire history as a nation into a sacred landscape and represent our supreme effort to canonize love of country. We do it with thousands of places and built artifacts across the land we call landmarks, which we have vowed to preserve lest we forget.

Meantime everywhere around us, undefended and unsung, lie dying the relics of our unsuccessful starts, our updated settings of life and work, our hit-and-run profiteering. The countryside is littered with abandoned farms, their barns and houses rotting, their once productive fields slipping back to untamed rangeland. In the Dust Bowl of our Great Plains the ruins of homesteads and windmills survive from the days when arid stretches were farmed as if they were lush prairieland; the precious soil was ruined, and with it the future of many of us. Long mournful lines of rusting railroad tracks west of the Alleghenies, clear across to the Pacific, are fringed with misbegotten towns. There are generations of abandoned one-room country schools; old silos and gas pumps; crumbling, hollow-eyed hulks of "housing projects" that warehoused the poor at the bleak edgeland of our great cities.

These too, of course, are monuments. But they have no markers, no visitors. They are too common to claim attention, or else too disgraceful to remember. Their presence is too diffuse. We like our memory compact and upbeat. We collapse the raw experience of thousands into single public gestures or picturesque stops spaced nicely along our recreational routes. A bloody battle becomes a plaque or a sculptured memorial; the grueling lives of our

An abandoned farm off County Road 1 in Otter Tail County, Minnesota.

mining past are consigned to gussied up ghost towns in Arizona or Montana we can buy an entrance ticket to. We drive unmindfully through miles of ravaged farmland, long reclaimed by nature under a blanket of second growth, to get to a "living historic farm" where you can be shown how cows once were milked and corn husked.

For most of us, indeed, memory has to be designed. Our minds have to be given selected stimuli to respond to. The same holds for public places. They have to be designed to help us come together: we won't fight odds to do it. Here, in this arrangement of the public realm, of monuments and communal stages, may lie the toughest challenge of American design. For architects and sculptors, planners and landscape artists, this may be the trickiest commission. Their client is the public, which means all of us, and it takes courage and a special gift to presume to speak for all

Office workers relaxing at the base of the statue of George Washington in Boston's Public Garden.

of us. Their program is tenuous—to make us proud of what we have done, to help us reflect on our social structure, to encourage us to live together. These are not sentiments that can be ordered with finality. They must be negotiated. Well-meaning official monuments by the score languish unattended. Grandly turned plazas that intended to formalize civility go to waste, while some scruffy corner lot with a trickle for a fountain, a leafy tree, and a bench or two brims with life. In societies like our own, commemoration wants to spring from the heart; participation needs to come about naturally. In the design of the public realm, that fit between structure and spontaneity is everything.

*Interior of the Dana-Thomas house, Springfield, Illinois. The house was built in 1902–4
for the socialite and women's activist Susan Lawrence Dana. It contains over one hundred
pieces of original Wright-designed furniture, two hundred fifty art glass doors, windows, and
light panels, and two hundred original light fixtures and skylights. The state of Illinois purchased the house in 1981 and maintains it as a museum.*

Top, left. *Rotch House in New Bedford, Massachusetts, 1846, by Downing's collaborator Alexander
Jackson Davis. The house is based on a Downing design, "A Cottage-Villa in the Rural Gothic
Style." The Downing-Davis collaboration began in the late 1830s and lasted until Downing's
death in 1852.*

Bottom, left. View of Glendale, *Ohio, ca. 1858–65; detail. Regular railroad commuter service was
maintained until 1927, when it was discontinued because of competition from the automobile.*

Overleaf. *Hearst Castle, San Simeon, California. One of the bell towers of the Casa Grande.*

Detroit Institute of Arts. Detail of the fresco Detroit Industry, *1932–33, by Diego Rivera.*

Right. *Strip farming southeast of Cedar Rapids, Iowa.*

Left. Abandoned head frame of a mineshaft, ca. 1880, Bodie, California. Gold was discovered here in 1859, and by 1880 the town had a population of nearly 10,000. Decline set in soon afterward. In 1962 Bodie was designated a State Historic Park.

Danbury, Connecticut. Union Carbide World Headquarters; aerial view.

Right. *Railroad Depot in Amboy, Illinois, built in 1876. This twenty-two room depot and railroad office building was rescued from demolition in 1976 and now houses a railroad museum.*

New York. The Bowery at Night, *a watercolor by W. Louis Sonntag, Jr., ca. 1895.*

*Bird's-eye view at night of
Burnham's proposal for the Chicago
waterfront, 1909.*

Left page. Sunset Street, *a painting by Wayne Thiebaud, 1985.*

Left. *A swan boat in Boston Public Garden. The boats are powered by pedals located in the body of the sheet-metal swan.*

Below. *Greenwood Cemetery, Brooklyn, shown in a contemporary print of 1852.*

Boston Public Library, 1887–95, by McKim, Mead & White. The library faces Copley Square.

Left. *Monument Avenue, Richmond, Virginia, with the Robert E. Lee Monument at center, 1890, Marius-Jean-Antonin Mercié.*

Overleaf. *Vietnam War Memorial, Washington, D.C., 1983, designed by Maya Ying Lin.*

JOHN F TYRRELL · VITALIO VELA Jr · ERNEST M WEATHERSBEE · WILLIAM D THOMAS · ORVILLE A SHEETS
JAMES W WILSON · SPENCER ADAMS · CHARLES L BAUGH · JOSEPH R WEAVER · ALBERT A TIPPETT
HARRY GENE BLOOMFIELD · ROBERT F BRULTE Jr · EMANUEL F BURROUGHS · JAMES H BENNETT
PETER COLICCHIO · KENNETH L CRYSEL · DONALD M DALE · LUNAS J DANIELS
MICHAEL M CADY · HERBERT C DAVIS · JAMES T DAVIS · WARREN M DIXON
DONALD L DYRESON · VERNON H LACKEY · RUSSELL J FAUSER Jr · MARION F FERGUSON
LESTER FREEMAN · SPENCER S FREESTONE · KENNETH L FULTON · JAMES T GAYNOR
JAMES M HILL · JOHN B HOGAN · EARNEST P HOLMES Jr · MARK E JAMES
ROBERT K KAWAMURA · DAVID E KEISTER · MICHAEL J KELLY · CHARLES W EGLIN III
CLAYTON LIGGINS · CHARLES F McGRATH · THOMAS J MARGLE · DOMENICO MORGERA Jr
CLYDE R McAFEE · MURAL McDANIEL · EARL MACK · RUSSELL W NAUGLE · BRUCE A NELSON
JOHN R PERRETTA · ANTHONY J PODEBRADSKY · GARRY R POWELL · EDWARD B QUILL Jr
RAMON S RODRIGUEZ · MELVIN H SANDERS · STEVAN R SARGENT · JIMMY L SILER
JAMES J STEWART · ROY F SWED · HENRY M TABET · WADE E THACKREY Jr · BRENT J TOSH
REX F TUTOR · BENJAMIN S UNDERHILL · DONALD W VAUGHN · RICHARD P VELLANCE
RALPH L WILLIAMS · ROGER C WILSON · JAMES L WOOD · ROBERT E ALEXANDER
CHARLES E ANDERSON · PAUL A JENSEN · WILLIAM BONEY · GERALD E GORDON
KENNY L COLTER · KEITH D E W COON · DONALD W DIXON · STEVEN E EMRICK
TAYLOR W FOREMAN Jr · ARTHUR T FRILEY · BOBBY F GALBREATH · DERYL R GARVICK
RICHARD L BOSWORTH · HAROLD P GRAY · WILLIAM L GREENWELL · BARRY N GRIGSBY
HERBERT D HAMMONS · DONALD A HIERLMEIER · ROBERT S HUTCHINSON II · PAUL M ASH
KENNETH R JOHNSON · JEROME R KELLY · ERNEST F LAWRENCE · WILLIAM A LEE
THOMAS L LITTLE SUN · ADOLFO LUNA · HARRY E MATTHEW · GERALD L MILBRODT
JACKIE M MORGAN · THOMAS H MORRIS · DONALD J WIELINSKI · BENNIE E McCORKLE
ROGER D PYNE · CULLEN W QUIN · JOHN H REYNOLDS · JOHN K RIPEL
HARRY W SCHNEIDER · WAYNE T SEVERINO · SANDY LEE SHULL
JOSEPH V SPELLMAN · DANIEL M STONE · PEARLY J THOMAS
VALENTINE B VOLLMER · ALEXANDER K WARD · JAMES D McALISTER
CLAYBORN W ASHBY Jr · FRANCIS S BECHTOLD · DAVID A BERNHEISEL · WILLIAM L DRAPER
FRANK A DAWSON · CHRISTOPHER G DELGADO · PAUL N DONATO
JAMES T GORDON · TERRENCE C GRAVES · HENRY GREGORY · BLAKE H HALFMAN
AMON F MOORE Jr · HENRY F HENDERSON III · FRANK L HOGE · JOHN F LEWIS
GEORGE M KIHNLEY · THOMAS W KLORAN · JAMES S KRAVITZ · THOMAS V MAYBURY
DENNIS J LULOFS · WILLIAM T MANGUM Jr · JAMES E MARTIN
JAMES F MEYER Jr · CHARLES P HEADLEY · RONALD L McELROY
DALE S McWRIGHT · GARY R SMITH · ANDRES SORCHINI · WILBURN E WESTER
DAVID H WARNER · JOSEPH C ANDREW · MICHAEL F AUSTIN
BONDROWSKI
BANAGA Jr
HEDLUND
LE BOMBARB
McDONALD
D L SMITH
J BREFCZYNSKI
ROBERT R GRAY
STURTEVANT
ANDERSON
A PINHEIRO
SWEENEY

Among the Sierra Nevada Mountains, California, *painted by Albert Bierstadt in 1868. This huge canvas, measuring more than six by ten feet, is now part of the collection of the National Museum of American Art in Washington, D.C.*

Overleaf, above. *Canal of the Central Arizona Project. This mammoth system, begun in 1973, will not be fully operational until the early 1990s. Walkways were built across parts of the canal for cattle and mule deer, and its banks were deliberately roughened to prevent small animals from slipping when they go down to drink.*

Overleaf, below. *Logging trails in Manchac Swamp, Louisiana. This swamp was a prime source of cypress around the turn of the century. The radial patterns reflecting sunlight are small canals that were used for floating logs to sawmills in the New Orleans area.*

5

The Shape
of the Land

The story of that marvelous construction called the Hoover Dam began in 1905 when the Colorado River, always prone to violent flash floods, burst its banks and inundated the prosperous communities of California's Imperial Valley. The unwelcome water ravaged the land for months. It left behind a permanent memorial, the thirty-mile long Salton Sea which filled an ancient lake sink. Over the next twenty-five years, attempts to contain the unruly river behind levees proved inadequate, or failed outright. Hoover Dam did the job.

They started in 1931. The dam site, in Black Canyon about thirty miles southeast of Las Vegas, had first to be unwatered. Through the rock walls of the steep, narrow canyon they drilled and blasted four huge tunnels with a combined length of 16,000 feet, lined them with concrete, and into them diverted the fast stream of the Colorado. To keep the working area dry, they bracketed the site with cofferdams, and protected the downstream cofferdam with a 54-foot high rock barrier.

Left page. *Hoover Dam, originally called Boulder Dam, built across the Colorado River on the Arizona-Nevada border from 1931 to 1936 by the Bureau of Reclamation. The highest of the federal dams in the West, it stands 726 feet from lower outlet level to its lip.*

Pressure-grouting jumbo completing the tunnel lining at the intake portal of Diversion Tunnel No. 4, Hoover Damsite, October 1932. Two tunnels on each side of the river were driven through the canyon walls to carry the flow of the river during construction. The tunnels have a circular cross section and were excavated fifty-six feet in diameter and lined with three feet of concrete to make a finished diameter of fifty feet.

Aerial view looking south to Hoover Dam, with the intake towers and Lake Mead in the foreground. The lake extends a hundred fifteen miles up the Colorado River.

Then the site was excavated to reach clean bedrock; about 200,000 cubic yards of gravel and loose rock were removed with crawler-mounted electric shovels to expose an inner gorge bordered by rock benches. The dam wall went up across the gorge in a sweeping arc—to a height of over 700 feet. Behind the curve of the dam crest rose pairs of intake towers, tall as skyscrapers and fitted with trashracks between radial fins. The water in the reservoir that the dam created would pass through these towers and would be released periodically into the spillways, where it would be held in check by floodgates; or else it would pass through penstock tunnels and into the two wings of the V-shaped power plant at the toe of the dam, where it would be converted to electricity.

This was only the beginning. About one hundred and fifty miles downstream, at the California-Arizona border, another dam was built, to harness the regulated flow of the Colorado. From an extensive reservoir at that point, Lake Havasu, the water passed into a capacious aqueduct which carried it for some 250 miles across Southern California to Riverside. From there it entered a network of secondary aqueducts and rushed to meet the daily needs of a number of cities, among them Los Angeles and San Diego.

The Imperial Dam on the Colorado River, three hundred miles below Hoover Dam. On the right are the sluiceway, headworks, and desilting basin for the All-American Canal system which runs through Southern California.

Still further downstream, the Colorado was dammed again and put through three immense desilting basins. The purified waters were then diverted into the All-American Canal and its branch, the Coachella Canal. From these they issued, through a system of irrigation channels, to green the fields of the Imperial Valley, reaching more than half a million acres of agricultural land. On the other side of the border, more recently, Arizona made its own claim on the Colorado River. From Lake Havasu across its desert it moved water almost two hundred miles, through an amazing system of concrete-paved aqueducts, pumping stations, siphons, and control gates, to Phoenix and Tucson. The water must pass through a seven-mile tunnel cut into the Buckskin Mountains and be lifted three thousand feet during its seven-day journey. This Central Arizona Project, or CAP, under construction for the last twelve years, has painted a bright blue ribbon on the tawny desert bed and will soon be supplying the state with a million and a half acre-feet of water annually, enough to flood that many acres of arid land. Six other states inside the Colorado River basin are entitled to its waters, and of them Utah has already put in a bid for its own share.

To tame nature and redesign it—to tap its forces and exploit its wealth for welfare and profit—this has been an obsession of Americans from the time of their first arrival. The land was new, obstreperous, inexhaustible. We set out to make it our own, to subjugate it, to shape it to our purposes. Never satisfied with the order we brought to the land, we needed to make it over and over, or abandon what we had first accomplished to push further out beyond the horizon and start our design in the fresh wilderness.

Americans, the Austrian traveler Francis Gund wrote in 1837, "treated nature as a conquered subject: not as a mother who gave them birth." Indeed so. We cut through mountains and altered the course and behavior of rivers. We spanned valleys and lakes, cleared forests and drained marshlands, pockmarked the earth's crust with sand and gravel and iron pits, and scored it with paved roads and the raw strips of coal-mining. We cut up the Indian homelands into speculative parcels and sold them to each other. "They could not at first love what was not theirs," Gund wrote

Circular fields irrigated with center-pivot systems near O'Neill, Nebraska. Most of the round fields in this photograph are planted with corn. The picture was taken from an altitude of about 270 miles by Skylab *astronauts in June of 1973.*

of us; "and when it became theirs, they had already changed its face."

The impressions we have made are indelible. From the air, we can see plainly the great orderly grid set upon two-thirds of the United States in accordance with the Land Ordinance of 1785; the finer patterns of cultivation within its undeviating matrix, from the earliest farm fields to the giant green circles of center pivot irrigation; waterways and highways; airfields, oil fields, salt ponds, and freeway exchanges; and, most widespread of all, the variegated blanket of our settlements. At closer range, we can see the monumental panoply of dams and levees; long-span bridges and the cooling towers of nuclear plants; the giant radio telescope dish antennas like the group of twenty-seven called the Very Large Array, each eighty-two feet in diameter, set across twenty-one miles of an ancient New Mexico lake bed; and testimonials of the now forgotten energy crisis, like the thousands of tall steel windmills on concrete plots on the grassy knolls of the Altamont Pass east of San Francisco, their rotorized heads spinning to generate electric current. Below ground, there are the caves blasted inside Cheyenne Mountain in the Rockies, not far from Colorado Springs, as the headquarters of the North American Aerospace Defense Command; the wind tunnel in Mountain View, California, where jets and bombers are tested; and the newly planned "Superconducting Super Collider," a sixty-mile long circular tunnel for the world's most powerful atom smasher.

For four hundred years we used the continent as our drafting table. We drew our lines freely, erased what we did not like. The achievement is awesome; the engineering feats, without parallel. Yet to scan the record of this all-encompassing design, to view the proud issue of its execution, is also to reflect on the very substance of civilized life. When do the benefits of civilization threaten the fundamental order of things? What are the limits of rearranging nature? Is it possible to overspend our inheritance? We should know. We have done it all. We have designed a continent. And we have done it brilliantly.

Indians and Colonists

The North American continent had its own ancient design—and earlier tenants than ourselves.

The architecture of our continent between its two ocean arms, with its roughly north-south grain, had a broad, stately composition. Beyond the comparatively congested East Coast—the barrier islands, the eastern coastal plain from New Jersey to Alabama, the narrow band of the Appalachians parallel to the coast—opened the lush prairie, a rippling lowland, silent, empty. At the Missouri River the land rose imperceptibly in a sweeping ramp for 600 miles toward the Rockies; this was the area of the Great Plains, vast and blizzard-prone. West of here, the young spread of mountains that started at the Rockies, covered nearly a third of the continent all the way to the Pacific. In the Southwest, the great desert basin, treeless grassland, arid and inhospitable.

The forces that created the design over geologic time left memorable scars: Meteorite Crater in Arizona, the Scablands of Washington, the great moraine of Long Island, the elongated glacial hills of Wisconsin, the Grand Canyon, the dunes of Death Valley. Other patterns were changeable, the meanders of the mighty rivers, for example, snaking back and forth across flat valley floors, or high land, like the oxbow bends of the Mississippi whose superseded loops live in the curved field patterns of the bayous.

This was the land that was home to the Indians for over ten thousand years before the Spaniards, the French, and the English first arrived. And their long occupation had made its own order. Tribal boundaries, means of communication, monuments testified to their presence. Organized into traditional societies, the Indians had their own cultural mold and government.

The tribe was the primary unit of society. Each tribe had a name, a territory, and a decision-making body. They were small, between 200 and 6,000 people, and there were many. The size of their territory ranged from a minimum of 500 square miles to as much as 20,000. East of the Rockies, these small entities sometimes came together to form confederacies, but the few Indian "nations" that the Europeans made known later on were by and large a fiction invented by them as an administrative convenience: it made it easier than having to deal with hundreds of small, shifting tribes, each possessed of its own land and sovereignty.

The limits of tribal territory were well marked and respected. They included not just the villages and their corn gardens but also hunting grounds. The only way a tribe lost control of its territory was to abandon it voluntarily or to have it taken by another tribe through conquest. This was different from the accepted practice of allowing another group to hunt in or tempo-

The Village of Secoton *in a view of 1585–87 by John White.*

rarily occupy your territory, usually in a dependent role; this may be what some Indians thought they were doing when they made the first deals with the newly arrived Englishmen.

Tribal boundaries usually followed natural features like rivers, lakes and ridges; or they were determined by time measures—for example, "the distance it takes to walk for half a day." There were boundary markers, but the physical nature of them is not clear. A Cayuga (Iroquois) chief, speaking in a land cession council in 1789, put it this way: "Our ancestors had certain Marks, each

The Great Serpent Mound of the Adena-Hopewell people, begun ca. 800 B.C. in what is now Adams County, Ohio.

Tribe had a certain Boundary or Line they called their own, of the Land the Great Spirit gave them." In a war between tribes—the Five Nations against the Illinois and Miami—the offended parties asserted that the others "had cut down the Trees of Peace, which were the limits of our Country." When the warring Iroquois and the Ottawa made peace about 1690, they hung "a sun at the strait between Lake Herier and Lake Huron, which should mark the boundaries between the two peoples." And we have the case of Baton Rouge. When Pierre Lemoyne d'Iberville and his party went up the Mississippi in 1699, they saw on the first bluffs a large red pole some thirty feet high decorated with bear and fish heads. This was the marker, they were told, that separated the hunting grounds of the Bayougoula Indians from those of the Houmas. The Indians called it Istrouma, or Red Pole; hence Baton Rouge.

Within the territory there were villages, small settlements organized into extended kin networks. But these were not fixed to a site. The villagers went where the food was, in accordance with the seasons, and the village went with them. In the east the houses, bent sapling frames covered with grass mats or bark, were designed to be taken apart and moved in a few hours. These wigwams, and most of the household goods, were owned by the women. Only farming Indians cleared the land and stayed put for a few seasons—perhaps eight to ten years, until the soil was depleted. In the unfenced fields corn was interlaced with other crops, like squash, pumpkins, and tobacco. The fields stood under leafless dead trunks, remnants of the forest trees whose bark was set fire to as a prelude to clearing.

The tribes moved on rivers in rafts and along the paths they made. They burned large sections of forest to simplify travel and hunting. On land they moved on foot, and they favored high ground along land ridges. They knew neither pack animal nor wheel, so the paths were very narrow. Some, like the Natchitoches Path from Louisiana to St. Louis, are still visible today, especially from the air. The Old Connecticut Path led from the vicinity of Boston to the upper Hudson Valley. The Iroquois Trail to the west crossed New York in the Mohawk Valley, cut across the watershed south of Lake Ontario, and ended at Niagara Falls. This first American transportation network would be perpetuated by the Europeans. The Warrior's Path of the Cherokee and Shawnee hunters that crossed the Appalachians through the Cumberland Gap became Wilderness Road, the most popular route of westward-bound immigrants from the Shenandoah Valley to the Bluegrass Basin and the lower Ohio Valley. The National Road incorporated Necamolin's Path and the Great Trail.

In the Midwest, along the Ohio Valley, an early people, the Adena-Hopewell, raised astounding earthworks for the rites of a mortuary cult. Mounds and ridges and earth-enclosed avenues, these built shapes were sometimes artfully layered in alternating tiers of sand, earth, and rock, covering areas of as much as four square miles. The earth was carried in baskets by individual workers, and the earthworks were built in phases, over a long period of time.

So the land of the Indians had a time-honed shape, roads and rituals, established uses. But to the invading Europeans it was a wilderness occupied by savages:

> A waste and howling wilderness,
> Where none inhabited
> But hellish fiends, and brutish men
> That Devils worshipped.

According to Western wisdom, a basic difference between savages and civilized people could be detected in notions of ownership, of private property. Indians, like all other savages, had no permanent attachment to the land. "Amonge them the lande is as common as the sonne and water: . . . Myne and Thyne . . . have no place with them," wrote Peter Martyr in the sixteenth century. Their claim to the land was "natural" rather than civil; that is, they held it in common, and people hunted and sowed where they pleased. Civil ownership meant enclosing the land to raise crops and cattle and to improve it. And in Puritan theory, supported by Old Testament references, land not being "improved" by the heathen was open to any Christian who would make use of it. In the eyes of the English colonists, cornfields were the only property Indians had improved sufficiently to call their own. The rest was up for grabs.

Alongside this material attitude toward the land went another prevailing European concept—the right of patent. It determined that a Christian monarch had full authority over lands discovered in his name, so long as the inhabitants were not Christian. The kings of England, France, and Spain in turn made grants of their American domain to proprietary governors or trading companies and their settlers, and these agencies decided how it was to be distributed. The tribal lands of the Indians, given to them by the Great Spirit and held in trust for the whole tribe by their chiefs, or sachems, in the colonialists' eyes became a pattern of fixed parcels with purely arbitrary boundaries that could be bought and sold.

With such long-entrenched European notions about savagery and civility, there was no way in which the two groups could live together in peace as equals. In Virginia the English had created a fortified line between themselves and the Indians as early as 1629.

Four scenes of the evolution of a New York frontier farm, 1849, from O. Turner's History of the Holland Purchase.

They cleared some 300,000 acres of land on the lower peninsula of its native population and built a palisade from the James River to the York. The Indians, confined west of the line and north of York, were formally granted lands, fifty acres to each male adult. The story was much the same in New England; survivors were forced to adapt. By the end of the seventeenth century many Indians were beginning to keep European livestock. In the next century the Indians of Maine had divided their lands into family hunting territories with hereditary ownership, following the English practice of inheritance.

With the change of hands came a change in shape. The European settlers had no love of nature. Out there was a threatening, evil element, and agricultural clearing was the prime way to cope with it. They were "insensible to the wonders of nature," de Tocqueville wrote, "and they may be said not to perceive the mighty forests that surround them till they fall beneath the hatchet." From the early seventeenth century until the end of the nineteenth, the act of a single man cutting down several acres of woodland and building himself a house in a clearing would be repeated a few million times in the eastern and northern portions of the country. By 1850, 115 million acres of the nation's land had been cleared; then, in a dramatic escalation, 40 million more in the ten years before the start of the Civil War. It was the first transfiguration of the American landscape, and it may have been the most momentous.

It took about thirty man-days to clear a forested acre, and in the aftermath, there were stumps and scorched trunks on the ground, and stacks of split logs and firewood. In the prairies, by comparison, you could break an acre of sod in one and one-half man-days, but then wood was scarce and had to be brought in by railroad. Around the cleared land you put up a fence. Until the invention of barbed wire in 1873 by a man named Glidden, this meant rock or stone or wood fences, fences made of split rails, and hedgerows, usually Osage orange, which could spread to a width of twenty feet or more and go up to thirty feet.

Forests were also burned for the ash used to manufacture soap and gunpowder, and potash, as it is known, became a major New England export. And of course forests were felled to fuel hearths and furnaces and to build houses and ships. The evidence of decades of logging still meets the eye in the landscape—the receding forest line where the dense timber stand abruptly ends, or the skid tracts, fanning out of a zigzag logging road on a mountain side, attesting to where logs were dragged to central loading points. (See color section.) Another early ritual of logging, the log drive, has left no traces. This carefully orchestrated group procedure was first tried in the headwaters of the Hudson River in about 1813. Loggers would push their marked logs downstream in the spring thaw, and then sort them out and reclaim them in huge pens near sawmills called booms.

So the land was redesigned. In New England, by the end of the Colonial period, the near-imperceptibly settled Indian landscape of heavy forests, open woods, salt marshes, and coastal plains, where mobility was the way of life, had been taken over by permanent townships, with the dividing line between them and pasture rigidly defined. In the countryside you found, as William Cronon puts it in his eloquent book, *Changes in the Land,* "the seemingly endless miles of fences, the silenced voices of vanished wolves, the system of country roads, and the new fields filled with clover, grass, and buttercups." The destruction of forests laid bare the land and dried up streams and springs. Indian paths were widened to accommodate carts and wagons. Their hunting grounds were subdivided. European wars and European diseases decimated their numbers. They became a subject people. "They are in a state of pupilage," Chief Justice John Marshall ruled in 1831. "Their relation to the United States resembles that of a ward to his guardian." As we moved West, Indians were in the way. Their sense of shared custody hampered expansion. Deals were made. They were driven to sell what the Great Spirit had given their ancestors at the beginning of their time. In the end, even the tribal identity we allowed them on reservations would not remain secure. The story of the detribalizing of the Narragansett by act of the Rhode Island state legislature reads like an elegy: "[The] relation which has existed for nearly 250 years [between the European stock and Indians] is now terminated and the name of the Narragansett tribe passes from the statute books of the State."

We resented them for occupying "useful" land, for being exempt from taxes, for being immune to debt suits. But above all, we never forgave them for their ignorance of the rules of private property. Teddy Roosevelt could repeat unblushingly the convenient Colonial creed three hundred years after Jamestown and Plymouth.

Where the game was plenty, there they hunted; they followed it when it moved away . . . and to most of the land on which we found them they had no stronger claim than that of having a few years previously butchered the original occupants.

The National Survey

On the thirtieth of September 1785, Thomas Hutchins, the first geographer to the United States, and his deputies set up their

Jacob's staff on the north bank of the Ohio River, at the convergence of Little Beaver Creek, where Pennsylvania, West Virginia, and the Ohio Territory met and they laid out a line exactly due east-west. In the next several weeks they hacked their way westward where Neville School now is in the town of Liverpool, Ohio, for six miles along this line. There they surveyed again and cut a north-south line down to the Ohio River. This was the beginning of a national survey of America's public domain which in a hundred years would affect the design of about seventy percent of the land in the continental United States. It was the most thorough and extensive cadastral survey in history, and it had a profound impact on every aspect of our life—our social and political structure, our taxation and election practices, the size of our farms, the placement and spatial order of our towns.

The idea was Thomas Jefferson's. Immediately following the Declaration of Independence, the original states holding western land claims, like New York, Connecticut, Massachusetts, and Virginia, began to cede them to the U.S. Congress. The federal government extended these vast territorial holdings with purchases of its own—from Indian tribes, and from the French who would sell us the territory of Louisiana outright in 1803. Jefferson wanted to make sure that the occupation of these newly opened stretches of the continent would be orderly and equitable and proposed that they be surveyed and divided into square townships. The Congress agreed. It authorized the establishment of the U.S. Public Land Survey with the Ordinance of May 1785. The plans were ready within three months, and Hutchins was dispatched in September of that year to initiate the extraordinary undertaking.

Until that time, the settlement pattern in the American colonies had been irregular. It was motivated by the push for choice acreage and controlled by the shape of the land. The division was made without proper surveying, by metes and bounds—"from the big oak to the river, and along the bank to So-and-So's farm," and so on. The imprecise demarcation of boundaries caused disputes, and since roads could not always coincide with these erratic boundaries, they very often had to cut through properties.

The French, whose settlements were strung along the rivers, favored long lots with water frontage for easy transport. These

Long-lot land division along the Bayou Lafourche, Assumption Parish, Louisiana. Bayou Lafourche is a delta branch of the Mississippi. Homesteads were closely spaced in line villages along both sides of the river, with narrow lots extending back from the water.

became narrower with time as the land was repeatedly subdivided to accommodate newcomers. When the river front was taken, a second row would be started behind the river lots, fronting a road that connected these new farms. The long narrow fields had at least one advantage: they minimized the number of times a farmer had to turn his plough. The French used the system in Canada and northern Maine, in Indiana along the Wabash, in Louisiana along the Mississippi. You can read it still in stretches of Louisiana farmland in the lower Mississippi Delta, like those at Empire, or along Bayou Lafourche in Assumption Parish, where the fields occupied the well-drained natural levees of sand and gravel created by floods, the only suitable sites for settlement, and extended as far as they could into the back swamps.

In the English colonies, the South followed the headright method of choosing land, which meant that each settler took the land best suited to his purposes. This appropriation ignored orderly outlines and contiguity with neighboring properties. In the North, the New England townships instituted a more controlled settlement form. The land was surveyed first and then divided. Here and in Pennsylvania there was a strict correspondence at first between your town lot and the farmstead you were assigned in the country—"proportionate ownership in town and country," as William Penn put it. But in the eighteenth century the trend was away from such compact, coherent settlements in favor of a more dispersed arrangement, as residents began to move out to their fields permanently and to start individual farmsteads quite separate from the towns and villages.

The Spanish too came with disciplined notions of colonizing. Theirs were square land claims, *sitios* as they were called. And the cities, along with their dependent countryside, were to be laid out in an articulated grid according to the detailed instructions of a planning document called the "Laws of the Indies," a set of 148 articles issued by Spain in 1573, codifying earlier ordinances. But in reality land division was quite irregular in the Spanish settlements of Texas, California, and the upper Rio Grande Valley, from Santa Fe north into Colorado. The ranchos, or large grants of grazing land assigned to the first families, were informally delimited, with natural boundaries like rivers and clumps of trees. In California there were about five hundred of these ranchos at the time of the American takeover, which was officially marked by the Treaty of Guadalupe Hidalgo in 1848; most of these were created by the Mexican administration.

In fact, the only regular land designations in Spanish California were the deliberately planned pueblos, or towns, like San Jose and Los Angeles, and the presidios (military encampments), like San Francisco. Both were entitled, according to the Laws of the Indies, to four square leagues of land, the area to be measured "in a square or prolonged form according to the character of the land." (A Spanish league was 2⅗ miles.) By the time the Americans were in charge, the inhabitants of pueblos and presidios were busy selling their land. All that Los Angeles, for example, has to show of its original patrimony today is Pershing Square, Elysian Park, and the old plaza.

It was to prevent the continuation of these arbitrary Colonial ways of parceling and occupying land that the National Survey was adopted. The Ordinance of 1785 provided that all prior claims, including Indian titles, be extinguished before the land could be surveyed. Furthermore, surveyors were instructed to keep field notes on land cover, the quality of soil, salt licks and other minerals, and waterpower sites; so the survey turned into a kind of crude land inventory.

The lines of the survey were determined using astronomical devices and were strictly oriented to the four cardinal directions. The lines ran straight, in complete disregard of the irregularities of the terrain, for thousands of miles. To compensate for the slight convergence of lines running true north toward the poles, the surveyors shifted the meridians a hundred yards to the west every now and then, so in a sense the great American grid is actually a number of separate grids slightly offset from one another. This solution was first put into effect in 1804 in southern Indiana. The baselines of the individual grids still serve as local streets today. A Baseline Road traverses Boulder, Colorado, and San Bernardino Baseline skirts Los Angeles to the north.

But these offsets or doglegs are hardly noticed on the ground or from the air. The unforgettable impression as you fly over the Midwest is of an undeviating regularity, a rational course that makes no exception and knows no obstacle. In this the survey differs from its historical predecessors. Roman centuriation, the division of the countryside into squares, each containing a hundred small landholdings, was never considered unconditionally continuous; often the parallels and meridians were adjusted to be in line with the prominent features of the topography. In Holland, where the polders, or lands reclaimed from the sea, were blocked out in large squares, no fanatically straight east-west, north-south field lines prevail. This example probably figured in the planning stages of the survey, since a member of the commission that drew up the Ordinance of 1785, the North Carolina delegate Hugh Williamson, had taken a medical degree in Utrecht and would have been familiar with Dutch practice. The foreign system closest to the survey was almost certainly unknown to commission members. This was Japan's *jori* system, introduced as early as the seventh century as a nonvarying square grid in the Nara Basin, but adjusted to the topography in other parts of the country.

Jefferson had proposed a metric system of measurement—an "American mile" divided into one hundred "chains." The checkerboard squares would measure ten of these miles on each side. But the ordinance specified six regular miles, or square "townships" of thirty-six square miles each. Every other township would be subdivided into 640-acre lots, called sections; there would be thirty-six sections with sides one mile long. These would be put up for sale, except one, Section 16, which was to be set aside for schools. But the law was revised later to allow for parcels smaller than a section to be sold, until the quarter-section (160 acres) became the standard unit for single landowners; after a time, it came to be viewed as the ideal size for the family farm.

So the pattern was set: four farms to the section. In the Midwest, fields, pastures, and woodlots were all bounded by section lines. Rectangular fields decreed straight-line tillage. To plow a straight furrow became a matter of pride for the farmer. The farmhouse, the barn, even ornamental trees followed this rectilinear matrix. So did the tree groves or shelterbelts in Iowa and Minnesota, planted on the north and west sides of farmsteads as protection against the strong northwesterly winds.

Over five million farms were plotted on public lands between 1800 and 1900. This was by and large a peaceful process, free of violent boundary disputes. For this we can thank the grid, and wonder what it would have been like if all of this terrain were to be divided in accordance with the old metes and bounds system. We have a glimpse of that eventuality in some pre-survey land grants, like the ones in the Virginia Military District of Ohio, that were designed to fulfill the warrants issued to soldiers who fought in the Revolutionary War. The warrants were for parcels of land, from 100 acres to 15,000 (the largest for the major general). They had no restriction as to shape, and a single warrant did not have to be a contiguous piece of land; so unsystematic, irregular patterns emerged. By contrast, federal scrip certificates followed the survey. These entitled the receiver to a select amount

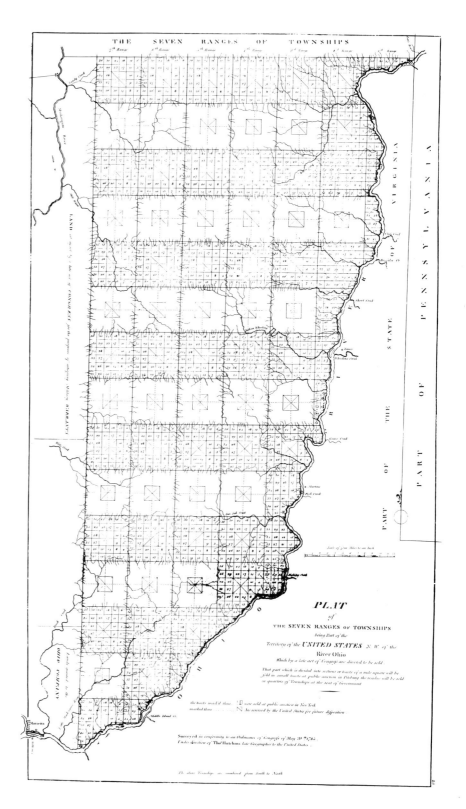

*"The Seven Ranges of Townships,"
1796; a plan of the first townships
surveyed according to the land
ordinance of 1785, in what was then
the Ohio Territory.*

Land division in Hancock County, Iowa.

of land in the public domain, and they were used as military bounty warrants, for agricultural college lands, and to indemnify those people whose land claims had been violated in some way. In the end, outside of land divisions in the Colonial period, Revolutionary land grants, and land grants made for canals and roads, the only major exception to the survey were the Indian reservations created by the treaties.

In Jefferson's vision at least, the majestic register of the survey was more than a device for the speedy and orderly occupation of newly opened lands. It was also a political diagram. It gave all of us, in theory, equal access to the land and buttressed an agricultural economy. Each section, in theory, was defined on all four sides by straight public roads whose purpose was to provide landowners with the means to get to the nearest town—to vote, pay taxes, worship, and conduct official business in the courthouse. Civil boundaries coincided with property lines, and the section lines were used in delimiting and organizing counties, or even states—for example, the boundaries between South Dakota and Wyoming and between Oklahoma and New Mexico. Election districts were dependent on townships, and so were taxes.

Yet the survey also denied us things. It denied us the sense of working with the shape of the land—its river bends and ridges, its curves and disjunctions. It scattered homesteads across the landscape instead of clustering them into villages, and so fostered that myth of the American as loner, boosting the frontier bravado in our character, that at its best nourishes us with the satisfaction of personal strength and self-reliance, and at its worst turns us against government and community.

The Spoils of Occupation

And so the origin of the survey was an uncharacteristic early initiative of national planning, while its follow-up is typical of the privatism we cherish.

No sooner did the Congress find itself in possession of unimagined stretches of public land, than it looked for ways to divest itself of its wealth. Some was sold, much was ceded away in the public interest. It has been reckoned that more than a billion acres of the original federal lands have since passed into private ownership or been alienated to the states. What remains is mostly arid, rough, or mountainous.

That we should all share in this bounty was an irresistible promise to land-hungry European immigrants. The Homestead Act of 1862 belatedly formalized the idea. It offered to give away

160 acres of land to any individual who would claim it and pay a nominal registration fee. All you had to do was live on the land for five years, cultivate and improve it, and you would receive title to a quarter-section of the public domain. The first tract to be claimed after the act was passed was in Beatrice West, Nebraska. The claimant's name was Daniel Freeman. A Homestead National Monument on the site commemorates the free land policy that was to govern the settlement of the West.

But only one in ten farms was acquired in this way. The act allowed land-grabbing, and in a short time large tracts were concentrated in the hands of wealthy individuals and speculative companies.

The common ideal of a nation of freeholders was always more myth than fact. From the start the Western frontier had plenty of landless farm laborers and tenant farmers, with their bosses controlling large landed estates. The act merely perpetuated this inequity. Already in the censuses of 1850 and 1860 a sharp increase is recorded in the number of farms that exceed five hundred acres, and in the number of hired hands and tenants paying rent to those who have variously been called "prairie landlords" and "capitalist estate builders." The nominal cost of homesteading may have been quite low, but the actual cost of farm-making was not. Many settlers attracted by the promise of free land found that they could not afford paid hands to break the soil or the labor-saving machinery they would need to do it themselves. You had to buy lumber for the house, the fencing, and the barn; the yoke of oxen, the plow, the seed, home furnishings, tools, and reserves to see the family through until the first harvest. All this could amount to a thousand dollars or more—a handsome sum of money. We hear a lot about the mortgaged farmer, but often it never got that far. A farmer simply hired himself out, or paid rent for a small tenant farm—in cash or with a share of his crop.

The corporate profiteers included railroad companies, granted land outright to run their lines where they wanted. They in turn sold off pieces of their grant to other companies and individuals, their one most successful expedient for this purpose being the creation of new towns at frequent intervals along the tracks. So many family farms did not end up being shares of our common bequest, as we had intended, but money-making parcels that fattened land and railroad companies; and the new towns of America were not genuine creations of communal space, but accommodations of real estate.

The federal government had decided almost from the beginning that America's transportation network would be left to the private sector. The first regional systems, like canals and toll roads, had no benefit of an overall plan. They ran where the companies, many of them tax-exempt "public-service corporations," thought the profits were. When the overland migrations to the Pacific Coast began around 1840 the wagons carrying fur traders, missionaries, gold seekers, and emigrants rutted their own trails across the prairie and the Great Plains. For twenty years until the Civil War, the Oregon Trail was the most popular route—2,000 miles from Independence, Missouri, to Oregon's Willamette River Valley and the terminus of Oregon City ten miles south of Portland, with a short alternate branch at Three Mile Crossing in Idaho. More than a quarter of a million people took the trail during that time. They set out in early spring from Independence, Council Bluffs, or St. Joseph and took six months getting across. On the rolling, featureless prairie expanse the wagons fanned out and made a long, unending trek until Scottsbluff in western Nebraska, on the banks of the North Platte River, where they again were channeled into a single track to go through Mitchell Pass. There the ruts of heavy wheels and axle scrapes are deepest, visible as they were more than a century ago, and they are visible again in the hard limestone spread near Gurnsey, Wyoming.

With the railroads, our first major interstate network, came an unparalleled federal largesse. Until the practice was discontinued by Congress in 1871, 1.5 million acres of the public domain went to them in grants. At first, the states were used as trustees and agents for these extravagant grants. But then the land began to go directly to the companies—a 400-foot wide roadway, and every alternate 640-acre section within the limits of twenty miles on each side of this right-of-way, to the sum of twenty sections per mile. The federal government also obligingly agreed to extinguish Indian titles where they conflicted with railroad titles. Later this intermittent ownership would make it extremely difficult for

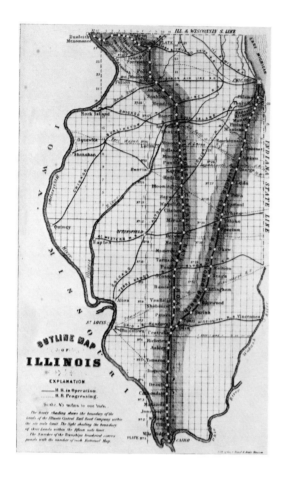

Lands and townships of the Illinois Central Railroad in Illinois, 1860.

any sort of regional planning without the assent of the railroad companies.

So great swaths of public land became the property of these private colonizing enterprises. One ran from Minnesota, through North Dakota, Montana, Washington, and down through Oregon; a second started one strand in Nebraska and another in Kansas and Colorado, then continued in a single fat band through Wyoming, Utah, and Nevada; a third traversed New Mexico and Arizona. All three met in California, which was provided for generously from north to south. Railroad companies determined the course and pattern of the colonization. They fixed the place of Western cities and mapped the limits of suburban sprawl. They were drawn to the coal in the Appalachians—the Pocahontas region of eastern Kentucky—the iron of the Mesabi range in Minnesota, and the phosphate rock of Florida. Their rails fitted a durable, shiny metal harness over the continent—dense in the industrial northeast, with long multiple-track sections from Cleveland to Philadelphia, from Washington to Albany, from Albany to Chicago; the two 2-track transcontinental lines of the Union Pacific and the Santa Fe; and the finely spun web of local lines fading out between the Mississippi and the Rockies.

Managing the Nation's Waters

It was when the West lay fully open in the closing decades of the last century that privatism showed its limitations. Transporting people out there was one thing; getting them to stay was another. The problem was water. In the enormous region between the Midwestern prairies and the coastal mountain ranges of the West the annual rainfall ranges from about five to eighteen inches. In the deserts west of the Rockies, there is hardly any rain at all. If we were to settle this region permanently, massive water management would be necessary.

A comprehensive program of irrigation held no appeal for private concerns, and in any case the scale of organization it required was far beyond their means. Federal involvement was mandatory. When a prolonged drought in the 1890s dried up local irrigation systems in Nebraska and Wyoming, the government was forced to act. In 1902 the Congress established the Bureau of Reclamation, as an agency of the Department of the Interior. Its charge was especially the arid Intermontane Region. The first reclamation dam was the Roosevelt Dam, built in the Salt River near Phoenix between 1906 and 1911. By 1950 the bureau had built 195 dams, 19,000 miles of canals and laterals, 47 power plants and 9,400 miles of transmission lines for the electicity they produced, 354 pumping plants to pump irrigation water to otherwise inaccessible areas, and some 200,000 irrigation structures of one sort or another. To date, the Bureau dams number 360, and the canals and laterals add up to 50,000 miles.

Water had always been our major resource. Quantities of water,

The High Bridge, built by John B. Jervis from 1839 to 1848, marked the completion of the Croton Aqueduct System. The bridge carried two iron pipes, thirty-six inches in diameter, and stretched 1,450 feet across the Harlem River. It still stands, the oldest extant bridge connecting the island of Manhattan to the mainland, although some of its piers have been removed to make room for shipping.

properly distributed, were needed in our cities and in the farm-land outside; early factories relied on water for their power; and river and canal traffic was critical to inland commerce. Municipal authorities had taken charge of their local water supply early in the nineteenth century. Philadelphia's waterworks, designed by Benjamin Latrobe, led the way. The system was planned in 1798 and built within the next two years. The Schuylkill River was dammed northwest of the city, at what is now Fairmount Park; the water was pumped by steam to an elevated reservoir and fed by gravity through wooden mains to hydrants throughout the city.

New York thirty years later was more ambitious. It decided to divert the water of the Croton River at some distance above its junction with the Hudson. This involved the building of a thirty-three mile aqueduct with long, difficult stretches of underground masonry conduits, bridges over twenty-five streams and many more brooks and reservoirs, and a 1,900-foot-long arched viaduct on Manhattan Island, beginning at the Harlem River and traveling

The Owens Valley-Los Angeles Aqueduct. Once the aqueduct passes the northern city limits it moves underground.

across the Manhattanville flatlands and down the West side near Tenth Avenue. It was the most impressive public works project of its day, and it was accomplished in the absence of advanced equipment and tools, through the manual labor of 3,000 men, most of them poor Irish immigrants.

Seventy years later, Los Angeles went 250 miles to the north, to the Owens River, for its water. That aqueduct entailed more than 40 miles of tunnel bored through solid rock. By this time American engineering was the most advanced in the world; the technology for such feats was at hand. This massive water diversion has not, of course, gone without controversy. Why should metropolitan areas with huge populations slake their thirst at the expense of small towns and farms? And going beyond local concerns, why should the needs of one region be allowed to diminish the quality of the environment for the rest of us? These conflicts of self-interest and environmental stability originate with the first federal agency to be charged broadly with the design of the land.

The Army Corps of Engineers was founded by Congress in 1795, more than one hundred years before the Bureau of Reclamation. The primary task of the Corps was to plan and build defensive works, especially seacoast fortifications. But by the 1820s, the army engineers were mapping territories, plotting canal routes, and designing bridges. Under French teachers, West Point became a topnotch school of engineering. Its graduates were constantly being lured away from the service by private companies, to supervise turnpike and railroad construction, systems of public utilities, and industrial plants.

In 1824, the Corps was given the task of making our rivers reliably navigable year-round. Initially this meant removing snags from the Ohio and Mississippi rivers, but these responsibilities were expanded over the years to include the regulation of tributaries, flood control, dredging, and the reinforcement of banks. An extensive program started with the Mississippi River in 1879, and then moved in the following decades to the Illinois, the Ohio, and the Missouri. Their more recent activity, since the Second World War, created the greatest system of inland waterways in

A concrete mat casting field in the Louisiana Delta. These mats are used to build revetments on the Mississippi's edges, particularly on the outside banks of bends in the river, where the water's attack is most destructive.

the world, involving rivers like the Allegheny, Cumberland, and Warrior, the Columbia and Arkansas, and brought about a renascence of water transportation that had been effectively killed off by the railroads a hundred years earlier.

It took decades to clear and canalize each river. Some are never finished. The Mississippi is the classic case. This restless river full of hidden, shifting snags, ever-widening meanders, a murky, unfathomable bottom, and treacherous eddies, was a test of a pilot's skills at the best of times. At its worst, the river would rage at everything in its way. Its floods would devastate huge areas of farmland and towns, disrupting commerce for weeks. Since the days of Mark Twain, the Corps built more than 2,000 miles of control structures along its course. The channel was dredged, cutoff channels were dug across meander loops to shorten the river's path, the inconstant banks were reinforced with mass-produced concrete mats, and a system of levees in the alluvial valley was enlarged and strengthened after the catastrophic floods of the Twenties, a project which must by now surely rank as the largest earth-moving project in human history. Today the Mississippi is a bustling waterway. In spite of competition from faster rail, truck, and air transportation, water shipment of bulk cargo—coal, ore, and grain—is still very economical.

But dams were the most prevalent architectural intervention. Navigation and flood-control dams regulated the rivers in times of drought and released water in a measured flow in times of plenty. To accommodate the whims of nature, many dams on a river and its tributaries would be coordinated by a system of locks to permit the water traffic to overcome the differences in water level at the dam sites.

The Corps originated two early types of dam and used them in the Ohio and Illinois rivers. The so-called "wicket" or "shutter dam," of which there are over forty in the original group of the Ohio, is simply a movable weir of steel-bound timber plates fixed to a concrete slab laid on the streambed. It is enough to impound a navigation pool, and in times of high water the hinged panels can be laid flat on the bed, so that the vessel can pass directly over the dam. The other type, the roller gate dam, is more sophisticated. A concrete wall is built across the stream, and on this

Wicket raising on the Ohio River in 1902. Today only two wicket dams remain on the Ohio River. The rest have been replaced by high-lift dams.

The Roller Gate on the dam at Gallipolis, on the Ohio River.

sit a series of concrete piers. Between each pair of piers is a hollow steel cylinder, or roller, which can be lowered to hold the water or raised to let the water through.

These are both low-head structures, suitable for broad, shallow streams that carry heavy loads of sediment. When it started, the

Bureau of Reclamation was not primarily interested in improving river navigation, for which the wicket and the roller were enough. Its assignment was threefold—flood control, irrigation, and the production of hydroelectric power. For these you had to build high-head storage dams that would hold water for irrigation and have the kind of pressure that would run electric generators.

The material was either earth or concrete. Earth dams have been around since ancient times. Their main advantage is that they can be constructed on poor rock and earth foundations; they can also use material excavated and compacted right on the site, or very close by. After 1870, instead of the traditional hand labor, the hydraulic-fill process used a stream of water to perform all major operations of building. Nowadays that process has been taken

Life *magazine's first cover showed Montana's Fort Peck Dam under construction, as photographed by Margaret Bourke-White. Employing 10,000 workers during the height of the Depression, this relief project was heralded as the largest earth dam ever built.*

Above, left. *Bartlett Dam on the Verde River, Arizona. This buttress dam is eight hundred feet long.*

Above. *Spillway of the Grand Coulee Dam as seen from the right power plant roof. This gravity dam on the Columbia River near Spokane, Washington, took from 1933 to 1943 to build.*

over by large earth-moving equipment developed primarily for the construction of highways. If you have to work with a broad valley or with excessive depth to bedrock, an earth dam is the answer. And these dams can never be wholly obsolete. The largest dam in the world, Fort Peck (Montana) on the Missouri River, is an earth dam, and so is one of the highest dams in the United States, Oroville on the Feather River of California.

Sometime before 1870 a kind of primitive concrete, a rubble-and-mortar mix, was invented starting a rapid shift in technology. By the 1880s concrete as we know it was in full use. Its application in dam construction was natural. For one thing, concrete dams are a good bit more watertight, and you can incorporate openings into their structure—for such things as outlet pipes—much more easily. But you need bedrock for the foundation level and very narrow canyons with good rock flanks. In terms of design, three basic types have been built by the Bureau. The "gravity dam" is simply a solid wall that relies on its own weight to resist water load—the Grand Coulee (1933–43) in the Columbia River near Spokane, Washington, is a famous example. Hoover in the Colorado River represents the "arch dam." Here the wall curves upstream and so transmits the major part of its water load to the canyon walls. Last is the "buttress dam"; it has a sloping upstream face, or deck, propped up by flat slabs between pairs of buttresses, or else the sloping face is made up of a series of arches, as you can see in the Bartlett Dam near Phoenix, Arizona (1936–39). The buttress dam is uneconomical because of the large amount of formwork and labor it requires, so it is not very common.

This is just the visible design of a dam. We do not see the maze within the concrete mass—the holes drilled into bedrock for the grout that strengthens the foundations; the cooling system of tubes that alleviates the tremendous heat generated by the hardening of thousands of tons of poured concrete; the web of galleries, shafts, and chambers for things like drainage and maintenance.

And we are not always alert to the complexity of dam components. In simple dams, whose sole purpose is to divert water for purposes of irrigation, there will be an overflow section, or weir, that serves to gauge the river flow and the excess water of floods; the sluiceway and sluice gates, to regulate the pool level above the dam and release the right amount of water into the canals; the headworks structure on one or both banks of the river that regulates this flow into the canal system, with trashracks to catch floating debris; wingwalls upstream and downstream, to connect parts of the diversion dam with the river banks and dykes.

In multipurpose dams, the composition is much more involved. There are the reservoirs upstream that store the water; the power plant downstream; the spillways that carry the water down to the plant, through open channels or through tunnels independent of the dam located in the abutments; and the desilting basins that clean the stream of its impurities.

To visit one of the great dam sites of the West today is to marvel, first, at the colossal scale of the architecture, the technical knowledge and precision, the superhuman effort. Only as this initial wonder subsides do we turn our thoughts to the far-reaching outcome of this vision. Miles and miles of canals, unseen from where we stand, carry the impounded water out to the fields, and partly buried aqueducts rush it to the kitchen and bathroom taps

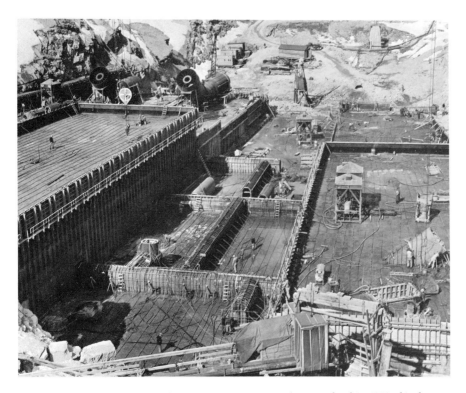

Hungry Horse Dam, Montana, under construction in 1950. When completed in 1953, this dam was one of the highest and largest in the United States. This photograph shows wooden forms set up in one of the dam's foundation blocks for the construction of galleries. Nearly one and one-half miles of tunnel-like galleries are buried within the three-million-cubic-yard structure. These galleries provide access to the foundation sections of the dam for inspection, grouting work, and for drainage.

of urban houses and businesses. Waterpower is converted into electricity by the humming generators in the power plant, and transmission lines carry this energy from the switchyards across the landscape to office towers and factories and hospitals and streets. Flash floods and deadly droughts are largely a thing of the past. We contemplate the many lives that are improved, the enhancement to the quality of life itself. And then they seem to us, these prodigies of water and wall, to be endowed, as it were, with the touch of Providence.

So indeed it seemed to the residents of a poor, depressed valley of the wandering Tennessee River, with its cotton fields and rows of tenant shacks on thin worn-out soil and its murky stream running red with the earth of the flatlands of Kentucky and western Tennessee. The river has five mountain tributaries as it moves through seven states, an area the size of England and Scotland combined. It is fed by the heaviest rainfall in the eastern United States, and in the days before the TVA, the Tennessee Valley Authority, this meant the punishing force of severe spring floods. The hilly terrain made farming difficult and was prone to soil erosion. Mountain barriers isolated the valley from the flow of commerce.

The federal government came in once, during the First World War. At Muscle Shoals, where the Tennessee drops swiftly through the slope of northern Alabama, they built the Wilson Dam to generate the cheap electricity that went into the production of synthetic nitrogen compounds used in munitions. But in the Twenties the nitrate plants stood idle, and the hydroelectric capacity of the Wilson Dam had been sold to a private company.

In May 1933, at the height of the Depression, President Roosevelt set his signature to a Bill of Congress that announced the creation of the TVA. This was a unique government agency that

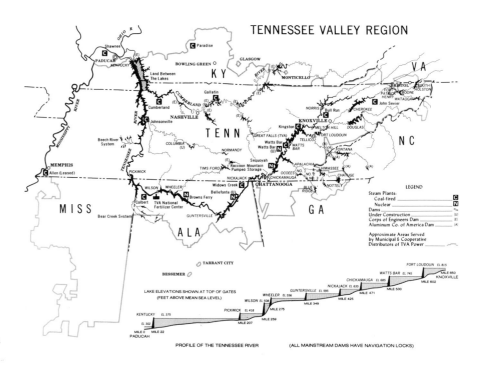

The Tennessee Valley Region.

Norris Dam and the surrounding area, the first TVA project. Facilities for visitors include an information center, a powerhouse reception room, and overlooks.

would be allowed to act much like a private corporation—without interference from federal bureaucracy and free also from local and state jurisdictions. It was our first experiment with comprehensive regional planning. This was not the usual dam by dam, levee by levee approach, but a blueprint for the development of a corner of America, the fifth largest river system in the country. And for a long while the experiment proved a resounding success.

There was some initial hardship of course. At least fifteen thousand families had to be moved so backwater areas could be flooded, and graveyards, schoolhouses, churches, even a few towns and villages had to be relocated. Moving at somebody else's behest is always traumatic. But the people did not go very far, and they could soon see changes that would benefit most of them. The people, the river, and the land, once bonded together in misery, now staged their own spectacular recovery.

In less than ten years, a whole system of dams was built, beginning with the Norris Dam on the Clinch River. The Tennessee turned deep blue. On its now regular course and that of its tributaries, a 640-mile-long navigable channel was created, on which

Drillers at the TVA's Fort Loudon Dam, August 1942.

freight could be carried nearly year-round. Hundreds of thousands of acres of land were cleared and turned into lakes. New highways and railroad lines were built, and old ones relocated. The tired soil was rebuilt with a mineral fertilizer which came from inert phosphate ore. The ore was melted in furnaces that were heated by the electricity the new dams made. Neatly undulating terraced hillsides produced rich harvests in the revitalized soil.

The TVA had its own staff of administrators. It marketed its own power. At the time of the Second World War this power contributed to the national defense by producing aluminum for military airplanes and, later on, by enriching uranium and assisting the atomic-energy program.

And the TVA—this "corporation clothed with the power of government but possessed of the flexibility and initiative of a private enterprise," as President Roosevelt had characterized it—is still in business today. It has withstood repeated attempts in Congress to dismantle it, yet Congress has also resisted all proposals to duplicate the model in other regions. In the Fifties the production of electric power became TVA's principal activity. As demands grew, it opted for coal-fired power and spurred a major upsurge in strip mining that had disastrous consequences for the land. In the last two decades the TVA has initiated a controversial program of nuclear-powered stream plants, thereby becoming embroiled in the most passionate debate of the Eighties. So what started more than fifty years ago as a concerted effort to revivify one of the nation's less fortunate regions—a symbolic olive branch to the South, some thought, for the deprivations visited upon it by the Civil War—has lived to demonstrate the cumulative benefits and far-reaching impact of comprehensive planning, as well as the corruptibility of entrenched institutions.

The glory of the TVA remains its first decade. That is the chapter writ large in the history of American architecture. The TVA had its own design and construction crews. From the very first buildings it put up, it created its own monumental style.

Prefabricated workers' housing at the Fontana Dam site, 1942.

There was much besides the dams of course. The town of Norris, built to provide workers' quarters, cast its modern house plans in the local vernacular; it is still largely intact, custom-tailored to its irregular site. For even more remote construction sites TVA-designed collapsible houses were trucked in, and the camps were enriched with community amenities like schools and recreational and medical facilities. You can find many of these prefabricated houses in the vacation resorts that have since replaced the camps.

But Americans, and the world, remember the dams. "Built for the People of the United States"—these are the words you find in each one of them, flanked by the dates when the dam was begun and completed. The first Chief Architect of the TVA was Roland Anthony Wank, an unsung master of manmade America. Wank was a Hungarian émigré who arrived in this country in 1924. He joined a firm that specialized in large railroad stations and cut his teeth with Cincinnati's Union Terminal. But Wank's dams for the TVA cannot be explained that simply. They created an American architecture as native and appropriately elegant as Sullivan's skyscrapers and the motorcar factories of Albert Kahn.

Roland Anthony Wank, 1898–1970. Wank was the TVA's first Chief Architect and served from 1933 to 1944.

Powerhouse and gantry crane at the Kentucky Dam. The Kentucky Dam, built from 1938 to 1944, is the largest of the TVA's main river dams.

Wonders of modern technology, the dams had a stripped down, archaic monumentality that recalled, as many observed, the pyramids and temple pylons of pharaonic Egypt. Rough formwork gave texture and substance to the concrete walls. Inside the powerhouses, in striking contrast, primary colors emphasized the eerie, humming world where water was turned into industry's version of gold in this modern epic of alchemy. The powerhouse at Pick-

Interior of the powerhouse at the Pickwick Landing Dam, built in the mid-1930s.

wick had generators of dark green and white metal, green tile wainscoting, and walls painted lemon yellow and light green. The dams were beautifully integrated with the reconstituted landscape of forests, rivers, and artificial lakes. This was engineering transcendent, anchored in the accommodating shapes of the land.

The Surpassing Bridges

The same partnership was being put to work during the Thirties on a generation of long-span suspension bridges for automobile traffic that were then, and still are, without peer.

The George Washington Bridge opened in 1931; it crossed the Hudson between Manhattan and the New Jersey Palisades at a point where it measures 3,500 feet from bank to bank. (The bridge was the first masterwork of the Swiss-born engineer Othmar Amman who would follow it with a glorious progeny over the next thirty-five years until the Verrazano-Narrows Bridge, which opened when he was in his Eighties.) In San Francisco, meanwhile, a bridge was heading across the 8-mile-wide Bay to Oakland. It had two end-to-end suspension spans, a tunnel through the rock of Yerba Buena Island, and a long cantilever bridge to the eastern shore. Its near-contemporary, the Golden Gate Bridge over the Bay's entrance, had a narrower leap—and an incomparable silhouette.

What followed is anticlimactic. The Tacoma Narrows Highway Bridge over Puget Sound, for example, was no contest. It connected the Olympic Peninsula with the mainland of Washington. A thin beautiful ribbon 2,800 feet long, it opened on the first of July 1940. Four months later, on November 7, "Galloping Gertie," as it was called because of its tendency to ripple, buckled violently for a few minutes—and plunged into the waters of the Sound. To counter the fears this spectacular disaster fueled, the bridge over the Straits of Mackinac between Lakes Huron and Michigan was grossly overbuilt. Big Mack they called it when it was completed in 1957. Finally, in 1965, the Verrazano-Narrows Bridge over New York Harbor captured the world's span-length

Below, left. *San Francisco-Oakland Bay Bridge, opened November 12, 1936. Originally, the lower deck had two sets of streetcar tracks and three truck lanes, while the upper deck's six lanes were for cars only.*

Below. *Golden Gate Bridge, San Francisco, California, opened in 1937.*

Union Pacific Railroad trestle bridge at Promontory, Utah, in a photograph of 1869 by A. J. Russell.

record by going the Golden Gate 60 feet better in width—but not necessarily in beauty. It culminated, for the present at least, the century-old saga of suspension bridges started at Niagara Falls and again at Brooklyn by John Augustus Roebling one hundred years earlier.

The chief feature of suspension bridges was of course their ability to cross water without resting on any supports that would impede the passage of vessels. The roadway was suspended from a giant bundle of twisted steel cables held aloft by two piers anchored in bedrock on the shore. But these bridges were notoriously unstable. The cables permitted much flexing, hence roadways were subject to vibration and sway from high winds. So suspension bridges did not become popular until the wide national acceptance of cars, which were not adversely affected by this erratic behavior.

The railroad companies, however, did not care for the suspension bridge. They wanted sturdy, steady bridges capable of carrying long lines of heavy freight cars. In the days of coaches, which weighed much less, you could get away with simple wooden bridges which spanned rivers where it was most convenient and least likely to impede water traffic. The railroad had an inflexible approach and needed a flat roadway; this limited placement possibilities. The wooden covered bridges of the turnpike era did not do the job, and even with the use of iron, which strengthened the trusses and roadways, the reinforced bridges kept collapsing.

Steel improved the situation. The first bridge to benefit was at St. Louis, a great upright triple arch of cast steel which crossed the Mississippi at Laclede's Landing. The Eads Bridge was conceived in 1867, when cheap methods of producing the new material were just being developed and it had not yet been tried in any large structure. There were two major obstacles for the bridge to overcome. Since the Mississippi teemed with water traffic, the bridge had to be built without timber falsework, which could obstruct the waterway. And it had to contend with a current that swept by at more than twelve feet per second at high water. The riverbed itself was notoriously inconstant; it shifted unpredictably and the bottom dropped several feet at a time. In winter ice floes raced down from the north and jammed the river, sometimes clogging it for as long as two or three months. Could the Mississippi be bridged at St. Louis?

Eads Bridge, St. Louis, completed July 1874.

James B. Eads, 1820–1887.

It was—because of the genius and tenacity of one man, Captain James Buchanan Eads. It is an unforgettable story.

Eads knew the Mississippi as a trapper knows his forest. Born in Indiana, he arrived with his family in St. Louis in 1833 at the age of thirteen, and five years later landed a berth on the *Knickerbocker* as a "mud clerk," or purser. A few months later the steamboat hit a snag and sank. It joined hundreds of other wrecks in the river bottom, the victims of such collisions and of fires and violent explosions to which these lightly built timber vessels with their high-pressure, wood-burning boilers were very susceptible.

Eads decided there was a living to be made salvaging the cargo of sunken steamboats and designed a boat equipped with derricks and pumps to do the job. This was a modified version of the common snagboat rigged with hoists and tackles, used for years to keep the channel clean. Eads called his boat the *Submarine*. He was then twenty-two. For the next eighteen years, until his retirement in 1860, Eads descended to the river bottom in his diving bell many hundreds of times, suspended upside down and supplied with air from pumps on deck, so he could examine a wreck, hook a line to some bit of its cargo—a whisky barrel or a pig of iron—and have his crew haul it up to the *Submarine* or one of its several successors. During the Civil War, Eads designed and built warships for the Union, the first ironclad gunboats in the history of the continent. Then in 1866 came his chance for immortality.

The first bridge over the Mississippi was the one at Rock Island, Illinois, built to carry the Rock Island Railroad to Iowa. It was a timber-truss bridge on stone piers, and the steamboat companies fought it all the way to the Supreme Court as an impediment to navigation. They lost. Meanwhile, the Illinois Railroad had reached East St. Louis, and the city saw its moment to strike in its bitter rivalry with Chicago. A bridge thrown across the river at St. Louis would make it possible to join the Union Pacific, which had started building furiously westward from Nebraska in 1865 on its way to meet the tracks of the Central Pacific pushing east from California.

A bridge company was formed and got the go-ahead from the legislatures of Illinois and Missouri. At the bridge site the river was fifteen hundred feet wide. The law required a main span of 500 feet, or two spans of 350 feet each. The company picked Eads, and Eads picked steel. While he pressured the manufacturing plants in Pittsburgh and Philadelphia to produce high-performance steel in quantity, he started work on the west abutment, in the heart of the busy waterfront. He cleared the under-river wreckage with a pile driver fitted with a huge steel-tipped chisel and built the abutment of solid masonry which rested on bedrock. This meant going about 50 feet down. But the feat seemed matter-of-fact compared to the east abutment on the Illinois shore where bedrock was at least 100 feet below mean high water. How could he get people working at that depth?

Eads found his answer on a trip to France. British and French engineers had pioneered a device called the "pneumatic caisson" to use in the construction of harbor works and bridges based in deep waters. Unlike the traditional open cofferdam, which Eads had used in sinking the west abutment, this was a sealed cham-

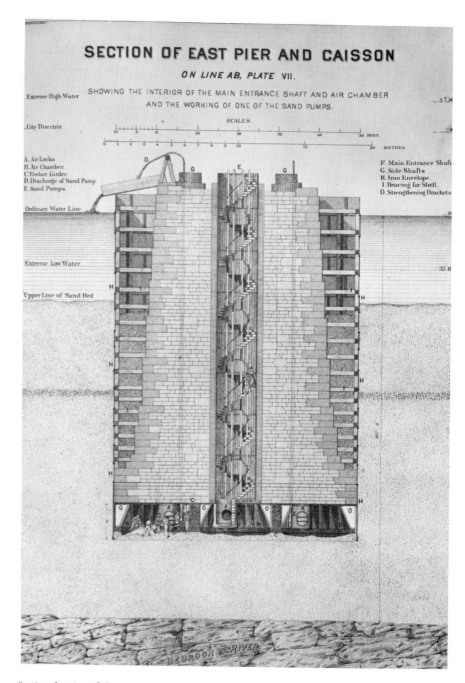

Section drawing of the east pier and caisson as designed by James Eads for the construction of the St. Louis Bridge. This drawing shows the interior of the main entrance shaft and air chamber and the working of one of the sand pumps.

Construction of the west and center arches of the Eads Bridge, St. Louis.

ber, filled with compressed air and equipped with an airlock. It had a floorless working chamber at the bottom. The workers went down a spiral stairway, entered the airlock and shut the door, then opened a valve to raise the pressure in the lock so that it equaled that of the working chamber below. Now they could enter the chamber, and at the end of their shift they would reverse the procedure to get back out.

Eads built two watertight wood caissons sheathed in iron. Each terminated in a floorless working chamber under an airtight bulkhead. Compressed air forced into the chamber kept the water out. Here the workmen shoveled the sand into pumps, which pushed it upward and out into the river. Meantime, masons laid the masonry foundation on top of the bulkhead that served as the roof of the working chamber. They laid it as a hollow shell, to be filled later with concrete. With the weight of the rising masonry, and the clearing of the sand below, the caisson would slowly sink—until it reached the river bottom. Eads used this installation first for the two mid-channel piers of his bridge, where the depth was moderate, in order to gain experience.

But as the chamber pushed its way down, his workers began to complain of symptoms of caisson disease familiar to European crews—stomach cramps and temporary paralysis. Then one day, when the air pressure reached forty-four pounds, a worker named James Riley came out of his caisson after a two-hour shift, keeled over, and died. Five more workers died in the next few days. A horrified Eads, and his personal physician, cut the working day into short watches with long rest periods in between, regulating the workers' sleep and diet.

It was the physician who, after suffering a terrible seizure himself from a visit to the caisson, hit upon the remedy—slow decompression—a remedy, incidentally, that had already been determined in Europe a few years earlier, and it is not clear why Eads, who was in touch with his peers across the ocean, was not properly informed. At any rate, the two piers could now be finished, but not before thirteen men had died and two had been crippled for life. By contrast, the most difficult of the four foundations, that for the east abutment, would be completed with only one fatality, even though Eads had to go more than 120 feet below mean high water to reach bedrock. To this day, it remains the deepest level at which compressed-air workers ever had to work.

Now came the arches—and more problems. There was no question of putting up centering—the timber falsework that would have helped in the building of the arches—since this would have interrupted river traffic for a long period of time, which was intolerable. So Eads built steel falsework *above* the abutments and piers as the arches were being raised from their two ends; he continued to extend these cantilever cables to meet the thrust of the slowly swelling arches. Once the arch halves were complete, Eads devised a screw that would join the final two steel tubes of each arch rib. Then he went to Europe without waiting for the arches to close. He was certain they would—and they did. "The laws which guide an engineer are immutable, and never deceive," Eads wrote. "Failures and disasters . . . result almost invariably from

Dedication of the Brooklyn Bridge, May 24, 1883.

the non-observance of these laws, or from a want of knowledge of them."

The magnificent triple arch was inaugurated with great fanfare on Independence Day in 1874. President Grant was in the reviewing stand. Eads's creation supported itself, a double railroad track, four lanes of roadway, and sidewalks. Nine years later, in May 1883, the single suspension span of Brooklyn Bridge between Manhattan Island and Brooklyn across the East River was opened to traffic. "With the completion of this bridge," an observer wrote that year, "the continent is entirely spanned, and one may visit, dry and shod and without the use of ferry boats, every city from the Atlantic to the Golden Gate." These two storied bridges of rival structural systems were paeans to modern technology, "a leap into a new consciousness," to use Hart Crane's expression in his commemorative poem on Brooklyn Bridge.

By the turn of the century, reinforced concrete had come into

The Russian River Gulch Bridge, Mendocino, California. This reinforced concrete bridge was constructed in 1940.

use. And by 1930 the sensational generation of long-span automobile bridges had gotten under way with the George Washington Bridge that in one fearless stroke doubled the previous record for span length of suspension bridges—and indeed the record for bridges of any kind. The practice was now to prolong the actual roadway by means of approach viaducts. Some new bridges combined suspension spans with conventional arched bridges; some used tunnels making it easier to cross navigation channels. In one celebrated contemporary instance—the Chesapeake Bay Bridge-Tunnel which opened in 1964—the system includes four artificial islands, two tunnels, two truss bridges over the waterways, and more than twelve miles of low-level trestled roadways over the shallower portions. It moves traffic across the mouth of the Bay

Chesapeake Bay Bridge and Tunnel.

where it meets the Atlantic Ocean, between Norfolk and the Delmarva Peninsula. This extraordinary hybrid structure crosses twenty-three miles of water in all.

Roads and Settlements

The lithe, generous sweep of the Chesapeake Bay Bridge-Tunnel hooks up smoothly at either end to join a flowing system of highways, of which it is a complement. Flow is the right word to use for our transportation conduits today. Since the arrival of the automobile, unencumbered movement across land and water has been our earthly charter. We have set about to countermand the stiff, unwieldly course of railroad lines; and slowly, ever slowly we have

Interstate 80 near Vallejo, California.

softened the once uncompromising routines of the National Survey. The roads we built for our new personal conveyances streamed across the landscape. They branched and proliferated, inscribed breathless curves, coiled around mountain slopes, and intricately intertwined. They gave us the exhilarating sense of floating freely over the shapes of the continent.

But this freedom came at a cost. The continuous ribbons of pavement, tens of thousands of miles from coast to coast, have completely made over the surface of the continent. There were more and more cars as the years went by, and they wanted to go faster and faster. To move huge volumes of traffic at high speed you must have lots of room to maneuver, and we took it as we needed it, without remorse. A simple cloverleaf interchange alone, it is reckoned, uses up about forty acres of land.

We have not always made aesthetic amends for the denuding we brought about, and for the ecological loss there is of course no possible redress. On the other hand, highway design at its best is much more sophisticated now, more sensitive to the prospects it traverses, than in the boom years of highway construction that preceded and followed the inauguration of the Interstate System. A good deal of emphasis is now placed on the continuity of alignment—those connections between straight or tangent stretches and simple curves that make for fluent highway lines. The deadly impact of the colossal roadbed, 120 feet of paved surface and the tributary strips of shoulder and embankment, is mitigated by resorting more and more to divided highways with landscaped median strips of varying width. And the harsh, businesslike way of cutting through the terrain, as if it had no valid mold of its own to take into account, is rarer now than it used to be. In the end, we have to bring about that difficult match between two sovereign systems of design: the highborn landscape forms of river and plain and mountain, and that implanted frame of tremendous strength and scale, with its on-ramps, interchanges, railings, and troughs on massive piers.

There is also the pattern of our settlements to consider. Here the challenge is of a different order. The landscape forms retain their sovereignty of course, but what we work into them now—in contrast to dams, long-span bridges, and highways—are tiny built objects, our houses, which can hold their own only if they are grouped with forethought and purpose. The urban mass, with its crowded central business district and closely spaced streets round about, has no problem setting up a focused presence. The skyline will be ragged or memorable, the dense residential core will be of varying effectiveness, but the city is there. We know it when we

A suburban development in Rodeo, California.

drive toward it or alongside it on the freeways, and at night, from the air, a tracery of lights picks out its character and announces its status.

Yet whatever there is of visual benefit to that compactness of buildings will dissipate at the edges, as the suburbs and the fringe beyond ooze out into the empty countryside at will, seemingly without rhyme or reason. It is at best a piecemeal accretion of subdivisions, this "slurbia" as it is sometimes called, and its course is determined at the whim of the real estate developer. Since nowadays it is the developer who builds the streets and provides the services, not the municipality, subdivisions tend to be small, scattered, and randomly shaped. They create a spotty carpet of even-grained parcels around an irregular rural road net.

The street scheme of these developed parcels was almost always a rectilinear grid until about 1950. Since then the housing market has favored curvilinear adaptations of the speculative grid, with roads for fast traffic distinguished from streets of local traffic and with loops and cul-de-sacs designed for the exclusive use of abutters. Detailed subdivision regulations now prescribe uniform set-back lines, uniform sideyards, rear yards, and lot sizes. But all of this is decided on the basis of the individual lot rather than the subdivision as a whole—and may well be one of the reasons for the numbing monotony of so many suburban layouts.

Yet the land is being gobbled up. With every subdivision, the space between cities is being filled in; the edges of one city reach out across what was once intervening countryside and touch the edges of another. So we get what are called urban regions or regional cities (the English call them "conurbations"), each megalopolis made up of several constellations. The Atlantic Urban Region of the Eastern Seaboard, for example, takes in New York, Boston, and Washington, and lesser towns like Hartford and New Haven in Connecticut. The Great Lakes Urban Region is spearheaded by Chicago, and the Pacific Urban Region stretches from the San Francisco Bay Area to the greater Los Angeles area. These huge concentrations of urbanites, and two or three others like coastal Florida, the Gulf Coast, and the Piedmont Urban Region from Atlanta and Athens to Raleigh, North Carolina, leave much of the country lightly populated in comparison. Gertrude Stein said it in her own way years ago, and it is still true that "in the United States there is more space where nobody is than where anybody is. That is what makes America what it is."

Design for Air Travel

To avoid the surface congestion of the urban regions and to move faster about the country, we have taken to the air. In the open skies, we have carved out our latest road system, invisible but real—two sets of overlapping airways, one for slow propeller-driven aircraft and the other for the speedy, high-flying jets. This time the federal government, which had stood back in the past and watched the private sector develop our major transportation systems—turnpikes, canals, railroads—kept a close eye on what was going on. As well it should. We are in danger once again, as we were with our highways, of overcrowding and making ineffective what we created to give ourselves freedom of motion. In 1980, commercial airlines carried 300 million passengers for about 200 billion passenger miles—six times as many miles as were logged by the railroads and busses combined.

The airways' imprint on the land is most apparent at our airports. There are 15,000 or so of them, most privately owned, but also about a hundred major hubs for scheduled airline service. The design of the airports is advanced, recurrent. There is the terminal area, surrounded by the ramps where aircrafts are parked for boarding; the taxiways, which provide access from here to the runways; the holding aprons or run-up pads where the planes wait

O'Hare Airport, Chicago. O'Hare is the world's busiest airport.

Terminal building at Dulles International Airport, Chantilly, Virginia, just outside of Washington, D.C., by Eero Saarinen & Associates, 1958–62.

for clearance; the control tower manned by a small army of controllers managing the growing traffic with the aid of radar and computers; and the runways themselves, oriented mainly toward the directions of the prevailing winds. These runways consist of one or a parallel set of reinforced concrete strips two miles or so in length; intersecting runways in other directions take care of the unusual wind conditions. The numbers at the ends of the runways, visible from the air, are derived from the compass direction of the particular runway. If the direction is 193 degrees, say, the runway number will be 19; if the direction is 261 degrees, the number will read 26.

With their approach roads, parking areas, large hangars for the storage and repair of aircraft, and hotels, our metropolitan airports are extensive but not very engaging landscapes. Their best aspect is the architectural accent of their terminals, at least the ones built back when air travel was relatively new and the thrill

Baling hay in Cache Valley, California.

was not gone. Then, structures like the Dulles Airport Building and the Trans World Airlines Terminal Building in New York's Kennedy Airport were out to convey the joy of flight—to turn the experience of flight into architecture. The architect of both of these was Eero Saarinen, who admitted as much when he said that he tried, in the design of the TWA building, "to express the drama and specialness and excitement of travel," and indeed the terminal is not a static, enclosed space, but a place of movement and transition. Four interacting vaults of slightly different shape spring from Y-shaped supports, and from certain angles the whole building seems poised to take off.

Furrows, Scars, and Pipelines

In the frame of our national history, this soaring is a recent adventure. Commercial air transport began in 1918 with the first carriage of mail from Washington, D.C., to New York City, and the first attempt at regular passenger service was made in Florida four years earlier, when the Tampa-St. Petersburg Airboat Line flew people across Tampa Bay in a Benoist flying boat.

Burrowing we have done much longer: it is as old as civilization, and we are at it still. For a long time, in farming and mining, we made do with hand tools and hand labor. Farm tools used in the Colonial period were the same as those in use for 2,000 years. Then in the half-century following the American Revolution came the scythe and the cradle attached to its blade, the steel

Plowing in Cache Valley, California.

plow, the cotton gin, and the mechanical reaper. But not until the shortage of farm labor caused by the Civil War was hand power broadly converted to horse power. With it started large-scale farming, which in turn brought a drastic change in the design of the land. When Oliver Dalrymple took over the management of undeveloped railroad lands in the Red River Valley in 1875, and added steam tractors to the machinery hauled by horses and mules, his wheat furrows ran straight for several miles. It was a premonition of things to come. Another labor shortage after the Second World War, and animal power would give way completely to electricity. The farm would turn into a factory in the fields.

Today not much is left to nature. Both soil and crops are manufactured. And the new rural landscape has no resemblance to that traditional scene of farmsteads with their barns and fenced fields, orchards and feedlots, one-room schools and small country towns. A mere ten million or so Americans now live on farms, compared to more than thirty million in the early part of the century. In 1850 farmers accounted for sixty-four percent of the nation's labor force; today, for just over three percent. Our own suitcase farmers live in the city and farm by machine. The occupied farming units are farther and farther apart. This dispersal, and the declining population in general, enfeebles country society and kills country towns by the hundreds. Churches, schools, banks, newspapers close, and leave their ruins on the land.

There are fewer, larger farms now. The barn is a totally mechanized, artificial environment which processes its contents. The farmstead is made of cement block, galvanized steel, aluminum, plastic. Bulldozers and other earth-moving equipment rearrange the soil, leveling and regulating it so tractors can move more easily. There are new kinds of rows, new patterns of irrigation.

We have come a long way from that first instance of modern irrigation farming 140 years ago, when the Mormons in Utah diverted the water of City Creek to their fields. For decades thereafter this gravity-fed system was what we worked with. We dammed streams and carried the stored water in open ditches to the level land, and through feeder ditches at the heads of furrows we got it to the crops. This system lives on, though the feeder ditches have now been replaced by sectioned pipe with multiple valves (called

*Center-Pivot Irrigator in Nebraska.
This type of irrigation apparatus was
first patented in 1952.*

"gated pipe"). But most everywhere farmers first switched to
movable systems with sprinkler nozzles, which are good mostly
for pasture and the hay crop since the pipe can damage taller
crops, and later to the trickle system, which uses plastic tubing
with small emitters. Three decades ago the newest gadget, introduced by a wheat farmer in Colorado, gained acceptance—the
center-pivot sprinkler. And that is the one that has inscribed the
most arresting irrigation patterns on the land.

Green circles, etched between the High Plains and the Sierra
Nevada, and especially from Texas to North Dakota, are there in
great clusters—lush circular fields of about 130 acres each, stamped
on the parched summer land. The idea is simple. Lift the tubing
of the sprinkler system above ground, so it can clear even the
tallest crops, and hook it up with underground wells or some
central source of irrigation water. What is actually involved are
one-quarter mile long sections of steel pipe about ten feet above
ground, supported and moved around a pivot point by seven to
eleven wheeled towers. The propelling was done by water turbines
once; now electric motors are commonly used, and more recently
hydraulic systems that work with oil. You can vary the speed and
have the moving end revolve around the circumference, which

Nebraska cornfields irrigated with center-pivot sprinklers. Most of the systems are designed to fit the conventional quarter section, or one hundred sixty acres. Until recently, the circular pattern skipped almost thirty of these acres at the corners, and the corner land was commonly used for dry-land crops, pasture, farmsteads, or grain storage.

measures about a mile or a mile and a half, in anything from twenty to two hundred hours.

The traces of mining are not so pretty. Nowadays we have been primarily absorbed by our search for coal, and if the mines are underground, as most of them were until the Second World War, the surface scars are not extreme. The typical underground coal mine is laid out as a grid, with empty spaces from which coal has been removed and large blocks of coal left standing to support the roof. Toward the end of the operation, you mine the blocks themselves, starting with the ones farthest in and letting the roof collapse as you work your way backward to the mine entrance. This is called "room-and-pillar mining." There is a recent underground alternative—longwall mining—where you extract a continuous block of coal, as much as one mile long, with a machine that planes or shears coal from the face of the block. The roofing is done using a system of movable supports which advances with the machine.

All the work goes on below the surface. But what we see is still bad enough—a desolate landscape of shafts and mine dumps, tailing ponds and railroad tracks. When the ore lies close enough to the surface to be mined from above ground, the picture changes. You dig an open pit, and work around it in ever-widening circles with a machine that chews at the walls in a series of concentric terraces. In Hibbing, Minnesota, at the heart of the Mesabi Iron Range, an open-pit mine occupies almost 13,000 acres; it is the largest of its kind in the world. As it grew the town of Hibbing had to be moved a mile further south from its original site. And then there are the giant pits of copper mines, like the one near Bingham, Utah, of the Kennecott Copper Corporation. Step by step, over the span of forty-five years, an entire mountain was removed and an amphitheater more than two miles in diameter was created in its place. Sometimes, as in the Esperanza Mine near Tucson, of the Duval Corporation, you don't dig a pit, but rather start at the summit of a copper-rich mountain and cut your way down in concentric terraces. In either case, and whatever the irreparable damage to the earth's crust, an enigmatic design appears

Kennecott Copper Mine, Bingham, Utah. Copper is the leading mineral produced by the state.

343

over time in the wilds of the West, in Utah or Nevada or Arizona, which rivals the design of the land, and like it, has no purpose to serve in the end beyond the act of its making.

But the harshest desecration is committed by strip mining. It is a relatively recent technique; it became feasible only after the invention of the large power shovel. Since the Second World War its use has become pervasive, primarily for coal, and now dominates the critical coal area of the Appalachian Plateau, from Ohio to Alabama. It's a crude method. You simply remove the overburden of rock and soil, as much as two hundred feet of it, from an underlying coal seam with draglines and excavators whose buckets can hold up to 180 cubic yards of earth material; you scoop up the exposed coal with enormous shovels and load it into trucks that can haul away 170 tons at one time. Or you mix the coal with water and send it via slurry pipeline; or put it on a special conveyor, like the prodigious ten-mile stretch that moves coal from the Black Mesa mines to a railroad ending in Page, Arizona.

The scars are hideous—spoil heaps of earth and rock that follow the contours of the coal seams in ragged, recursive lines. Little grows on the acid, mined surface, and nothing on the windrows of overburden which erode with rain and are scored with the effects of gullying and sheetwash. Stagnant water collects in the exposed ditches. It is a scene of devastation—of death. Today the law no longer permits it. Now you have to restore the land after your scrappers and power shovels and draglines have done their worst. You fill in the ditches, recontour the land, return the topsoil, and replant it. It makes a difference. It covers the traces of human exploitation and gives the rent land a chance to reconstitute itself. For most of us today, and our agencies of government, the well-being of the planet that sustains us is no longer a matter of insouciance.

Indeed, our celebration of progress has been tempered lately with concern for its consequences. The once heroic monuments of our enterprise as a nation, our brave, unapologetic landscape of industry and the power it consumes, now are not above contention; to some at least they seem unequivocally benighted. Nuclear plants, imposing structures to look upon with their container domes and cooling towers, inspire respect and fear in equal measure. The

Watts Bar Nuclear Plant, Tennessee. The plant's two nuclear reactors and their containment buildings are visible to the right of the cooling towers.

spectacle of illuminated oil rigs along the Gulf Coast is coupled in the mind with its familiar, tragic counterpart—beaches after the visitation of an oil spill.

Once the nation could rejoice carefree at the opening of the Erie or Panama Canal, the completion of Eads Bridge or Brooklyn Bridge, the spanning of America with the great transcontinental lines of the Union Pacific and the Santa Fe. Against the thrill of these national adventures, we recall the story of the Alaska pipeline. In the abstract, that is our own contemporary wonder, as astounding a technological feat as any our history has witnessed. For 800 miles across the bleak tundra at the edge of the Arctic Circle, from the rich oil fields of Prudhoe Bay to the port of Valdez, the pipeline zigzags its way. It passes through three mountain ranges and under some 350 rivers and streams, hoisted bravely above ground for more than half of its course to guard against melting the permafrost. And it was built in frantic haste. At peak times, a work force of as many as 20,000 put in 12-hour days seven days a week, often working in subzero cold. They built bridges, drill pads, and air strips; and workers' camps sealed tight from the elements. Atop the permafrost, north of the Yukon River,

The Alaska Pipeline. In addition to allowing wildlife to pass underneath, the heat-exchanging fins which support the pipeline help keep the permafrost around the supports frozen.

they laid an all-weather gravel road 360 miles long in just five months, to help them haul the 80-foot sections of steel pipeline. It was a lightning conquest of America's last frontier.

But there was little public jubilation. This was so, in part, because we have become inured to our technological prowess. Nothing much surprises us since the walk on the moon. We are also more circumspect now about the wisdom of open-ended growth. Most of all, we worry about the effect of our undertakings on the design of nature. The trans-Alaska pipeline would bring prosperity to many and cheaper oil to many more. But in the public debate these gains were pitted against the fate of the peregrine falcon and the salmon of the Delta River, and the engineers took the extra trouble to raise portions of the pipelines in deference to the migrating habits of the caribou.

The Polite Wilderness

"The most distinctive, and perhaps the most impressive, characteristic of American scenery is its wilderness," wrote the painter

Thomas Cole in 1836. It was a time, a hundred and fifty years ago, when we first began to question our harsh dominion of the continent. For two centuries we had hacked our way through forests, disciplined rivers, and put them to work. We had battled the wild prospects in order to settle them. Out there was danger of beast and savage, a barrier to progress and prosperity, an unreclaimed waste where evil lurked. Wilderness was the foe of godliness: we were sure of that.

Then, as we advanced ever more cockily westward in the name of our God, our race, and our ambition, a handful of city-bred intellectuals thought to ask whether we had not been fighting the wrong adversary. There was something sublime in the architecture of the Adirondacks, in the uncharted reaches of Maine and Minnesota. There was, in fact, something of God in undisturbed nature. "The groves were God's first temples," as William Cullen Bryant put it in "A Forest Hymn." And to the extent that the American landscape was unparalleled anywhere in the Old World, it was also an aspect of our national identity, our American-ness. Literary figures now set their pen to praising the wilderness; painters like Cole, Asher B. Durand, Thomas Moran, and Albert Bierstadt sought remote, romantic landscapes to celebrate. They called their paintings "Twilight in the Wilderness" and "View Near Ticonderoga" and explored the Grand Canyon, Yosemite, and Wyoming's Teton Range.

This celebration of the wilderness fueled thoughts of conserving it. And the conservator could be no other than the federal government, since the public land had been entrusted to its custody. So it was an act of novel import when in 1864 a federal grant of land was made, not for the customary purpose of settlement or the advance of railroads, but "for public use, resort and recreation." This was Yosemite Valley, about ten square miles of wilderness which was being turned over to the State of California for the enjoyment of its people. Several years later, on March 1, 1872, President Grant signed a bill which specified that two million acres in northwestern Wyoming were to be "reserved and withdrawn from settlement, occupancy, or sale . . . and set apart as a public park or pleasuring ground," and the Secretary of the Interior was instructed to "provide for the preservation . . . of all timber, mineral deposits, natural curiosities or wonders within said park . . . in their natural condition." So started Yellowstone National Park, the world's first example of protecting a bit of nature from human designs.

But before long things went awry. The visitors were followed by businesses catering to their needs, and Yosemite and Yellowstone began to lose their wild character. We were caught on the horns of a dilemma. To conserve the wilderness you had to regulate its use. You had to control the flow of people and their behavior. And the more you did of this the more you compromised the basic democratic premise of these retreats—that they were, unlike the European precedent of royal hunting preserves and the gardens of noble families, places of unrestricted access. How can you leave nature untouched when thousands descend upon it every month? It is a dilemma we have not yet resolved.

This problem is linked to another controversial question. What happens when we are presented with some legitimate demand to exploit the resources resident in a national park? When in 1883 a railroad company petitioned for a right-of-way through Yellow-

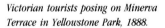
Victorian tourists posing on Minerva Terrace in Yellowstone Park, 1888.

Yosemite Valley in an Ansel Adams photograph.

stone Park to help some nearby mines find access to markets, the company argued before Congress that "the rights and privileges of citizenship, the vast accumulation of property, and the demands of commerce" could not yield to "a few sportsmen bent only on the protection of a few buffalo." But for once this standard defense for progress was turned down. "Never before," writes our finest student of natural conservation, Roderick Nash, "had wilderness values withstood such a direct confrontation with civilization."

Yet a similar request a little later was decided in favor of civ-

Theodore Roosevelt and John Muir on Glacier Point, Yosemite, 1906.

ilization. At issue was the Hetch Hetchy Valley in Yosemite on the Tuolumne River. San Francisco wanted to have access to it for city water and hydroelectric power. There was a great national debate, with eloquent conservationists on either side. Gifford Pinchot made the case for the city. John Muir strenuously objected to any interference with the native condition of park lands. The final arbiter had to be the president—Teddy Roosevelt. Reluctantly he sided with Pinchot and against his friend Muir. He wrote Muir that, though he would do all he could to protect the national parks, they could not be allowed to "interfere with the permanent material development of the State."

President Roosevelt's is a fitting name to evoke in concluding a review of our designs on the land we made our own. It was he who justified the taking of this land from its prior inhabitants, reaffirming the traditional Western view that those who do not materially "improve" what they occupy have no lasting claim to it. But this was the same man who grew to regret the disappearance of frontier virtues, the exhaustion of open land, the transfor-

Mesa Verde, American Indian Cliff Dwellings preserved under the Preservation of Antiquities Act of 1906.

mation of the modern American into an "overcivilized man." He urged communion with the wilderness. When he signed the Act for the Preservation of Antiquities in 1906, which put an end to the gross vandalism of Indian remains like the cliff dwellings and pueblos of the Southwest, he attested, as it were, to a kind of atonement for the impetuousness of our past.

Once, we saw only an empty, unaccommodating waste where

a gentle pattern had been lodged before us, and we harshly civilized what we could not comprehend. And often thereafter, in the course of our long tenancy, we shaped the land unfeelingly, out of need or rapacity, oblivious to the toll we exacted and the patches of ugliness we left behind. We were impatient. We had a continent to settle and values to anchor there—values of home and work and prideful nationhood. But, as often, we did things right.

The business of designing our environment is of course never finished. Every generation must remake in its turn the arrangements of its time. Wisdom resides in making sure that our handiwork respects what it inherited, that it matches verve with decency, and that it fortifies the best impulses in the long pageant of creating America by design.

A Selection
of Readings

The bibliography for this book cannot pretend to be comprehensive: my subject is too far-ranging, and many of the topics commented upon have their own extensive literature. The purpose of the following is to cite source material that is especially pertinent to the text, and on which I lean most heavily. I also include some references that would take the reader further along the lines of my discourse, or else provide a divergent perspective. The selection throughout is, therefore, minimal and, of course, rather arbitrary. The organization is thematic, and the order follows that of the book.

The American House

There are several recent general histories, among them D. F. Handlin, *The American Home, Architecture and Society, 1815–1915* (Boston: Little, Brown, 1979); G. Wright, *Building the Dream, A Social History of Housing in America* (New York: Pantheon, 1981); and C. E. Clark, Jr., *The American Family Home, 1800–1960* (Chapel Hill: University of North Carolina Press, 1986), which appeared after we had gone into production. All three have full bibliographies. V. Scully's distinctive view is best sampled in his essay "American Houses: Thomas Jefferson to Frank Lloyd Wright," in E. Kaufmann, ed., *The Rise of American Architecture* (London: Pall Mall, 1970). J. B. Jackson has written a number of beautiful essays on Americans and their houses over the years, among them "The Westward-Moving House" (E. H. Zube, ed., *Landscapes*, Amherst: University of Massachusetts Press, 1970, pp. 10–42); "The Domestication of the Garage" (*The Necessity for Ruins*, Amherst: University of Massachusetts Press, 1980, pp. 103–11); and "The Movable Dwelling and How It Came to America" (*Discovering the Vernacular Landscape*, New Haven: Yale University Press, 1984, pp. 89–101).

For more contemporary issues, some titles worth reading are T. Kidder, *House* (Boston: Houghton Mifflin, 1985); P. Langdon, "The American House," *The Atlantic*, September 1984, pp. 45–73; C. Moore, D. Lyndon, and G. Allen, *The Place of Houses* (New York: Holt, Rinehart and Winston, 1974); D. Hayden, *Redesigning the American Dream* (New York: Norton, 1984), a trenchant critique of our traditional attitudes toward the house; and W. F. Wagner, Jr., *A Treasury of Contemporary Houses* (New York: McGraw-Hill, 1978), an anthology of architects' designs.

On the Hearst mansion, see K. Murray, *The Golden Days of San Simeon* (Garden City, N.Y.: Doubleday, 1971); P. Failing, "William Randolph Hearst's Enchanted Hill," *Art News* 78, No. 1, January 1979, pp. 53–59; and T. R. Aidala and C. Bruce, *Hearst Castle, San Simeon* (New York: Harrison House, 1981). For Hearst's architect, the best place to begin is R. Longstreth, "Julia Morgan: Some Introductory Notes," published originally in *Perspecta* 15, 1975, pp. 74–86, and reprinted as *Julia Morgan, Architect* by the Berkeley Architectural Heritage Association in 1977.

For the Williamsburg houses, the standard work is M. Whiffen, *The Eighteenth-Century Houses of Williamsburg* (Williamsburg, Va.: 1960). More recently, E. Chappell, "Williamsburg Architecture as Social Space," *Fresh Advices*, November 1981. A broader survey is D. Upton's "Vernacular Domestic Architecture in Eighteenth-Century Virginia," *Winterthur Portfolio* 17, No. 2/3, 1982, pp. 95–119.

Apposite references for Thomas Jefferson include F. D. Nichols and J. A. Bear, Jr., *Monticello, A Guidebook*, 2nd ed. (Monticello: Thomas Jefferson Memorial Foundation, 1982), with an excellent bibliography. See also W. H. Pierson, Jr., *American Buildings and Their Architects*, Vol. 1 (New York: Oxford University Press, 1986), Chapter VIII.

On rowhouses, see N. W. Shivers, *The Old Placid Rows: The Esthetic Development of the Baltimore Rowhouse* (Baltimore: Maclay & Associates, 1981); K. Ames, "Robert Mills and the Philadelphia Rowhouse," *Journal of the Society of Architectural Historians* 27, No. 2, 1968, pp. 140–46; W. J. Murtaugh, "The Philadelphia Row House," *Journal of the Society of Architectural Historians* 16, No. 4, 1957, pp. 8–13; and for the English precedent, J. Summerson, *Georgian London* (New York: Scribner's, 1946, reissued by Penguin Books in 1962, and Barrie and Jenkins, London, in 1970).

Andrew Jackson Downing's *The Architecture of Country Houses* of 1850 and *Cottage Residences* of 1842 are available in reprints (New York: Dover, 1969 and 1981, respectively). Additional sources on Downing include G. B. Tatum, *Andrew Jackson Downing, Arbiter of American Taste* (unpublished Ph.D. dissertation, Princeton University, 1950), and W. H. Pierson, Jr., *American Buildings and Their Architects*, Vol. 2 (New York: Oxford University Press, 1986), especially Chapter VII. See also C. E. Clark, Jr., "Domestic Architecture as an Index to Social History: The Romantic Revival and the Cult of Domesticity in America, 1840–1870," *Journal of Interdisciplinary History* 7, 1976, pp. 33–56. On house construction in Downing's time, see R. Jensen, "Board and Batten Siding and the Balloon Frame," *Journal of the Society of Architectural Historians* 30, 1971, pp. 40–50, and D. Upton, "Traditional Timber Framing," in B. Hindle, ed., *Material Culture of the Wooden Age* (Tarrytown, N.Y.: Sleepy Hollow Press, 1981).

Downing's writings about yards include his *A Treatise on the Theory and Practice of Landscape Gardening* (1841; facsimile ed., New York: Funk, 1967), and "A Chapter of Lawns" in *Rural Essays* (1853; reprint, New York: Da Capo, 1974). A later source is T. Baker, *Yard and Garden* (Indianapolis: Bobbs-Merrill, 1913). M. T. Watts discusses the changing taste in domestic plantings in her *Reading the Landscape of America* (rev. ed., New York: Collier, 1975).

For American suburbs in general, the best account is now K. T. Jackson, *Crabgrass Frontier* (New York: Oxford University Press, 1985). For the early suburbs, see also J. Archer, "Country and City in the American Romantic Suburb," *Journal of the Society of Architectural Historians* 42, No. 2, May 1983, pp. 139–56; S. B. Warner, *Streetcar Suburbs* (Cambridge, Mass.: Harvard University Press, 1969, 1982); and R. G. Wilson, "Idealism and the Origin of the First American Suburb: Llewellyn Park, New Jersey," *American Art Journal* 11, October 1979, pp. 79–93. The Glendale Heritage Preservation's publication committee has a handy guide to this early Ohio suburb (1976). For Riverside, Illinois, see W. L. Creese, *The Search for Environment* (New Haven: Yale University Press, 1966), pp. 153–57.

For the furniture in the Asa Packer mansion, see K. Ames, "George Henkels, Nineteenth-Century Philadelphia Cabinetmaker," *Antiques*, October 1973, pp. 641–50. A. C. and F. H. McArdle's *Carpenter Gothic* (New York: Watson-Guptill, 1978) has brief descriptions and good photographs of New England's gingerbread houses.

Catharine Beecher by K. K. Sklar (New Haven: Yale University Press, 1973) is a good biography of the nineteenth-century reformer and author. Beecher's ideas about the arrangement of kitchens are found in *The American Women's Home* (1869), which she wrote with her sister Harriet Beecher Stowe. For information about the interior of the American house, the classic source is still S. Giedion, *Mechanization Takes Command* (New York: Oxford University Press, 1948); see also S. M. Strasser, *Never Done: A History of Housework in the United States* (New York: Pantheon, 1982), and R. S. Cowan, "The 'Industrial Revolution' in the Home," *Technology and Culture* 17, No. 1, January 1976, pp. 1–23.

The layout of the American house is analyzed most cogently in the following: D. Upton, "Pattern Books and Professionalism," *Winterthur Portfolio* 19, No. 2/3, 1984, pp. 107–50; V. Scully, *The Shingle Style* (New Haven: Yale University Press, 1955); J. Lane, "The Period House in the Nineteen-Twenties," *Journal of the Society of Architectural Historians* 20, 1961, pp. 169–78; J. Vlach, "The Shotgun House: An African Architectural Legacy," in D. Upton and J. M. Vlach, eds., *Common Places* (Athens, Ga.: University of Georgia Press, 1986), pp. 58–78. See also F. Kniffen, "Folk Housing: Key to Diffusion," *Annals of the Association of American Geographers* 55, No. 4, December 1965, pp. 549–77. On bungalows, see most recently C. Lancaster, *The American Bungalow, 1880s–1920s* (New York: Abbeville Press, 1985).

There is of course an enormous bibliography on the houses of Frank Lloyd Wright. The handiest references are H.-R. Hitchcock, *In the Nature of Materials: The Buildings of Frank Lloyd Wright, 1887–1941* (New York: Duell, Sloan and Pearce, 1942, reprinted by Da Capo, 1973); G. C. Manson, *Frank Lloyd Wright to 1910, The First Golden Age* (New York: Reinhold, 1958); and W. A. Storrer, *The Architecture of Frank Lloyd Wright* (Cambridge, Mass.: MIT Press, 1974, 2nd ed. 1978). See also R. C. Twombly, "Saving the Family: Middle-Class Attraction to Wright's Prairie House, 1901–1909," *American Quarterly* 27, 1975, pp. 66–69. There is an excellent monograph on the Robie House by Joseph Connors (Chicago: The University of Chicago, 1984). On the Tomek House, see also M. Moran, "In the Garden with Frank Lloyd Wright," *Inland Architect,* March/April 1984, pp. 27–29. On the Dana-Thomas House, see also R. C. Melotte and R. R. Morse, "The Dana-Thomas House: Symbol of a Revolution," *Stained Glass* 77, No. 3, 1982, pp. 267–68. The Ardmore houses are discussed in R. Sherwood, *Modern Housing Prototypes* (Cambridge, Mass.: Harvard University Press, 1978).

On the early apartment house, see A. Alpern, *Apartments for the Affluent* (New York: McGraw-Hill, 1975), and W. De Wit, "Apartment Houses and Bungalows: Building the Flat City," *Chicago History,* Winter 1983/84, pp. 19–29. For a contemporary reaction to New York's Dorilton, see "Architectural Aberrations: The Dorilton," *Architectural Record* 12, No. 2, 1902, pp. 221–26. "Apartment Hotels in New York City," *Architectural Record* 13, No. 1, January 1903, pp. 85–91, discusses apartment hotels as a new building type and explains how they differ from apartment buildings.

For tenements and public housing in general, some useful references include A. Jackson, *A Place Called Home* (Cambridge, Mass.: MIT Press, 1976), which gives the story for New York; R. Pommer, "The Architecture of Urban Housing in the United States during the Early 1930s," *Journal of the Society of Architectural Historians* 37, 1978, pp. 235–64; R. Plunz, *Housing Form and Public Policy* (New York: Praeger Scientific, 1980). On slums, see T. L. Philpott, *The Slum and the Ghetto* (New York: Oxford University Press, 1978), and G. Osofsky, *Harlem: The Making of a Ghetto* (New York: Harper & Row, 1966).

R. Bender gives a general review of prefabrication in *A Crack in the Rear-View Mirror* (New York: Van Nostrand Reinhold, 1973). On mail-order houses, see J. L. Garvin, "Mail-Order House Plans and American Victorian Architecture," *Winterthur Portfolio* 16, No. 4, 1981, pp. 309–34, and T. Snyder, "The Sears Pre-Cut," *Fine Home-Building,* No. 28, August/September 1985, pp. 42–45. For mass-produced houses, see B. Kelly, *The Design and Production of Houses* (New York: McGraw-Hill, 1959); H. J. Gans, *The Levittowners* (New York: Vintage, 1967); and N. Eichler, *The Merchant Builders* (Cambridge, Mass.: MIT Press, 1982). Mobile homes are discussed in S. Davis, ed., *The Form of Housing* (New York: Van Nostrand Reinhold, 1971), pp. 217–42.

The American Workplace

There are no convenient general histories of the American workplace—a singular lack. For the early period, good places to begin are J. Stilgoe, *Common Landscape of America, 1580 to 1845* (New Haven: Yale University Press, 1982), with brief reviews of mines and mills, farms and logging camps; S. B. Warner, *The Private City* (Philadelphia: University of Philadelphia Press, 1968), which documents, for one important American city, the separation of home and work after 1800, and the slow change of the downtown from an environment of small shopkeepers to a business district of large concerns. For the period just after the Civil War, the best introduction would be J. B. Jackson, *American Space: The Centennial Years* (New York: Norton, 1972). For the later period, D. T. Rogers, *The Work Ethic in Industrial America, 1850–1920* (Chicago: University of Chicago Press, 1978) provides the proper background for the discussion of the physical setting of the workplace.

On the farm environment, I have benefitted from the following: S. Giedion, *Mechanization Takes Command* (New York: Oxford University Press, 1948); B. D. Halsted, ed., *Barn Plans and Outbuildings* (1881, republished as *Barns, Sheds, and Outbuildings* [Brattleboro, Vt.: Stephen Greene Press, 1977]), an excellent source of illustrative material for things like cattle shelters, piggeries, poultry houses, granaries, and corn cribs; A. G. Noble and G. A. Seymour, "Distribution of Barn Types in Northeastern United States," *The Geographical Review,* April 1982, pp. 155–70; J. F. Hart, *The Look of the Land* (Englewood Cliffs, N.J.: Prentice-Hall, 1975); and N. C. Teter and H. Giese, "Power and Livestock," in the United States Department of Agriculture, *Power to Produce* (1960), pp. 218–30.

The plantation of the South is enjoying new scholarly attention. See, for example, C. Anthony, "The Big House and the Slave Quarters," *Landscape* 20, No. 3, 1975, pp. 8–19 and 21, No. 1, pp. 9–15; E. Chappell, "Slave Housing," in *Fresh Advices,* November 1982, pp. i–iv; and to my mind the most important contribution for the physical and social world of the plantation, D. Upton, "White and Black Landscapes in Eighteenth-Century Virginia," *Places* 2, No. 2, pp. 59–72. Also interesting, for details about the work force and the economic picture in general, is the case study presented in P. G. E. Clemens, "The Operation of an Eighteenth-Century Chesapeake Tobacco Plantation," *Agricultural History* 49, No. 3, July 1975, pp. 517–31. The accommodation of urban blacks in the nineteenth century is discussed in R. C. Wade, *Slavery in the Cities* (New York: Oxford University Press, 1964), especially Chapter 1 ("The Urban Perimeter") and Chapter 3 ("The Quarters and the House").

On warehouses, see, among others, L. Eaton, "Warehouses and Warehouse Districts in Mid-American Cities," and "Winnipeg: The Northern Anchor of the Wholesale Trade," *Urban History Review* 11, No. 1, June 1982, pp. 17–26 and No. 2, October 1982, pp. 17–30; also see Eaton's "Oscar Eckerman: Architect to Deere & Company, 1897–1942," *RACAR—Canadian Art Review,* No. 11, 1977, pp. 89–99. See also J. Vance, *The Merchant's World: The Geography of Wholesaling* (Englewood Cliffs, N.J.: Prentice-Hall, 1970). There is a useful architectural guide to Laclede's Landing in St. Louis by C. H. Toft and O. Overby (published by the Landmarks Association of St. Louis, 1977).

Of company towns, those connected with the textile mills of New England have been the most persistently studied—from J. Coolidge's classic account (*Mill and Mansion,* New York: Columbia University Press, 1942) to S. Dunwell's *The Run of the Mill* (Boston: Godine, 1978) and D. Macaulay's *Mill* (Boston: Houghton Mifflin, 1983), with its wonderful illustrations of mill construction. T. K. Hareven and R. Langenbach's *Amoskeag* (London: Methuen, 1979) gives a complete picture of life and work in one of these mill towns, down to the present day, through a series of interviews with people who once managed the mills and worked there.

For other sorts of company towns, some recent references include C. E. Stoehr, *Bonanza Victorian, Architecture and Society in Colorado Mining Towns* (Albuquerque: University of New Mexico Press, 1975), and S. Dallas, *Colorado Ghost Towns and Mining Camps* (Norman: University of Oklahoma Press, 1985). The University of Oklahoma has also published books on the ghost towns of Arizona and New Mexico (both by J. E. and B. H. Sherman), and Oklahoma (by J. W. Morris). A handy encyclopedia, L. Florin's, *Ghost Towns of the West* (New York: Promontory, 1971), covers thirteen states and British Columbia. J. S. Garner's *The Model Company Town* (Amherst: University of Massachusetts Press, 1984) looks at New England in general, but focuses on Hopedale, Massachusetts. The best book on Pullman is still S. Buder's *Pullman* (New York: Oxford University Press, 1967).

A good introduction to Taylorism is S. Haber, *Efficiency and Uplift, Scientific Management in the Progressive Era, 1890–1920* (Chicago: University of Chicago Press, 1964). Also essential is H. Braverman, *Labor and Monopoly Capital* (New York: Monthly Review Press, 1975). For Taylor's own words, one must turn to his *Principles of Scientific Management,* first published in 1911. On Henry

Ford, the definitive work is still A. Nevins and F. E. Hill, *Ford,* 2 vols. (New York: Scribner's, 1954, 1957), but see also K. Sward, *The Legend of Henry Ford* (New York: Rinehart, 1948).

Albert Kahn deserves more study. At present, the best account of his architecture is G. Hildebrand, *Designing for Industry, the Architecture of Albert Kahn* (Cambridge, Mass.: MIT Press, 1974); but it should be supplemented with W. H. Ferry, *The Legacy of Albert Kahn* (Detroit: Detroit Institute of Arts, 1970), and for an insider's account, G. Nelson, *Industrial Architecture of Albert Kahn* (New York: Architectural Book Publishing, 1939).

For the twentieth-century industrial plant, see J. F. Munce, *Industrial Architecture* (New York: F. W. Dodge Corp., 1960); K. Baynes, *Industrial Design and the Community* (London: Lund, Humphreys, 1967); O. W. Grube, *Industrial Buildings and Factories* (New York: Praeger Publishers, 1971); and J. Drury, *Factories: Planning, Design and Modernization* (London: Architectural Press, 1981). Much of the literature merely describes and illustrates buildings; a proper history of the building type remains to be written. The conversion to electricity is discussed in R. B. Du Boff, "The Introduction of Electric Power in American Manufacturing," *The Economic History Review* 20, No. 3, December 1967, pp. 509–18.

The literature of the office environment has long been dominated by the architectural history of the skyscraper. For this side of the story, some major titles will suffice: C. Condit, *The Chicago School of Architecture* (Chicago: University of Chicago Press, 1964); P. Goldberger, *The Skyscraper* (New York: Knopf, 1982); and for the more recent crop, A. L. Huxtable, *The Tall Building Artistically Reconsidered* (New York: Pantheon, 1984). Louis Sullivan's contribution to the development of the tall office building has also been amply commented upon. Consult the standard monographs about his work by H. Morrison (1935, 1962), Albert Bush-Brown (1960), W. Connelly (1960), S. Paul (1962), M. Kaufman (1969), and N. G. Menocal, *Architecture as Nature, The Transcendentalist Idea of Louis Sullivan* (Madison: University of Wisconsin Press, 1981). Frank Lloyd Wright's Larkin Building and the Johnson Wax Administration Building are in all the standard books on this architect. I might mention some less obvious sources: N. K. Smith, *Frank Lloyd Wright, A Study in Architectural Content* (Englewood Cliffs, N.J.: Prentice-Hall, 1966), pp. 136–48, and "Wax Research and Development Tower," *Architect and Engineer,* December 1950, pp. 20–24.

For legal and economic issues affecting the tall building, E. Schultz and W. Simmons, *Offices in the Sky* (Indianapolis: Bobbs-Merrill, 1959) is worth reading. The best review of the office as a workplace is L. Gatter, "The Office, An Analysis of the Evolution of a Workplace" (unpublished Master of Architecture thesis, MIT, 1982).

On Kevin Roche's buildings for Union Carbide and General Foods, see W. McQuade, "Union Carbide Takes to the Woods," *Fortune* 13, December 1982, pp. 164–74; "Restructuring the Corporate Habitat," *Architectural Re-*

cord, October 1983, pp. 110–17; and A. O. Dean, "Corporate Contrast in the Suburbs: Kevin Roche's Union Carbide and General Foods Headquarters," *Architecture,* February 1985, pp. 60–69.

The American Street

The history of American roads has been recounted several times, more or less competently: J. Labatut and W. J. Lane, eds., *Highways in Our National Life* (Princeton: Princeton University Press, 1950); C. Borth, *Mankind on the Move* (Washington, D.C.: Automotive Safety Foundation, 1969) and G. Hindley, *A History of Roads* (Secaucus, N.J.: Citadel, 1972), both with a fair portion devoted to the American story; J. Robinson, *Highways and Our Environment* (New York: McGraw-Hill, 1971); and the semi-official account by the historian of the United States Bureau of Roads, A. C. Rose, *Historic American Roads* (New York: Crown, 1976). But there is no equivalent history of our urban streets, which still has to be pieced from a very diverse and incomplete assortment of sources.

On the alleys of Washington, D.C., see J. Borchert, *Alley Life in Washington* (Urbana: University of Illinois Press, 1980). On L'Enfant's Washington and the planning history of the city in general, J. Reps, *Monumental Washington* (Princeton: Princeton University Press, 1967) and F. Gutheim, *Worthy of the Nation* (Washington, D.C.: Smithsonian, 1977) contain all the pertinent information and bibliography.

A good description of river cities is in P. Kramer and F. L. Holborn, eds., *The City in American Life* (New York: Capricorn, 1971), pp. 95–118. On our waterways, see the general road histories cited above and also L. Harris, *Canals and Their Architecture* (London: Godfrey Cave, 1969, 1980), which gives the English side of things, and W. H. Shank *Towpaths to Tugboats, A History of American Canal Engineering* (York, Pa: American Canal and Transportation Center, 1982). The American Canal and Transportation Center has a long list of publications on individual canal systems like the Chesapeake and Ohio, or C.&O., and the people involved with them. There is a good new book on the Albemarle and Chesapeake Canal: A. C. Brown, *Juniper Waterway* (Charlottesville: University of Virginia Press, 1981). The quotations from Charles Dickens come from his *American Notes,* first published in 1842. Another early traveler who left an account of canal journeys is Philip Nicklin, alias "Peregrine Prolix," whose book of 1835 is edited by W. H. Shank in *Journey through Pennsylvania* (York, Pa.: American Canal and Transportation Center, 1975).

Popular studies of toll roads include R. N. Parks, *Roads and Travel in New England* (Sturbridge, Mass.: Old Sturbridge Village, 1967), and A. L. Reist, *Conestoga Wagon* (Lancaster, Pa.: Forry and Hacker, 1975). The old National Road has been looked at in some detail in P. D. Jordan, *The National Road* (Indianapolis: Bobbs-Merrill, 1948, 1966); T. B. Searight, *The Old Pike* (Orange, Va.: Green Tree Press, 1971); G. R. Stewart, *U.S. 40* (Boston: Houghton Mifflin, 1953); and T. R. and G. R. Vale, *U.S. 40 Today* (Madison: University of Wisconsin Press, 1983), which retraces Stewart's itinerary and matches his photographs to highlight the changes that took place in the thirty-year interim. See also J. D. Van Trump, "National Stone: The Cumberland Road and American Architecture," *Antiques,* August 1962, pp. 165–67.

On the bridges along the old roads, see F. Kniffen, "The American Covered Bridge," *Geographical Review* 41, No. 1, January 1951, pp. 114–23; E. Sloane, "The First Covered Bridge in America," *Geographical Review* 49, No. 3, July 1959, pp. 315–21; M. V. Mish and D. T. Cottingham, *Bridges: Our Legacy in Stone,* the catalog of an exhibition by the Washington County Museum of Fine Arts, Maryland, August/September 1965; J. Gies, *Bridges and Men* (Garden City, N.Y.: Doubleday, 1963), Chapter 11, "The Yankee Bridge"; and R. S. Allen, *Covered Bridges of the Northeast,* rev. ed. (Brattleboro, Vt.: Stephen Greene Press, 1974). On early national highway policy, see C. Goodrich, "National Planning of Internal Improvements," *Political Science Quarterly* 63, No. 1, March 1948, pp. 16–44.

The books by John Reps are the prime resource material for the design of early American cities: *The Making of Urban America* (Princeton: Princeton University Press, 1965); *Tidewater Towns* (Williamsburg, Va.: The Colonial Williamsburg Foundation, 1972); *Town Planning in Frontier America* (Princeton: Princeton University Press, 1969), among others. See also P. Groth, "Street-grids as Frameworks of Urban Variety," *The Harvard Architecture Review* 2, Spring 1981, pp. 68–75, and R. Pillsbury, "Urban Street Patterns and Topography: A Pennsylvania Case Study," *The Professional Geographer* 22, 1970, pp. 21–25. An excellent survey that goes beyond the physical aspects of urban form is C. N. Glaab and A. T. Brown, *A History of Urban America,* 2nd ed. (New York: Macmillan, 1976). On Savannah's grid, the best recent commentary is S. Anderson, "The Plan of Savannah and Changes of Occupancy during Its Early Years," *The Harvard Architecture Review* 2, Spring 1981, pp. 60–67. For a pictorial history of the city, see M. Lane, *Savannah Revisited,* 3rd ed. (Savannah: Beehive Press, 1977).

Bibliography for rowhouses is suggested above, under "The American House." Frances Trollope's remark appears in her *Domestic Manners of the Americans,* first published in 1832.

The impact of the railroad on the design of cities still needs investigation. An aspect of this story is covered brilliantly in J. Stilgoe, *Metropolitan Corridor* (New Haven: Yale University Press, 1983). Railroad towns have been studied by: J. B. Hedges, "The Colonization Work of the Northern Pacific Railroad," *Mississippi Valley Historical Review* 13, December 1926, pp. 311–42; P. W. Gates, *The Illinois Central Railroad and Its Colonization* (Cambridge, Mass.: Harvard University Press, 1934); T. Harvey, "Railroad Towns: Urban Form on the Prairie," *Landscape* 27, No. 3, pp. 26–34 (on Minnesota's Red River Valley).

Main Street is now a popular subject. I note only a few entries of more than routine interest: R. V. Francaviglia, "Main Street USA, The Creation of a Popular Image," *Landscape* 21, No. 3, 1977, pp. 18–22; C. Rifkind, *Main Street: The Face of Urban America* (New York: Harper & Row, 1977); P. Schrag, "Is Main Street Still There?" *Saturday Review* 17, January 1970, pp. 20–25; and L. Atherton, *Main Street on the Middle Border* (Bloomington: Indiana University Press, 1954). Elm Street and Millionaire's Row have yet to find their scholars. On street lighting, there were frequent articles published in *The American City* at the time of the City Beautiful Movement; see, for example, E. L. Ellitt, "The New Street Lighting," May 1910, pp. 254–58; C. L. Eshleman, "Modern Street Lighting," February 1912, pp. 510–17; and J. A. Corcoran, "The City Light and Beautiful," July 1912, pp. 46–49. For more recent sources, see S. P. Noreen, "Public Street Illumination in Washington, D.C.," *George Washington University Studies* 2, 1975, and K. Bolton, "The Great Awakening of the Night," *Landscape* 24, No. 2, 1980, pp. 41–47.

Transportation has its own voluminous literature. On the other hand, the effect of transportation on street design has received little attention. On the history of urban transportation, consult J. P. McKay, *Tramways and Trolleys* (Princeton: Princeton University Press, 1976), for the European background; B. Bobrick, *Labyrinths of Iron* (New York: William Morrow, 1981, 1986), for subways; and J. Vance, *Capturing the Horizon* (New York: Harper & Row, 1985). The elevated design in Chicago has been treated by J. L. Davis, "The Elevated System and the Growth of Northern Chicago," *Northwestern University Studies in Geography*, No. 10, 1965. The most detailed account of street pavements is by C. McShane, "Transforming the Use of Urban Space: A Look at the Revolution in Street Pavements 1880–1924," *Journal of Urban History* 5, 1979, pp. 279–307. For the scene below the street, the best visual source is D. Macaulay, *Underground* (Boston: Houghton Mifflin, 1976). See also P. Jones, *Under the City Streets* (New York: Holt, Rinehart and Winston, 1978), a history of subterranean New York.

The Chicago Fair of 1893 is currently being reassessed. See, among others, A. Trachtenberg, *The Incorporation of America* (New York: Hill and Wang, 1982), especially Chapter 7. The standard recent work on Daniel Burnham is by T. Hines (*Burnham of Chicago,* New York: Oxford University Press, 1974). On the City Beautiful, current scholarship is represented by W. H. Wilson, "The Ideology, Aesthetics and Politics of the City Beautiful Movement," in A. Sutcliffe, ed., *The Rise of Modern Urban Planning, 1800–1914* (London: Mansell, 1980), pp. 165–98, and R. E. Foglesohn, *Planning the Capitalist City* (Princeton: Princeton University Press, 1986).

The highways of the automobile age have a prodigious bibliography. For the early period, I found J. Interrante, "You Can't Go to Town in a Bathtub: Automobile Movement and the Reorganization of Rural American Space, 1900–30," *Radical History Review,* Fall 1979, pp. 151–68, extremely provocative; see also M. Foster, "City Planners and Urban Transportation, The American

Response, 1900–1940," *Journal of Urban History* 5, 1979, pp. 365–96, and P. J. Hugill, "Good Roads and the Automobile in the United States, 1880–1929," *Geographical Review* 72, No. 3, July 1982, pp. 327–49. On the Pennsylvania Turnpike, there is the popular account of W. H. Shank, *Vanderbilt's Folly* (York, Pa.: American Canal and Transportation Center, 1973), and a fond description of Old U.S. 1 by B. Dale will be found in *The National Geographic,* December 1984, pp. 790–817. The roadside environment is best sampled in W. J. Belasco, *Americans on the Road* (Cambridge, Mass.: MIT Press, 1979), and C. H. Liebs, *Main Street to Miracle Mile* (Boston: Little, Brown, 1985), which covers everything from auto showrooms and gas stations, to miniature golf courses and drive-in theaters. D. Brodsly's *L.A. Freeway* (Berkeley: University of California Press, 1981) is a perceptive critique of this phenomenon.

The Public Realm

A special issue of *The Public Interest* (No. 74, Winter 1984), entitled "Architecture and Public Spaces," is a good starting point for the themes taken up in this chapter. Also rewarding are R. Sennett's classic essay, *The Uses of Disorder: Personal Identity and City Life* (New York: Knopf, 1970), and A. Koetter, "Monumentality and the American City," *Harvard Architecture Review* 4, 1984, pp. 167–84.

There is, to my knowledge, no detailed history of Boston Common, although surveys of Boston, like W. M. Whitehill's topographical history, and guide books, like the excellent recent one by D. Lyndon (*The City Observed,* New York: Random House, 1982), have something to say about it. A useful reference for American squares is A. Heckscher, *Open Spaces* (New York: Harper & Row, 1977). For the Spanish plaza, see D. P. Crouch, D. J. Garr, and A. I. Mundigo, *Spanish City Planning in North America* (Cambridge, Mass.: MIT Press, 1982). The New England common has been treated in J. D. Cushing, "Town Commons of New England, 1640–1840," *Old-Time New England* 51, No. 3, January–March 1961, pp. 86–94, and J. Stilgoe, "Town Common and Village Green in New England: 1620–1981," in R. L. Fleming and L. A. Halderman, eds. *On Common Land* (Cambridge, Mass.: Harvard University Press, 1982), pp. 7–36.

My discussion of the county courthouse square is based on the following: E. T. Price, "The Central Courthouse Square in the American County Seat," *Geographical Review,* January 1968, pp. 29–60; J. B. Jackson, *Discovering the Vernacular Landscape* (New Haven: Yale University Press, 1984), pp. 77 ff.; and M. M. Ohman, "Diffusion of Foursquare Courthouses to the Midwest, 1785–1885," *Geographical Review* 72, No. 2, April 1982, pp. 171–89. The Pennsylvania origins are discussed in W. Zelinsky, "The Pennsylvania Town," *Geographical Review* 67, No. 2, April 1977, pp. 127–47, and R. Pillsbury, "The Market or Public Square in Pennsylvania, 1682–1820," *Proceedings of the*

Pennsylvania Academy of Sciences 41, 1967, pp. 116–18. On the Confederate monument of courthouse squares, see S. Davis, "Empty Eyes, Marble Hand," *Journal of Popular Culture* 16, No. 3, 1982, pp. 2–21, and J. J. Winbery, " 'Lest We Forget': The Confederate Monument and the Southern Townscape," *Southeastern Geographer* 22, No. 2, November 1983, pp. 107–21, where the Lumberton inscription we quote is recorded.

Much is written on the American cemetery in general, and the picturesque rural cemetery in particular. Two introductory essays are R. V. Francaviglia, "The Cemetery as an Evolving Cultural Landscape," *Annals of the Association of American Geographers* 61, No. 3, September 1971, pp. 501–9, and J. B. Jackson, "The Vanishing Epitaph: From Monument to Place," *Landscape* 17, No. 2, Winter 1967/68, pp. 22–26. On the rural cemetery, see T. Bender, "The Rural Cemetery Movement: Urban Travail and the Appeal of Nature," *New England Quarterly* 47, No. 2, June 1974, pp. 196–211; D. E. Stannard, "Calm Dwellings—The Brief, Sentimental Age of the Rural Cemetery," *American Heritage,* August/September 1979, pp. 43–55; and M. J. Darnall, "The American Cemetery as Picturesque Landscape," *Winterthur Portfolio* 18, No. 4, Winter 1983, pp. 249–69, dealing mostly with Bellefontaine Cemetery in St. Louis. Mount Auburn, among others, is discussed by S. French, "The Cemetery as Cultural Institution: The Establishment of Mount Auburn and the 'Rural Cemetery' Movement," *American Quarterly* 26, No. 1, March 1974, pp. 37–58, and J. Zanger, "Mount Auburn Cemetery: The Silent Suburb," *Landscape* 24, No. 2, 1980, pp. 23–28. Selected references on monuments and tombstones should include A. Ludwig, *Graven Images* (Middletown, Conn.: Wesleyan University Press, 1966); E. Dethlefsen and J. Deetz, "Death's Heads, Cherubs, and Willow Trees: Experimental Archaeology in Colonial Cemeteries," *American Antiquity* 31, No. 4, April 1966, pp. 502–10; and K. L. Ames, "Ideologies in Stone: Meanings in Victorian Gravestones," *Journal of Popular Culture* 14, No. 4, Spring 1981, pp. 641–56.

Recent surveys of urban parks include G. Cranz, *The Politics of Park Design* (Cambridge, Mass.: MIT Press, 1982); see also a provocative essay by R. Rosenzweig, "Middle-Class Parks and Working-Class Play," *Radical History Review* 21, Fall 1979, pp. 31–46, where the emphasis is on Worcester, Massachusetts. Frederick Law Olmsted, who has been accorded an excellent biography (L. W. Roper, *FLO,* Baltimore: Johns Hopkins University Press, 1973), a scholarly edition of his papers by C. C. McLaughlin (1977 ff.), and several monographic studies (e.g., A. Fein, *Frederick Law Olmsted and the American Environmental Tradition,* New York: Braziller, 1972), is now in the process of revisionist updating. See, for example, R. Starr, "The Motive Behind Olmsted's Park," *Public Interest,* No. 74, Winter 1984, pp. 66–76. On Central Park, see A. Fein, ed., *Landscape into Cityscape* (Ithaca, N.Y.: Cornell, 1968).

The Brooklyn Museum's catalog for an exhibition entitled *The American Renaissance, 1876–1917* (1979) is a fine introduction to that subject. The standard survey of state capitols is H.-R. Hitchcock and W. Seale, *Temples of*

Democracy (New York: Harcourt Brace Jovanovich, 1976). For the Statue of Liberty, see M. Trachtenberg, *The Statue of Liberty* (New York: Viking, 1976).

On department stores, see S. P. Benson, "Palace of Consumption and Machine for Selling: The American Department Store, 1880–1940," *Radical History Review* 21, Fall 1979, pp. 199–221. The changing scale and profile of the American city are described most imaginatively by C. Tunnard and H. H. Reed in their *American Skyline* (Boston: Houghton Mifflin, 1955).

On the need to remember and the ways of doing it, I have read with benefit D. Lowenthal's work, especially "Past Time, Present Place," *Geographical Review* 65, No. 1, January 1975, pp. 1–36, where I saw the reference to the John Steinbeck quote I use on p. 248, and his "Age and Artifact: Dilemmas of Appreciation," in D. W. Meinig, ed., *The Interpretation of Ordinary Landscapes* (New York: Oxford University Press, 1979), pp. 103–28. See also A. Brandt, "A Short Natural History of Nostalgia," *Atlantic Monthly* 242, December 1978, pp. 58–63.

The preservation movement has its own voluminous literature. For a history of the movement, see C. B. Hosmer, Jr., *Presence of the Past* (New York: Putnam, 1965), dealing with the period before Williamsburg, and his *Preservation Comes of Age, from Williamsburg to the National Trust, 1926–1949,* 2 vols. (Charlottesville: University of Virginia Press, 1981). For an unofficial view of the Williamsburg and Greenfield experience, see M. Wallace, "Visiting the Past: History Museums in the United States," *Radical History Review* 25, 1981, pp. 63–96. The official publication for Greenfield Village is by G. C. Upward, *A Home for Our Heritage* (Dearborn, Mich.: Henry Ford Museum Press, 1979). A catalog of replicas of historic buildings around the country has been put together by S. S. Brown (*Remade in America,* Salem, Oreg.: Old Time Bottle Publishing, 1972). For theme parks, see M. Hall, "Theme Parks: Around the World in 80 Minutes," *Landscape* 21, No. 1, 1976, pp. 3–8.

A whole issue of *Progressive Architecture* (November 1985) is devoted to "Restoration and Reuse." See also the articles on South Street Seaport in New York, Washington's Old Post Office, and others in *Architecture,* November 1983. On Rouse and his company, see W. Fulton, "The Robin Hood of Real Estate," *Planning,* May 1985, pp. 4–10, and "Roundtable on Rouse," *Progressive Architecture,* July 1981, pp. 100–06. For similar projects by others, see P. Lemov, "Celebrating the City," *Builder,* February 1984, pp. 90–97.

A report on the competition for the St. Louis Memorial Arch can be found in *Progressive Architecture,* May 1948, pp. 51–59; see also the May 1963 issue, pp. 188–91, for the engineering of the Arch, which is also discussed by M. J. Crosbie in *AIA Journal,* June 1983, pp. 78–79. The Vietnam Memorial has had extensive comment. The best reviews are by S. N. Blum in *Arts Magazine* 59, No. 4, December 1984, pp. 124–28; K. Andersen in *Time,* 15 April 1985, p. 61; A. C. Danto in *The Nation,* 31 August 1985, pp. 152–55; and C. M. Howett in *Landscape* 28, No. 2, 1985, pp. 1–9. For the

Roosevelt Memorial, see T. Creighton, *The Architecture of Monuments: The Franklin Delano Roosevelt Memorial Competition* (New York: Reinhold, 1962).

The Shape of the Land

The subject of this chapter is addressed in one recent general book, W. Sullivan's *Landprints* (New York: New York Times, 1984), but the attention there is mostly on geological formations. The natural design of the continent is analyzed also by J. H. Paterson, *North America,* now in its 7th edition (New York: Oxford University Press, 1984). B. J. Richardson, *Atlas of Cultural Features* (Northbrook, Ill.: Hubbard, 1972) uses aerial photographs and tracings to study a sample of land designs. The most complete pictorial narrative of land use as it applies to farming is still F. J. Marshner, *Land Use and Its Patterns in the United States* (Washington, D.C.: U.S. Department of Agriculture, 1959). See also the broad-ranging essay by D. Lowenthal, "The American Scene," *Geographical Review,* January 1968, pp. 61–88. A brilliant new book, D. W. Meinig's *The Shaping of America* (New Haven: Yale University Press, 1986), dealing with Atlantic America up to 1800, appeared too late to do our story any good.

The Indian order on the land can be gleaned from the following: J. M. Cooper, "Land Tenure among the Indians of Eastern and Northern America," *The Pennsylvania Archaeologist* 8, 1938, pp. 55–59; A. L. Kroeber, "Nature of the Land-Holding Group," *Ethnohistory* 2, 1955, pp. 303–14; R. A. Manners, "Tribe and Tribal Boundaries: The Walapai," *Ethnohistory* 4, 1957, pp. 1–26; A. F. C. Wallace, "Political Organization and Land Tenure among the Northeastern Indians, 1600–1830," *Southwestern Journal of Anthropology* 13, 1957, pp. 301–21; and E. Boissevain, "Detribalization and Group Identity: The Narragansett Indian Case," *Transactions of the New York Academy of Sciences,* March 1963, pp. 493–503. The relationship of the Indians with the arriving Englishmen is studied in two remarkable books: B. W. Sheehan, *Savagism and Civility, Indians and Englishmen in Colonial Virginia* (Cambridge: Cambridge University Press, 1980), and W. Cronon, *Changes in the Land: Indians, Colonists, and the Ecology of New England* (New York: Hill and Wang, 1983). Also worthwhile is A. T. Vaughan, *New England Frontier, Puritans and Indians, 1620–1675* (Boston: Little, Brown, 1965). For Indian paths, see the bibliography for roads given above for our "Street" chapter (Borth, Labatut and Lane, etc.).

The colonists' attitude toward the wilderness is discussed in R. Nash, *Wilderness and the American Mind* (New Haven: Yale University Press, 1957), and H. Huth, *Nature and the American* (Berkeley: University of California Press, 1957), where the verses we quote (p. 289), by Michael Wigglesworth, are to be found. The New England colonial land pattern gets a fresh interpretation in J. S. Wood, "Village and Community in Early Colonial New England," *Journal of Historical Geography* 8, No. 4, 1982, pp. 333–46. The

Spanish impact, at least as far as one state is concerned, has been dealt with by W. W. Robinson, *Land in California* (Berkeley: University of California Press, 1948). See also S. G. McHenry, "Eighteenth-Century Field Patterns as Vernacular Art," published originally in *Geographical Review*, January 1968, now reprinted in D. Upton and J. Vlach, eds., *Common Places* (Athens, Ga.: University of Georgia Press, 1986), pp. 107–45. On our deforestation efforts, my information comes from M. Williams, "Clearing the United States Forests," *Journal of Historical Geography* 8, No. 1, 1982, pp. 12–28.

The National Survey has been thoroughly studied. The best account is H. B. Johnson, *Order upon the Land* (New York: Oxford University Press, 1976), but I also found the following useful: N. J. W. Thrower, *Original Survey and Land Subdivision* (Chicago: Rand McNally, 1966), which deals with a small section of northwest Ohio and contrasts land subject to the survey lines with the irregularities of land belonging to the Virginia Military District of Ohio; W. D. Pattison, *Beginnings of the American Rectangular Land Survey System, 1784–1800* (New York: Arno Press, 1979); and V. Carstensen, "Patterns on the American Land," *Surveying and Mapping*, December 1976, pp. 303–9.

The section we call "The Spoils of Occupation" is based in part on P. W. Gates, "Frontier Estate Builders and Farm Laborers," in W. D. Wyman and C. B. Kroeber, *The Frontier in Perspective* (Madison: University of Wisconsin Press, 1957), pp. 143–63.

On the Philadelphia waterworks, see T. F. Hamlin's biography of Benjamin Latrobe (New York: Oxford University Press, 1955), and W. H. Pierson, Jr., *American Buildings and Their Architects: The Colonial and Neoclassical Styles*, pp. 357–60. The story of the Croton water system is most conveniently found in P. Jones, *Under the City Streets*, already cited above for "The American Street" (pp. 38–66). For California's water systems, see, for example, R. A. Nadeau, *The Water Seekers* (New York: Doubleday, 1950), with a good account of the Owens Valley project; R. De Roos, *The Thirsty Land* (Stanford, Calif.: Stanford University Press, 1948), on the Central Valley project; and for the recent controversy over the Los Angeles water diversion policies, R. D. James in *The Wall Street Journal*, 4 and 12 February 1981.

The Bureau of Reclamation records its own activities. See, for example, its *Dams and Control Works*, 3rd ed. (Washington, D.C.: Department of the Interior, 1954), which has an introductory essay on the Bureau and its history. See also M. C. Robinson, *Water for the West, The Bureau of Reclamation, 1902–1977* (Chicago: Public Works Historical Society, 1979). Dam types and construction are neatly reviewed in C. Condit, *American Building* (Chicago: University of Chicago Press, 1968, 1982).

There is a vast amount of published material on the Tennessee Valley Authority. The best general accounts are probably J. Huxley's *TVA, Adventure in Planning* (Cheam, Surrey: Architectural Press, 1943); D. Lilienthal's very partisan *TVA, Democracy on the March*, first published in 1944 and with a new

"Twentieth Anniversary Edition" (New York: Harper) in 1953; and another insider, G. R. Clapp's *The TVA, An Approach to the Development of a Region* (Chicago: University of Chicago Press, 1955). From an architectural point of view, most important are: a special issue of *Architectural Forum*, August 1939, devoted to the TVA; J. H. Kyle, *The Building of TVA, An Illustrated History* (Baton Rouge: Louisiana State University Press, 1958); and the catalog of a recent exhibition, edited by M. Moffett and L. Wodehouse—*Built for the People of the United States, Fifty Years of TVA Architecture* (Knoxville: University of Tennessee Press, 1983)—with a study by W. Jordy of the new Raccoon Mountain installation (pp. 48–58) and an interesting essay entitled "The TVA as an Allegory" by W. L. Creese (pp. 59–63). Remarkably, there are as yet no serious published studies of Roland Anthony Wank and his work.

The chief popular account of bridges is J. Gies, *Bridges and Men,* cited already. A. Trachtenberg's *Brooklyn Bridge: Fact and Symbol* (Chicago: University of Chicago Press, 1965, 1979) is unsurpassed. On the Eads Bridge, besides the account given in Gies, see Q. Scott and H. S. Miller, *The Eads Bridge* (Columbia, Mo.: University of Missouri Press, 1979), mostly a pictorial history; these and all other retellings of the story are ultimately drawn from C. M. Woodward, *A History of the St. Louis Bridge* (St. Louis: G. I. Jones and Company, 1881).

The classic presentation and analysis of the patterns of modern roads and settlements is C. Tunnard and P. Pushkarev, *Manmade America* (New Haven: Yale University Press, 1963). On suburbia, we now have K. T. Jackson's *Crabgrass Frontier,* cited above for "The American House," and two reviews of the current literature in *American Quarterly* 37, No. 3—M. H. Ebner's "Rereading Suburban America" (pp. 368–81) and C. O'Connor's "Sorting Out the Suburbs" (pp. 382–93). On freeway design, see also the impressionistic but thoughtful *Freeways* (New York: Reinhold, 1966) by L. Halprin.

For airports and airfields, a technical source is R. Horonjeff and F. X. McKelvey, *Planning and Design of Airports,* 3rd ed. (New York: McGraw-Hill, 1983). A more accessible reference, with a workmanlike survey of the major airports, is E. G. Blankenship, *The Airport* (New York: Praeger, 1974).

The landscape of farming has a venerable tradition of scholarship. We have referred to some principal sources above—Marshner's *Land Use,* Stilgoe's *Common Landscape of America,* J. B. Jackson's *American Space* and his pieces in *Landscape,* especially, for our own time, "The New American Countryside, An Engineered Environment," 16, No. 1, 1966, pp. 16–20. Let me add here R. K. Sutton, "Circles on the Plain, Center Pivot Irrigation," *Landscape* 22, No. 1, 1977, pp. 3–10, and W. D. Rasmussen, "The Mechanization of Agriculture," *Scientific American,* September 1982, pp. 76–89.

Mining patterns are discussed in Sullivan's *Landprints,* pp. 283 ff. See also E. W. Miller, "Strip Mining and Land Utilization in Western Pennsylvania," *Scientific Monthly,* August 1949, pp. 94–103; D. B. Luten, "Western Coal Mining," *Landscape* 24, No. 1, 1980, pp. 1–2; and a clear account by R. L.

Marovelli and J. M. Kahrnak, "The Mechanization of Mining," *Scientific American,* September 1982, pp. 90–102.

On the trans-Alaska pipeline, see R. Corrigan, "Alaska Embarks on Its Biggest Boom," *Smithsonian* 5, October 1974, pp. 38–49. National parks have been studied by J. Ise, *Our National Park Policy* (Baltimore: Johns Hopkins University Press, 1961), and R. Nash, "The American Invention of National Parks," *American Quarterly* 22, No. 3, Fall 1970, pp. 726–35.

Illustration Credits

Chapter 1

Page 4, Hearst San Simeon State Historical Monument; *5, top*, Hearst San Simeon State Historical Monument; *5, bottom*, Werner Schumann; *6*, National Archives; *7, left*, Werner Schumann; *7, right*, Jennifer Gruber; *8*, Werner Schumann; *11, top*, Colonial Williamsburg Foundation; *11, bottom*, Werner Schumann; *12, top*, Werner Schumann; *12, bottom*, Werner Schumann; *13*, The Earl Green Swem Library, College of William and Mary in Virginia; *14*, Thomas Jefferson Memorial Foundaiton, Inc./James Thatch; *15*, Copyright © by the White House Historical Association, photograph by the National Geographic Society; *18*, Werner Schumann; *19*, Boston Athenaeum; *20*, The Library Company of Philadelphia; *22, left*, Library of Congress; *22, right*, Library of Congress; *25, top*, Henry Francis du Pont Winterthur Museum Library, Collection of Printed Books; *25, bottom*, Werner Schumann; *27*, Glendale Heritage Preservation, photograph by Werner Schumann; *29*, Copyright © 1984 David King Gleason, from *Over Boston* (Louisiana State University Press); *30*, Werner Schumann; *32*, The Stowe-Day Foundation; Hartford, Connecticut; *34*, The Stowe-Day Foundation, Hartford, Connecticut; *36–37*, Richard Tobias; *38*, Wayne Andrews; *39*, Douglas S. MacDonald; *40*, Photograph by Frederick L. Hamilton, from A. McArdle and D. B. McArdle, *Carpenter Gothic* (New York, Whitney Library of Design, 1978, Watson-Guptill); *41*, Wayne Andrews; *42*, The Frank Lloyd Wright Home and Studio Foundation, Oak Park, Illinois; *43*, The Frank Lloyd Wright Home and Studio Foundation, Oak Park, Illinois; *47, top*, Copyright © The Frank Lloyd Wright Foundation 1962, Courtesy of The Frank Lloyd Wright Memorial Foundation; *47, bottom*, Copyright © The Frank Lloyd Wright Foundation 1962, Courtesy of The Frank Lloyd Wright Memorial Foundation; *49*, Photograph by Byron, The Byron Collection, Museum of the City of New York; *50*, Werner Schumann; *52*, National Archives; *54*, Library of Congress; *56*, Library of Congress; *58*, Copyright © William A. Garnett, Napa, California; *59*, Copyright © William A. Garnett, Napa, California; *61*, Werner Schumann; *62*, Werner Schumann; *63*, Werner Schumann; *64*, Copyright © 1956 Ezra Stoller, ESTO; *65*, Hedrich Blessing; *67, top*, Jennifer Gruber; *67, bottom*, Copyright © 1986 Douglas S. MacDonald; *68*, Werner Schumann.

Chapter 2

Page 70, Werner Schumann; *71,* Collections of Henry Ford Museum and Greenfield Village, Neg. No. 55282 A; *73,* Courtesy of Sears, Roebuck and Co., photograph by Hedrich Blessing; *74,* Werner Schumann; *76,* Werner Schumann; *77,* Werner Schumann; *78, top,* Moorland-Spingarn Research Center, Howard University; *78, bottom,* Werner Schumann; *81,* Department of Special Collections, F. Hal Higgins Library of Agricultural Technology, University of California, Davis; *82,* Library of Congress; *83,* Library of Congress; *84–85,* Library of Congress; *86,* Werner Schumann; *87,* Missouri Historical Society, photograph by W. C. Persons, St. Louis, Neg. Interiors 100; *88,* Werner Schumann; *90,* Werner Schumann; *91,* Werner Schumann; *92,* Copyright © 1968 Randolph Langenbach; *94, top,* National Archives; *94, bottom,* Museum of American Textile History; *96,* Library of Congress; *98–99,* Chicago Historical Society; *98, bottom,* Chicago Historical Society; *99, bottom,* Werner Schumann; *102,* Photograph by Elias Goldensky, National Museum of American History, Smithsonian Institution; *103, top,* National Museum of American History, Smithsonian Institution; *103, bottom,* Frederick W. Taylor Collection, Stevens Institute of Technology, Hoboken, New Jersey; *105,* Collections of Henry Ford Museum and Greenfield Village, Neg. No. 27330; *107,* Smithsonian Institution; *108,* Collections of Henry Ford Museum and Greenfield Village, Neg. No. 895; *109,* Albert Kahn Associates, Inc.; *111,* Werner Schumann; *112, left,* Werner Schumann; *112, right,* Werner Schumann; *113,* Collections of Henry Ford Museum and Greenfield Village, Neg. No. 6577; *115,* HABS, Library of Congress; *116,* Photograph by Byron, The Byron Collection, Museum of the City of New York; *118,* The Frank Lloyd Wright Memorial Foundation, Scottsdale, Arizona; *119, top,* Werner Schumann; *119, bottom,* Werner Schumann; *120,* Werner Schumann; *121,* Chicago Historical Society; *122,* Werner Schumann; *123, left,* Werner Schumann; *123, right,* Julius Shulman, Los Angeles, California; *124,* Werner Schumann; *125,* Werner Schumann; *126,* Copyright © 1956 Ezra Stoller, ESTO; *127, left,* Haworth Inc., Holland, Michigan; *127, right,* Werner Schumann; *128,* Copyright © 1984 Chas McGrath, courtesy John Burgee Architects with Philip Johnson; *129,* Union Carbide Corporation; *130,* General Foods Corporation; *131,* Werner Schumann; *132, San Francisco Examiner,* photograph by Craig Lee.

Chapter 3

Page 136, Grace Stix Guggenheim; *137,* Werner Schumann; *138,* Werner Schumann; *140,* Library of Congress; *141,* Collections of The Cincinnati Historical Society; *142,* C&O Canal National Historic Site, National Park Service; *143,* Werner Schumann; *144,* Smithsonian Institution; *146, top,* Werner Schumann; *146, bottom,* Werner Schumann; *148,* Werner Schumann; *149,* From G. E. Kidder Smith, *The Architecture of the United States; 150,* Smithsonian Institution; *152, top,* Collections of the Georgia Historical Society; *152, bottom,* Collections of the Georgia Historical Society; *153, top,* Collections of the Georgia Historical Society; *153, bottom,* Georgia Historical Society, photograph by Werner Schumann; *155,* Werner Schumann; *156–157,* Museum of the City of New York; *158,* Museum of the City of New York; *160,* Werner Schumann; *162, top,* Amon Carter Museum, Fort Worth, Texas, Mazzula Collection, R. Benecke, photographer, St. Louis, Missouri; *162, bottom,* Illinois Central Railroad Collection, Vol. 12, Baker Library, Harvard Business School; *163,* New York Historical Society, Bella C. Landauer Collection; *164,* Library of Congress; *165,* Library of Congress; *166,* Werner Schumann; *167,* Copyright © 1986 Douglas S. MacDonald; *168,* Werner Schumann; *169,* The Metropolitan Museum of Art, Purchase, Joseph Pulitzer Bequest, 1942 (42.138); *170,* Chicago Historical Society; *171,* Chicago Historical Society; *172,* A.T.&.T. Corporate Archives; *174,* Missouri Historical Society, Swekosky Collection, Neg. No. 72, Street Scenes; *175,* Smithsonian Institution; *176,* Brown Brothers, Sterling, Pennsylvania; *177,* Library of Congress; *179,* Werner Schumann; *180–181,* Illustration from *Underground* by David Macaulay, copyright © 1976 by David Macaulay, reprinted by permission of Houghton Mifflin Company; *184,* Library of Congress; *185,* The U.S. Commission of Fine Arts, Washington, D.C., photograph by Werner Schumann; *186,* Werner Schumann; *187,* Copyright © Jane Lidz, photographer, Courtesy Skidmore, Owings & Merrill; *189,* W. P. Snyder, *Harper's Weekly,* 1879; *190,* Library of Congress; *192,* Library of Congress; *195, top,* Werner Schumann; *195, bottom,* Werner Schumann; *196, top,* Courtesy of the Seaver Center for Western History Research, Natural History Museum of Los Angeles County; *196, bottom,* Reibsamen, Nickels and Rex, Architects, photograph by George R. Szanik; *198,* Howard Johnson Franchise Systems, Inc.; *200, bottom,* Werner Schumann; *200–201,* Words and Music by Bobby

Troup, copyright © 1946, Renewed 1973, Assigned 1974 to Londontown Music, All Rights Reserved; *203, left,* Copyright © Douglas S. MacDonald; *203, right,* Copyright © Douglas S. MacDonald.

Chapter 4

Page 206, Copyright © 1986 David King Gleason, from *Over Boston* (Louisiana State University Press); *207,* Werner Schumann; *208,* Boston Athenaeum; *209,* State of New Mexico, Economic Development and Tourism Department, Santa Fe; *210,* Copyright © 1986 David King Gleason, from *Over New Orleans* (Louisiana State University Press); *212,* The Beinecke Rare Book and Manuscript Library, Yale University; *213,* The New Haven Colony Historical Society; *214,* Werner Schumann; *215,* Library of Congress; *218,* Daniel Farber; *220,* Copyright © 1986 David King Gleason, from *Over New Orleans* (Louisiana State University Press); *221,* Werner Schumann; *222,* National Park Service, Frederick Law Olmsted National Historic Site, Brookline, Massachusetts; *223, top,* Parks Photo Archive, Museum of the City of New York; *223, bottom,* The J. Clarence Davies Collection, Museum of the City of New York; *224, top & middle,* Werner Schumann; *224–225, bottom,* New York City Parks Photo Archive; *225, top,* Werner Schumann; *228,* Virginia State Library; *229,* Werner Schumann; *230,* Werner Schumann; *231,* Springfield, Illinois Convention and Visitors Bureau; *232,* Werner Schumann; *233, top,* Library of Congress; *233, bottom,* Werner Schumann; *234,* Minute Man National Historical Park, National Park Service; *235,* Library of Congress; *237,* The Port Authority of New York and New Jersey; *238, top,* Library of Congress; *238, bottom,* Werner Schumann; *239,* Boston Public Library; *240,* Union Station Redevelopment Corporation, Copyright © 1986 Carol Highsmith, Photographer; *242, top,* Copyright © 1987 Macy*s New York, Inc.; *242, bottom left & right,* Copyright © 1987 Macy*s New York, Inc.; *243, top,* Copyright © 1987 Macy*s New York, Inc.; *243, bottom,* Werner Schumann; *245,* Douglas S. MacDonald; *250,* Werner Schumann; *253,* Greenfield Village, Dearborn, Michigan; *254,* Great America theme park, Santa Clara, California; *255,* Copyright © The Walt Disney Company; *256,* Werner Schumann; *257,* Jennie Moffitt; *259,* Library of Congress; *261, left,* Werner Schumann; *261, right,* Werner Schumann; *262,* Werner Schumann; *264,* The Rouse Company; *266–267, top,* Missouri Historical Society, Neg. River 112G–112H; *266, bottom,* Werner Schumann; *268,* Werner Schumann;

269, Richard N. Murray; *270,* Grace Stix Guggenheim; *271,* Grace Stix Guggenheim; *272,* Grace Stix Guggenheim; *274,* Copyright © 1985 Helen Lundeen Whittemore; *275,* Douglas S. MacDonald.

Chapter 5

Page 278, Library of Congress; *279,* U.S. Department of the Interior, Bureau of Reclamation, photograph by B. D. Glaha; *280,* U.S. Department of the Interior, Bureau of Reclamation, photograph by E. E. Hertzog; *281,* U.S. Department of the Interior, Bureau of Reclamation, photograph by E. E. Hertzog; *283,* NASA; *286,* Courtesy of the Trustees of The British Museum; *287,* Ohio Historical Society; *290,* Smithsonian Institution; *294,* U.S. Department of Agriculture; *298,* Ohio State University Libraries; *299,* U.S. Department of Agriculture; *303,* Manuscripts and University Archives, Cornell University Libraries; *305,* The J. Clarence Davies Collection, Museum of the City of New York; *306,* Los Angeles Department of Water and Power; *307,* Mississippi River Commission, U.S. Army Corps of Engineers; *309, top,* Ohio River Division, U.S. Army Corps of Engineers; *309, bottom,* Ohio River Division, U.S. Army Corps of Engineers; *310,* Margaret Bourke-White, *Life Magazine,* Copyright © 1936, 1964 Time Inc.; *311, left,* U.S. Department of the Interior, Bureau of Reclamation, photo by E. E. Hertzog; *311, right,* U.S. Department of the Interior, Bureau of Reclamation, Grand Coulee Project Office, photograph by Bob Isom; *313,* U.S. Department of the Interior, Bureau of Reclamation; *314,* Tennessee Valley Authority; *315,* Tennessee Valley Authority; *316,* Library of Congress; *317,* Tennessee Valley Authority; *318,* Tennessee Valley Authority; *319,* Tennessee Valley Authority; *320,* Tennessee Valley Authority; *321, left,* California Department of Transportation Library, Sacramento; *321, right,* Werner Schumann; *322,* Union Pacific Railroad Museum Collection; *323,* Werner Schumann; *324,* Missouri Historical Society, Neg. Portraits E-16; *326,* Missouri Historical Society; *327,* Missouri Historical Society, photograph by Robert Benecke, Neg. River 272; *329,* The J. Clarence Davies Collection, Museum of the City of New York; *330,* State of California, Department of Transportation, Sacramento; *331,* Chesapeake Bay Bridge and Tunnel District, Cape Charles, Virginia; *332,* State of California, Department of Transportation, Sacramento; *334,* Copyright © 1983 Barrie Rokeach; *336,* O'Hare Airport, Courtesy of the City of Chicago, O'Hare Development Program; *337,* From

G. E. Kidder Smith, *The Architecture of the United States;* *338*, Copyright © 1981 Barrie Rokeach; *339*, Copyright © 1981 Barrie Rokeach; *341*, Lindsay Manufacturing Company, Lindsay, Nebraska; *342*, Lindsay Manufacturing Company, Lindsay, Nebraska; *343*, Copyright © 1984 Don Green, Courtesy of Kennecott Copper Corporation, Salt Lake City, Utah; *345*, Tennessee Valley Authority; *346*, Chevron Corporation, San Francisco, California; *348*, F. Jay Haynes photograph, Haynes Foundation Collection, Montana Historical Society, Helena, Montana; *349*, Ansel Adams, *350*, Library of Congress; *351*, From G. E. Kidder Smith, *The Architecture of the United States.*

Color Section (in order, following page 180)

Plate 1, Werner Schumann; *plate 2*, Werner Schumann; *plate 3*, Glendale Heritage Preservation, photograph by Werner Schumann; *plate 4*, Werner Schumann; *plate 5*, Diego M. Rivera (Mexican, 1886–1957), *Detroit Industry*, 1932–33, Fresco, 33.10N, Detail (Detroit Institute of Arts and the Founders Society Purchase, Edsel B. Ford Fund and Gift of Edsel B. Ford); *plate 6*, Copyright © William A. Garnett, Napa, California; *plate 7*, Werner Schumann; *plate 8*, Union Carbide Corporation; *plate 9*, Werner Schumann; *plate 10*, Museum of the City of New York; *plate 11*, Chicago Historical Society; *plate 12*, San Francisco Museum of Modern Art, Purchased with the aid of funds from public subscription, William L. Gerstle Fund, Fund of the 80's, and Tom Weisel, 86.6; *plate 13*, Douglas S. MacDonald; *plate 14*, Library of Congress; *plate 15*, Metropolitan Richmond Chamber of Commerce; *plate 16*, Copyright © David King Gleason, from *Over Boston* (Louisiana State University Press); *plate 17*, Grace Stix Guggenheim; *plate 18*, Steve Northrup/*Time Magazine*; *plate 19*, Copyright © David King Gleason, from *Over New Orleans* (Louisiana State University Press); *plate 20*, National Museum of American Art, Smithsonian Institution/Bequest of Helen Huntington Hull.

Index

The italic page numbers refer to illustrations.